A PRACTICAL GUIDE TO

PUPPETRY

A PRACTICAL GUIDE TO
PUPPETRY

Mark Down

THE CROWOOD PRESS

First published in 2022 by
The Crowood Press Ltd
Ramsbury, Marlborough
Wiltshire SN8 2HR

enquiries@crowood.com
www.crowood.com

This impression 2025

British Library Cataloguing-in-Publication Data
A catalogue record for this book is available from the British Library.

For product safety-related questions, contact
productsafety@crowood.com

ISBN 978 0 7198 4101 9

Acknowledgements
My heartfelt thanks first to Fiona Clift, who has read and discussed and listened and advised and who features in many of the photographs. To Edward Docx, who enthused and encouraged and gave me a non-alcoholic beer at crucial moments. To Caroline Down, Ruth Paton and Giulia Innocenti, who read several chapters and gave helpful feedback. To Philip Haas, Peter Down, Carolyn Choa, my mum Maddy and my brother Jim, who are always supportive.

To Nick Barnes, who founded Blind Summit Theatre in 1997 and with whom I learned everything I know about puppetry. He made many of the puppets in this book. To all the people in the photographs, and behind the puppets in the photographs, whose remarkable work has inspired me for twenty-plus years making puppetry. To the current board of Blind Summit: Eddie Berg, Henrietta Duckworth, Jane Morgan and Wojtek Trjinski.

And I am extremely grateful to everyone who gave permission to use their photographs: Bertha Elizondo, Helen Foan, Antonella Carrara, Edmund Collier, Lorna Palmer, Odetta Riskute, Nick Barnes, Patrick Baldwin, Richard Blomshield, Susanna Neves, Aga Blaszczak, Harry Zundel and Stephanie Wickes.

Typeset by Shane O'Dwyer

Cover design by Sergey Tsvetkov

Printed and bound in India by Thomson Press India Ltd

CONTENTS

INTRODUCTION: WHAT IS PUPPETRY?

'I dream about puppets all night. I see strings on people.' (Trey Parker)

PUPPETRY IS NOT A SINGLE THING

A little man walks around on a table top complaining about his life, a cast of characters dance in a miniature theatre, a giant Wizard grows mightily into the air in a sports stadium, the shadow of an old lady changes into a bird, a pair of glove puppets fight, a miniature person watching TV is swallowed alive by their sofa, a detective multiplies into five tiny detectives, a firebird flies over the heads of the audience in a concert hall, a pair of red shoes walk up the wall in a dark caravan, two balloons 'vogue' to a contemporary soundtrack, a giant 'Gulliver' travels into a town on a barge.... Seeing these things is magical. They are puppetry.

There are many types of puppetry and hundreds of different puppets. There are giant puppets and tiny puppets. There are puppets that require lots of people to operate them and puppets that can be operated on one finger. Some puppets are beautifully sculpted or painted, while others may be traditional and rather crude in style. Simple everyday objects, which are not actually puppets at all, can be used by puppeteers to take the shape of living things. Some puppets are controlled by strings, rods, gloves, shadows or remote control, or a combination of all of these, or none of these.

OPPOSITE: Suki in *Citizen Puppet* (Blind Summit).

Some puppets work in miniature, others on a giant scale. They appear in theatres, on the street, on specially built stages, in stadiums, at the beach. Sometimes they are part of telling a story. At others they are a special effect. Some are specially invented for a particular show, while others may be part of a tradition that is hundreds of years old.

What all puppets have in common is that the protagonist in the scene – the character that the audience is watching – is played by a something that is not alive: a specialized object; a puppet. It only looks like it is alive because it is being moved by a puppeteer. Puppeteers, working behind the scenes, make everything happen.

However, the fact is that none of these things have happened at all. It just *looked* like they happened.

PUPPETRY IS AN ILLUSION

Puppetry is a kind of magic trick. The puppeteer brings life to an object that the observer knows is not alive. As with magic, the excitement for the people in the audience lies in whether the puppeteer can convince them with their skill. Can they make them see the puppet come alive? Can they make them believe it is alive? The trick is everything. Just as we know that there is no such thing as magic – it is a trick – we are all too aware that a puppet is not actually alive. But....

Where magic is about 'misdirection', puppetry is about 'direction'. While the magician tries to make the observer look away, so that they can do the trick without being seen, the puppeteer encourages the audience to look at the puppet and to see the trick. Puppetry is a magic trick done in plain sight.

When a magician pulls a live rabbit out of a seemingly empty hat, or a puppeteer makes fur move so that it looks like a living animal, the event happens in the imagination of the audience. Watching a magic act, the audience sees a non-existent rabbit magically come into existence, apparently out of nothing. Watching a puppeteer, the audience imagines that the fur is moving on its own and is able to overlook the fact that it is the puppeteer who is doing it.

Puppetry is the art of moving something with your hands so that it looks like it is moving on its own – like it is alive.

The puppeteer's hand holds the Rubik's Cube in the puppet's hand.

DUPLICATION

There is a difference between what the puppeteer does and what the audience sees. In puppetry, everything is duplicated. There is the puppet's world and the puppeteer's world. There is the puppet's head and hands and feet, and the puppeteer's head and hands and feet. There is the puppet's action and the character's action, and the puppeteer's action. There is what the puppet does, what that looks like, and what it means. And there is what the audience sees and what the audience understands from what it sees.

It would be wrong to say that the puppeteer 'does the movement of the puppet'; they do not. There is a difference between the movement that the puppet does, and the movement that the puppeteer does to make the puppet do that movement. The puppeteer makes the puppet move using their hands. When the puppeteer moves their hand holding the puppet's head, what the audience sees is the puppet move its head.

Consider a glove puppet picking something up. It bends over, it reaches out for the item, and it picks it up. At least, that is what it appears to do and that is what the audience understands it to have done. What actually happened, of course, is that the puppeteer made the puppet appear to bend over by flexing their hand. The puppeteer then moved the puppet in such a way that it appeared to reach out, then moved it again so that the puppet appeared to pick up the item in its arms. Actually, it was the puppeteer who picked it up in their hand.

Furthermore, different puppets would do it in different ways. A string puppet picks something up using a string rigged to pull into its hand. A three-person table-top puppet picks something up using the puppeteer's hand. In a shadow show, the item might be controlled on another stick, or the puppet might be swapped with another puppet that is already holding it, and so on.

What the puppeteer does, what the puppet does and what the audience sees are all different.

THE VIEW OF THE AUDIENCE

What this all comes down to is that there are two points of view in puppetry: the view from in front and the view from behind. The audience sees the puppet from in front and the puppeteer sees it from behind. The puppet has no point of view.

If the show is to be understood, it is the view of the audience – the view from in front – that matters. What the audience *imagines* the puppet is doing when they watch the show is what the puppet *is* doing. If they do not understand what the puppeteer wants them to see, and if they do not see what the puppets do, then to all intents and purposes it might as well never have happened.

Throughout this book, the audience – that is, the person watching from in front of the puppet

– is the arbiter of 'what happened'. What the puppet thought and did is what the audience *believes* it thought and did. What the audience sees and hears, and what they interpret from that, is what happened. There is no other view.

The only 'truth' in puppetry is what happens in the imagination of the audience.

PUPPETS ARE OBJECTS THAT PERFORM

A puppet of a dog walks on stage and the audience gasps. It looks just like a real dog, they say. It is more real than a real dog.

Notice that they do not say that they think it is a real dog. They are not fooled by it. They don't make that mistake. But they do say that it is even more real than a real dog.

It is more real than a real dog because it is acting. In other words, it is not behaving like a real dog at all, but like an acting dog. It is like a dog that has learned its lines and rehearsed beforehand. A real dog would bark at the audience, wag its tail, come and go as it wanted, lift a leg on the stage, and so on. A puppet dog does not do this. It is there to serve the story. It moves in sympathy with the storytelling, it learns and repeats the role, it listens and thinks and moves as the director directed it. It might even talk. It gives a written performance, like a dog actor.

Although, of course, it is not the dog that does it; it is the puppeteers.

SEEING THE PUPPETEER'S WORK

Although they do not realize it, the audience is really there to watch the puppeteers, not the puppets. As soon as someone sees a puppet, they know that there is someone behind it – or above or below. The puppeteers may or may not show their faces, or even appear on stage, but the audience knows they are there. The observer may or may not talk about the puppeteers – they may only talk about the puppet – but they know that the puppet did not do it on its own.

Without a puppeteer, a puppet is an incomplete object. Whether it is lying in a box or hanging on a hook, its joints will be floppy and its body will not hold it up. It may not have legs or hands; it may be just a pile of rags and a lifeless head. Without the puppeteer, the puppet cannot even stand up. It is only half there. The puppet becomes complete only when the puppeteer picks it up and brings it to life.

The puppet takes the physical space of a character in the show. The puppet is what the audience watches, but it is the puppeteer who learns the role and who makes the puppet do the performance. Equally, it is the puppeteer who is nervous before the show and who may be inspired in the performance.

And it is the puppeteer's work that the audience comes to see, mediated through the puppet.

THE DISAPPEARANCE OF THE PUPPETEER

When a puppet 'comes alive', in fact it does not change at all. It is the puppeteer who changes.

When a puppeteer brings a puppet on stage in a box, they are a person with a box. If the audience does not know what is in the box, they do not know whether the person is a puppeteer or not. They cannot say any more at this point.

If the puppeteer goes on to open the box and take out a puppet, then the audience will assume that they are a puppeteer, and that they are going to make the puppet come alive. To the audience, the person is a puppeteer, out of character, holding their puppet. (They could be wrong, of course. For example, if the person gives the puppet to someone else and leaves the stage, the audience might guess that they are in fact a stage manager or the puppeteer's roadie. However, the result is the same.)

Then, in order to bring the puppet to life, the puppeteer goes 'into character' as a puppeteer

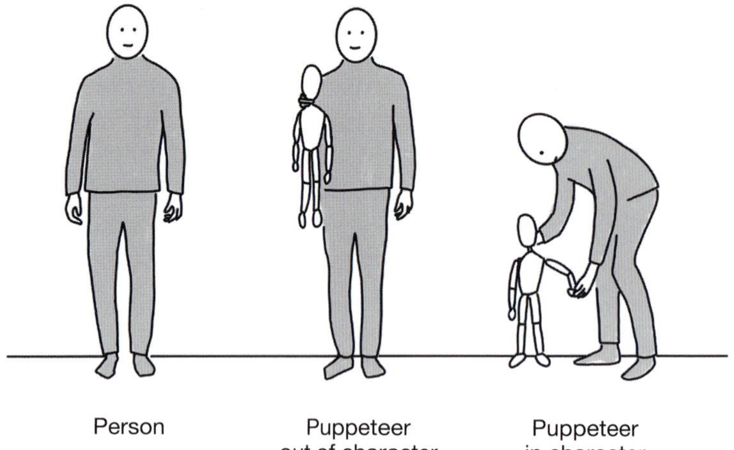

Three states of a puppeteer.

and begins to puppet it. The puppet comes alive and the audience no longer looks at the puppeteer. Although the puppet remains unchanged by all these developments, the puppeteer has gone through a series of changes.

Puppeteers do puppet shows, not puppets.

MOVEMENT: THE LANGUAGE OF PUPPETRY

The only thing a puppeteer can make a puppet do is move. Movement is the most basic sign of life. Animation is the absolute essence of a living thing. Through movement, the puppeteer can make the puppet appear to breathe, look about, walk, run, jump, see things, hear things, touch things, think and feel. Through movement, the puppets can appear to meet other puppets, to talk, to get into an argument, to fall in love. Movement transforms the puppet in the mind of the audience into a living thing.

A SPECIAL STAGE

When a string puppet performs on the street, as it comes alive, the world changes from a human world into a puppet world. The street stops being a street and becomes a stage for the puppet to perform on. The real elements behind the puppet – like the puppeteer's legs or body, a wall, shop-fronts – change into a landscape in which the puppet exists. They become a backdrop for the puppet. The onlookers are now watching a tiny person in a giant world.

If an audience member looks up at the puppeteer, the puppet becomes a puppet again. The puppet stage disappears and the world goes back to normal. Now they are watching a person with a puppet.

The puppeteer kills the puppet, and the puppet kills the puppeteer.

PUPPETRY IS TOTAL THEATRE

When someone decides to put on a show with puppets, they are making a highly eccentric choice: to tell a story with things that are not alive. The aim is to create a world where those items can come to life and tell the story.

To do this, they need to think carefully about the sight-lines, the text, the lighting. They must control where the audience is looking, to direct them to watch the puppets, and not look where they do not want them to look: at the puppeteer. The audience needs to be taught about the conventions of the puppetry of each show: how to watch the puppets, how to interpret their movement, and how to understand what they mean. The creator of a puppet show must recreate every aspect of theatre for the puppets.

Puppets do not go to the theatre. Puppets do not watch puppet shows. A puppet show is done by people who show puppets to other people.

A puppeteer needs to be able to make a puppet look like it is thinking, or walking, or talking; like it has ambition, or is falling in love, or learning to ride a bicycle – whatever the story needs the audience to see them doing – because the audience will only understand what the puppet is doing if the puppet looks like it is doing it.

How to do that is what this book is about.

PART I – TECHNIQUES

1
BRINGING OBJECTS TO LIFE

A puppet is an object that is used to do puppetry. It can take almost any form. It may be a simple, non-articulated, single object or a complex, multi-part construction made up of lots of objects held together with joints. It may be an ordinary, everyday object, such as a spoon, a piece of newspaper or a cardboard box, which has another purpose outside of being puppeted, or it may be a specialized object that is recognizable as a 'puppet', which has no purpose other than to be puppeted in a puppet show.

In this chapter you will work with simple, everyday objects, and learn how, by moving them, you can change them into puppet characters. You will learn to give them life, character, emotions, thoughts and joints, simply by moving them, so that they transform into living characters.

The objects do not of course actually 'come alive', except in the imagination of the viewer – your audience. For this reason, these exercises put equal emphasis on your role as an audience, in seeing how the objects change, as on your role as a puppeteer, in moving them. As you do the exercises, make sure that you also practise becoming a good audience, as well as a good performer. Watching puppetry to see what works and what does not work is as valuable in learning how to do it as is actually doing it.

You can practise these exercises on your own, with someone else, or in groups. It is always best to have someone who can watch you doing them, and whom you can watch. You can use any kind of objects or puppets that you are able to handle on your own.

OPPOSITE: He Liyi and his father in *Mr China's Son* (Blind Summit).

MEETING AN OBJECT FOR THE FIRST TIME

(Adapted from a lesson with puppeteer Steve Tiplady.)

When you first pick up an object, before you start moving it, you may not be able to see any potential in it. However, as soon as you start to play with it, and make it move, features will begin to appear: first, eyes, then a head, then a body, and so on. This exercise is a structured 'free exploration' of objects to see what emerges when you start to move them around. There are no 'wrong' puppets and no 'wrong' ideas: you try things and see what comes. You 'coax' characters out of the objects.

This is a really good way to approach an object, or puppet, when you pick it up for the first time. You can use it in exploratory workshops, for devising material and in trying to find the character of a puppet.

The Exercise

Everyone chooses an object and sits in a circle on the floor. The object can be anything you like: a pen, keys, a phone, a cup, a box, a piece of screwed-up paper, glasses, a shoe, a jumper, a cloth.

STEP 1: Close your eyes and pick up the object. Explore the object with your hands. See what it feels like. See if it makes any sounds. See if it moves or bends. Shake the object. Squeeze it. Put it against your cheek to see if it is hot or cold. Smell it. What are its material qualities? Does it remind you of anything? Does it stimulate any thoughts or feelings?

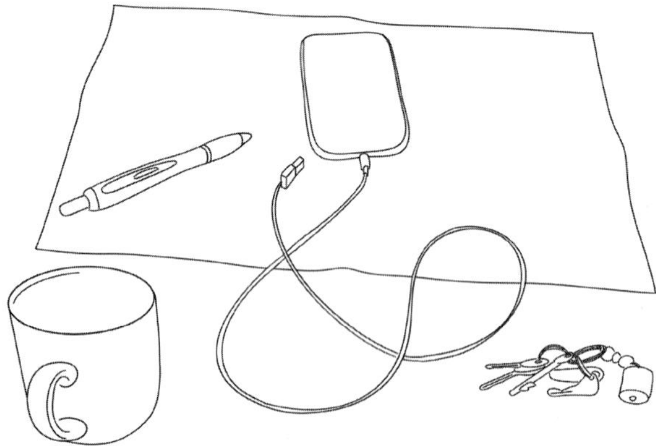

Choose any object: cup, pen, newspaper, mobile phone, keys... whatever.

Try to think of what the object makes you think of other than its purpose.

STEP 2: Now place the object on the ground in front of you. Keep your eyes closed, bend forwards so you are close to the object, and take a 'snapshot' of it by opening and closing your eyes very quickly like a camera. Move a bit further back and take another snapshot.

STEP 3: Open your eyes and look at your object. 'Focus' on it.

STEP 4: Put your hand on the object. Don't move it.

STEP 5: Begin to make the object breathe. Move it gently up and down on the ground and use your own breathing to make the sound of its breath.

STEP 6. Make the object 'wake up', sit up, stand.

STEP 7: Now imagine it has eyes. Decide where they are and make it start to look around. It sees where it is. It becomes aware of the floor, the ceiling, the room. It notices the other puppets in the room, but it does not interact with them yet.

STEP 8: Now make your object start to move around. Think about how it moves. Does it have legs? Or wheels? Does it slide on its belly? Or fly in the air? Or hover, or float, or swim? Does it run everywhere? How many legs does it have? Two, four, six, eight? Or 40? Does it stand up to walk, and then lie down when it arrives where it was going? Does it hop, jump, slither, crawl?

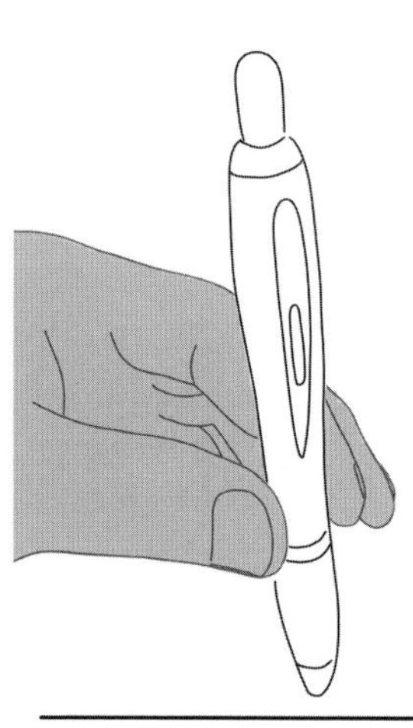

LEFT: STEP 6: The object stands up.

RIGHT: STEP 7: Hold a floppy object, such as a set of keys (*right*) or a sheet of newspaper (*far right*), with two hands – one at the 'head' and one at the 'feet'.

STEP 9: Decide where it is. Is it on ground, in the air, or in water? Is it inside or outside? Is it hot or cold? Is it in danger, or in a safe place? All the time make sure you keep it breathing, and looking at things.
STEP 10: Give your puppet a voice. What sort of voice does it have? Where does it come from? Is it loud or soft? Kind, or rough or aggressive? Does it bark, or meow, or hiss, or tweet, or growl? Does it speak or make words? What sort of language does it speak?
STEP 11: Think about what mood your puppet is in. What is it feeling? Is it happy or sad? Angry or relaxed? Frightened? Excited? Aroused? Whatever you see in it, go with that. If you don't see anything, try something.

Develop the 'mood' of your puppet. Make the emotion bigger and bigger. If it is sad, make it cry. Make it wail with sadness. If it is happy, make it laugh, and then roll around with hysterics. If it is angry, build the mood until it screams with fury. Breathe the feeling deeply into the puppet and let the emotion pour out.
STEP 12. Let the room become a madhouse of shouting, wailing, laughing puppets.
STEP 13: Then stop. Turn everything on its head and try the opposite of everything. Turn your object the other way up. Change the mood to the opposite. If your puppet was happy, make the new one sad. If it was angry, make it relaxed. If it was frightened, make it confident. Develop the new emotions until you have another cacophony.

Then relax.

Tips for Doing It Better

Try to form a clear image of the puppet that your object becomes As you get to know the character of your puppet in the improvisation, be as specific as possible with yourself about what it is. Try to visualize it. See where the eyes are, where the head begins and ends, where the body begins, and where the feet are. Think of your object as taking on a 'skin' to become the puppet. The puppet will be made up of the object, and imaginary, invisible extra parts. Be clear what part of the puppet your object is and how it moves in relation to the imagined parts of your puppet. When you show it to an audience, this is what they will be looking at, and they will want you to be consistent.
Keep your focus on the 'head' of your puppet Look at the head and make the puppet look at things. Don't break your focus on the head when you move it around, and make sure you always know what the puppet is looking at.

Things to Notice

You need to work with the natural qualities of your object An object has its own centre of gravity, its own way of moving and responding to impulses, and its own purpose and use. When you puppet it, you give the object a new centre to move around, you change the purpose of it, and you make it breathe and live. And yet the object's true qualities

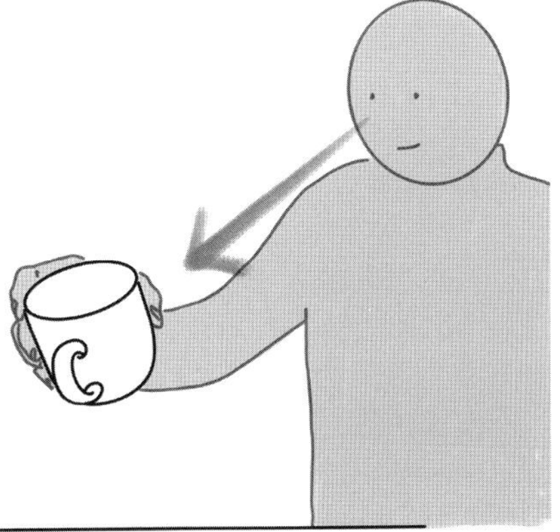
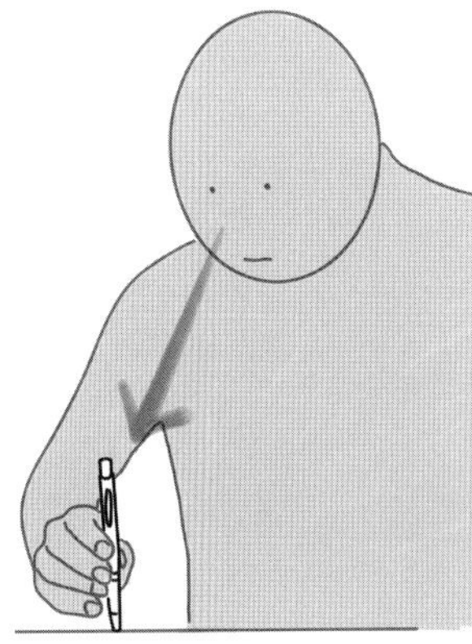

Focus on the head of the puppet – in the first image it is played by the cup, in the second it is the top of the pen.

are still there. A pen, for example, being small and thin, is easy to control but quite hard to see. A chair, on the other hand, being bigger and heavier, is easier to see, but will have its own way of moving, which you will need to work with.

Remember, there are lots of ways to see an object When you first look at it, you might think you know what it is going to do, but when you start to try things, other possibilities will offer themselves. The handle of a cup might make a nose one way up, but if you turn it round it could be a ponytail, or a handle to puppet with. A mobile phone with a cable could be the head and body of a snake one way round, or the body and head of a long-necked dinosaur the other way round. Both can work. You might change from one to the other to represent a change of character, or a change of expression.

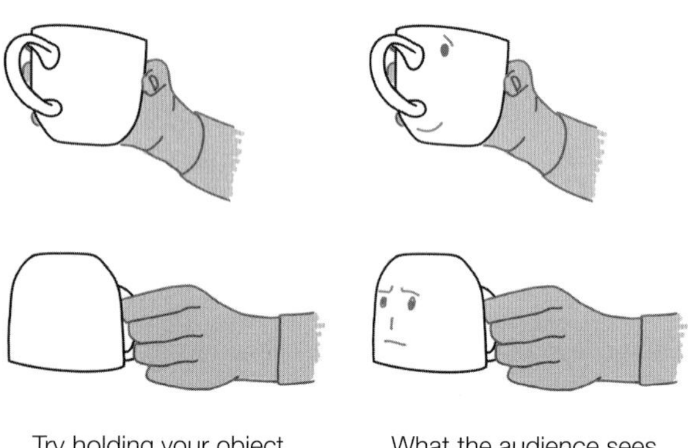

Try holding your object in different ways.

What the audience sees.

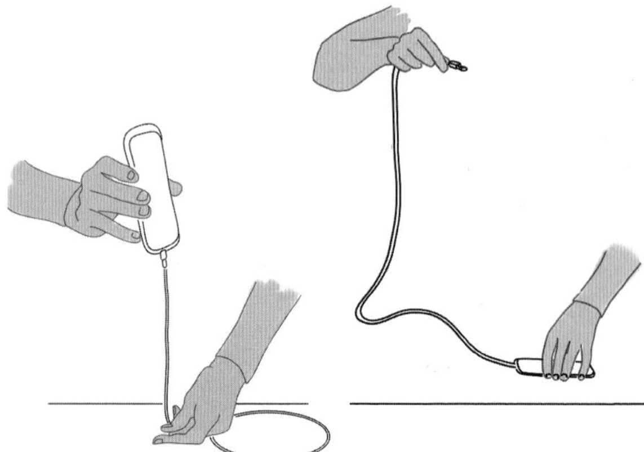

The phone and cable as a snake.

The phone and cable as some kind of long-necked creature.

Be aware of the way in which the puppet exists in relation to the floor When the object comes alive, it takes on an imaginary skin and extra 'invisible' features, such as arms, legs, eyes, which are filled in by the imagination of the audience. For example, when the pen walks on the floor, you imagine that there are legs of some kind that it is walking on. You do this because of the gap you make between the pen and the floor where you can imagine those legs. The relationship between the object and the floor, the puppet and the puppet stage, is an essential part of the transformation of the object into a puppet.

Variations on the Exercise

- Use different materials: instead of using objects, give each person a sheet of newspaper (inspired by an exercise with Improbable Theatre). Go through the steps of the exercise in the same way, starting with flat sheets of newspaper lying on the ground in front of you, and ending up with a scrunched-up, torn, raggedy collection of fabulous newspaper beasts running about and filling the room with life.
- Use props/puppets/materials you want to explore: this exercise can empower everyone to try things in an open, non-directed way. It is a very good structured way to get to know puppets or materials for the first time.

The audience fills in the gap between the object and the table top with this…

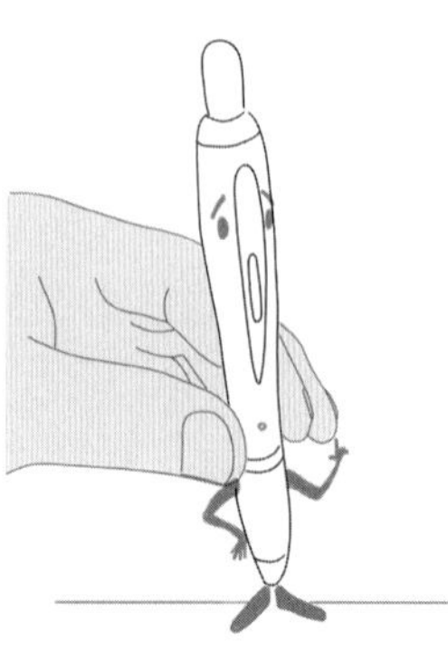

… or this. Or something else.

- Pass the object to your neighbour: at STEP 2, after feeling your object with your eyes closed, pass it to the person on your right, keeping your eyes closed, and receive one from the left. Repeat the exercise and pass the object on again. Then either continue passing the objects until they have gone all the way around the circle and your first one has come back to you, or pass two or three times and then continue the exercise with someone else's object. It is very interesting to explore objects with your eyes closed to see how they make you think and feel differently about them.
- Combine puppets to make a monster: at STEP 11, after making your individual objects walk and talk, make them meet the puppet next door to them. After meeting, make the two puppets join to make a two-part puppet. One of the objects becomes the feet and legs of the new puppet, and the other becomes the body and head. Then make the two-part puppets meet another two-part puppet, and make a four-part puppet. Keep joining the objects together until they are all involved, making a giant, multi-puppet 'monster'.
- Name the puppets and make them talk: at STEP 11, another way to develop the end of the exercise is to name the puppets and give them a voice. Make them meet their neighbour puppets and start a dialogue. Naming the puppets makes them more real, and gives you something to refer back to later in the day.

MAKING YOUR OBJECT PERFORM

(Inspired by a class with puppeteer Steve Tiplady.)

A puppet only really comes alive when you show it to an audience. It moves in your hand, but it only really lives in the imagination of the audience. They are your co-creators and you need to involve them in your creative process. This exercise gives you a structure for presenting your object improvisation to an audience in rehearsal, and for finding out from them what you've got. You create a puppet stage, present your object in a miniature performance, and invite the audience to help you find its puppet character.

When you are the one who is in the audience, you watch the puppet come to life and can give feedback afterwards. Watching other people's improvisations will inspire what you want to see the objects do, and will help you learn how to do what you want the audience to see.

The Exercise

Set up the room with the audience on one side and a stage area on the other. Everyone in the group makes up the audience, and you take it in turns to go on stage. When it is your turn to present your puppet, do it in the following way.

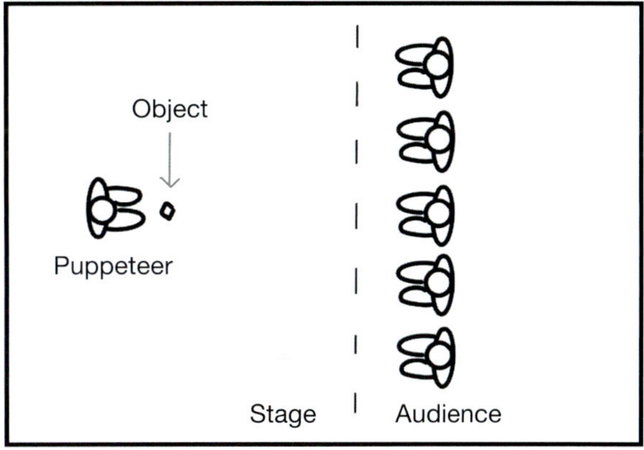

Set up the space with a stage and an audience.

STEP 1: Come on stage, kneel on the ground, put your object on the floor in front of you, and look up at the audience.
STEP 2: 'Collect' the eyes of the audience members. Look at each of them one by one, until you have everyone's attention.
STEP 3: Look down at your object and feel the audience follow your focus, so they are also looking at the object.
STEP 4: When you can feel everyone is looking at your object, reach out and take hold of it. Make sure that you don't move it as you take hold of it.

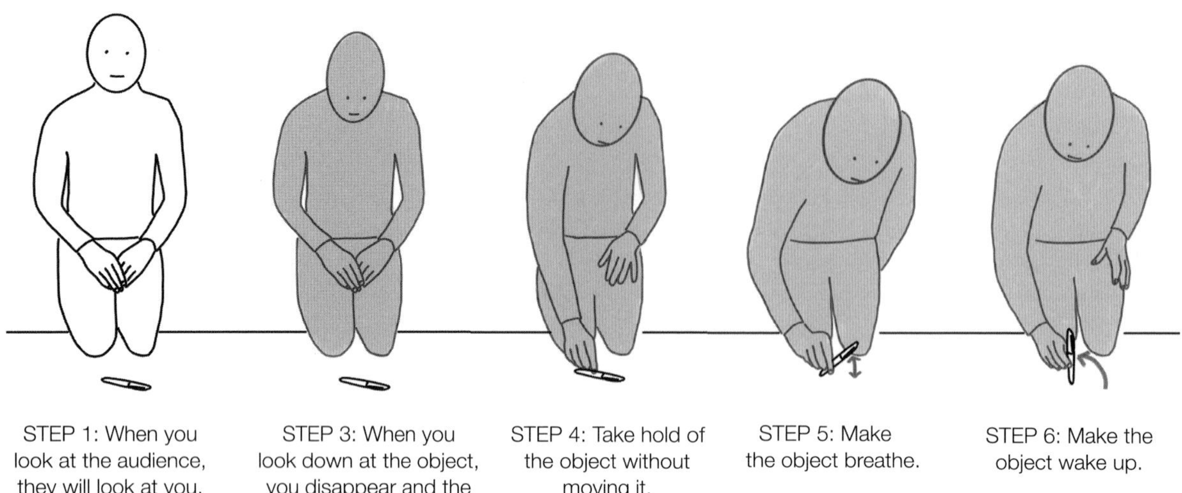

STEP 1: When you look at the audience, they will look at you.

STEP 3: When you look down at the object, you disappear and the object comes into focus.

STEP 4: Take hold of the object without moving it.

STEP 5: Make the object breathe.

STEP 6: Make the object wake up.

STEP 5: Start to make the object breathe, bringing it alive.
STEP 6: Make your object wake up.
STEP 7: Find its eyes and make it look around the room. Make it breathe, move, think, feel. Make it see the audience and react. Maybe it says 'hello'.
STEP 8: Begin to develop the emotion just as you did when improvising with it in the previous exercise. Show the audience the emotional extremes and movement of the object.
STEP 9: Keep the improvisation going until you are told to stop. Usually this is 2–5 minutes.
STEP 10: Finally, listen to the audience feedback on what they saw, what they understood from what they saw, what they like, and maybe what they did not like.

Tips for Doing It Well

Hold the object the way you want the audience to see it Show them which is the front of the puppet and which is the back. They will expect you to hold it from behind.

Hold a stiff object as close to the 'character centre' as possible: this gives you good control and means that the audience will be able to see both the feet and the head.

Hold a floppy object at the head and the feet Holding the object with two hands will give you as much control as possible. Use your dominant hand to hold the 'head'.

Don't change your grip Once you have taken hold of the object, maintain the same grip. Changing the grip or passing the object from hand to hand will draw attention to you and break the focus of the audience on the puppet. Move yourself about rather than changing your grip.

Take your time: don't be rushed Build expectation. Invest in each stage of development before moving on to the next. At the very beginning, make sure everyone is looking at you. Wait long enough for all of them to look at the puppet before you put your hand on it. Leave your hand on the puppet long enough before you start to move it. Wait for each moment to come before moving forwards. You only get one chance to do each stage and you cannot go back.

Use the audience as a 'mirror' While you are performing, try to understand what the audience are seeing. Listen for their reactions, for example, silence or laughter. If something you make the puppet do gets a reaction, try doing it again. Try to 'see' what they are seeing. Where are they seeing the puppet's eyes? How do they see the puppet walk?

After your presentation, ask your audience specific questions: Where are the eyes? Where is the puppet looking? Are these the feet? Is it too tall or short?

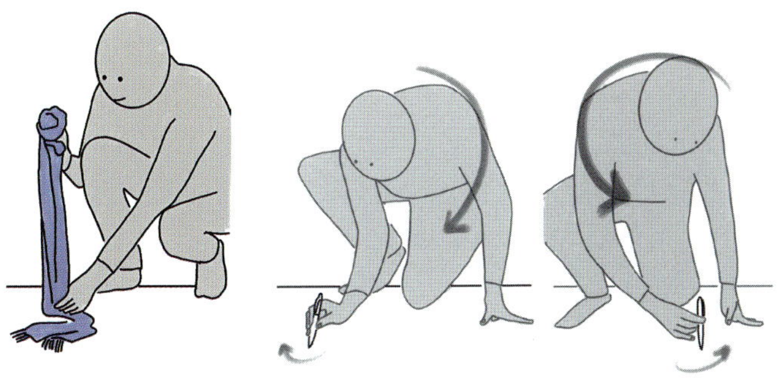

FAR LEFT: Hold a floppy object such as a scarf with two hands – one at the 'head' and one at the 'feet'.

LEFT: Move yourself around the object so that you can keep the same grip.

If you look up from your object, the audience will look at you.

Things to Notice

The object comes alive when you look at it At that moment, before you even go to take hold of it, you create a new reality. The audience sees the object in a different light: it has become a 'puppet'. At the same time, the floor becomes the object's stage, and you become an invisible puppeteer. This is why it is important not to move the puppet when you first take hold of it, because it is already alive in the mind of the audience, and you are reaching out to touch a living thing. If you move it when you go to take hold of it, then you become visible again, and the puppet will turn back into an object. It will die.

Avoid doing things that draw attention to you The illusion is delicate. Anything that you do that draws attention away from the puppet, and onto you, will break the illusion. If you take a moment to adjust your leg, or break your focus, or change your grip on the object, the audience will look up at you, and stop seeing the puppet as a living being.

HOW TO GIVE FEEDBACK

Watching is as important as 'doing' in puppetry and it is always valuable to take a moment after a presentation for everyone to talk about what they have seen. Watch each other's performances critically, paying attention to the things that make the object live, and the things that make it die. Anything that distracts you from seeing the puppet is a problem.

When giving feedback, try to be as precise as possible about what you are seeing. For example, when someone has puppeted a pen, you might say, 'I saw a very tall thin man, with a long face on the top half of the pen, with a sort of beanie hat and a roll-neck sweater on.' If they have used a scrunched-up piece of newspaper, you might let them know that you have seen 'a Victorian lady in a cape and hood', and so on.

Showing is the best way to explain what you mean by your feedback, and to learn to do it yourself. Swap places with the person, take their object, and show them what you saw in their puppet. By changing places between audience and performer you develop your ability to do what you want to see, and to see what you are doing.

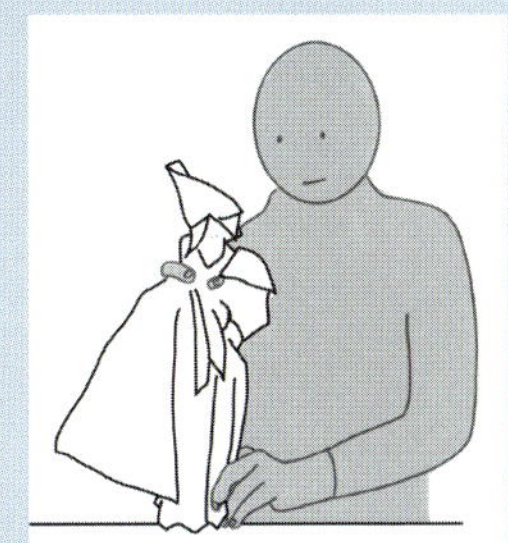

LEFT: 'It's a little man, the ring in the middle of the pen is a collar and the top is a fez....'

FAR LEFT: 'It's a Victorian lady in a cape and a hood....'

Sad and lonely, Mildred from *Low Life* (Blind Summit).

PUPPETING EMOTION

When the audience watches your object come to life they will look for what it is feeling. They will identify emotions whether you put them there or not. They will deduce what the puppet is feeling from the story they watch, and from the way you move it.

In this exercise, you let the audience guide you to develop the emotion of your object. The audience tells you what emotion they see in your puppet and you work to make it grow bigger, using movement and voice.

The Exercise

Set up the room so that you have an audience and a stage area. Participants will then go up one by one to do the exercise in front of the rest of the group.

STEP 1: The puppeteer places their object on the floor of the stage in front of the audience and brings it to life. They make it breathe and look around the space.

STEP 2: The audience members say what emotion they see in the object. Usually, they will agree on this. Sometimes, however, the emotion may be subtle and there will be a disagreement. In this case, they choose one and, once that choice has been made, that becomes the emotion.

STEP 3: The puppeteer then tries to make their object feel that emotion more. They make it breathe in that emotion, move with that emotion, and make the sound of that emotion. For example, if the puppet is sad, they can make it begin to cry; if it is happy, it can be made to laugh; if it is afraid, it may begin to shake; if it is excited, it might begin to pant.

STEP 4: Now the puppeteer pauses the improvisation and asks the audience if they know what the emotion is about. Where is the puppet looking? Is the emotion directed at someone in the audience? At something in the room? At itself? At the door? At a mark on the floor? It does not matter what it is directed at, as long as the puppeteer has chosen a focus for it.

STEP 5: The puppeteer develops the emotion further, making sure that the object keeps referring to the focus of the emotion. If it is sad, maybe it will turn away from the focus. If it is happy, perhaps it will want to come closer. If it is afraid, perhaps it will run away, and so on.

STEP 6: As the object becomes increasingly emotional the audience watches to make sure that the emotion is developing and not altering. It should become deeper and bigger rather than becoming different. For example, the breathing of the object could get noisier, the movements more dramatic. If the puppeteer gets stuck and does not know how to progress, they can pause the improvisation and ask the audience for suggestions of what they could do next.

STEP 7: The puppeteer takes the emotion as far as they think they can, keeping it consistent, and focusing on the same thing. If the puppet is sad, it should now be howling with grief. If it is happy, it should be rolling on the floor with laughter. If it is afraid, it should scream and run away. If it is excited, it should be leaping up and down and running around with enthusiasm. Eventually, the object will become exhausted by the emotion and the puppeteer can relax.

STEP 8: The audience gives feedback on what they have seen. Did the emotion go as far as they imagined it could or was there further to go? Was the puppet convincingly exhausted? What emotion does the object feel in the aftermath?

STEP 9: The next person moves up to have a go and explore a different emotion.

Tips for Doing It Better

Stick to one emotion The challenge in this exercise is to develop one emotion, directed at one thing, for as long as possible, and to take it to its extreme. It is like making a colour chart of that emotion. The purpose is to discover the full range of movements that relate to the one emotion so that you can draw on them later.

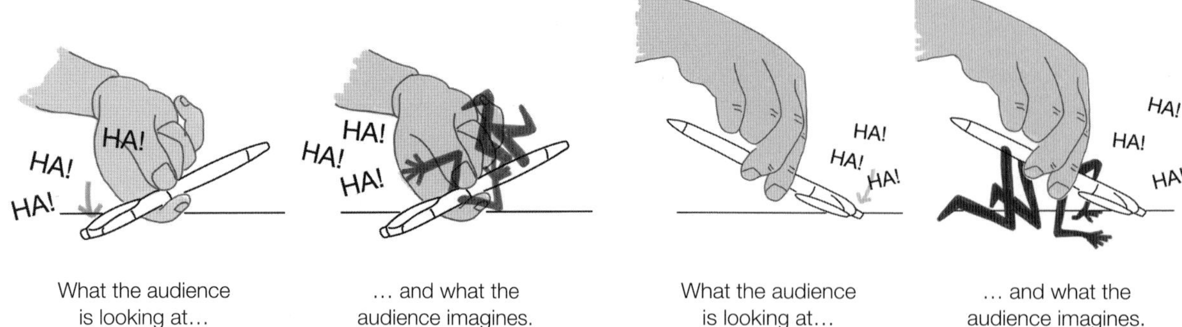

What the audience is looking at… | … and what the audience imagines. | What the audience is looking at… | … and what the audience imagines.

Visualize the puppet character See the puppet's eyes, mouth, legs and arms. Imagine how long its limbs are, how they work, and be consistent about where they are and how they work. Try to be aware of what you are making the audience see. For example, if your object is a pen, try to visualise a tiny laughing 'pen person'.

Move the object around the centre of the character In order to make it look as if the object is breathing, laughing or crying, you must move it around the centre of the imagined character (which may or may not be in the object itself). As the emotion grows and the movements get bigger, take care not to start movements centred on your wrist or elbow. The object should look like it is moving wildly, driven by its emotion, not like it is being wildly waved about by an emotional puppeteer.

Maintain the focus of your object Moving and shaking the head of the puppet can break its focus. As the breathing or movement becomes bigger, it can be difficult to maintain the focus and to be aware at all times of where the puppet is looking. A character who is convulsed with emotion will find it hard to control what they are looking at. Make the object look around at specific things between convulsions of laughter, in the suspensions of the breath.

Things to Notice

You need to make the breathing sounds You move the object with your hand, and do its breathing with your mouth. If they match up well, the audience puts the two together and believes that the object is breathing, experiencing the emotions, laughing, crying, screaming, grunting, whining…whatever.

Emotion is always building up or fading away Feelings generate movements, which create new feelings, which create new movements. Thoughtfulness becomes sadness, which becomes depression, which becomes crying, which becomes rage. Contentment becomes happiness, which becomes elation, which becomes laughter, which become painful, hysterical contortions. A mild feeling of discomfort becomes anxiety, which becomes agitation, which becomes nausea, which becomes vomiting. Fear begins as butterflies in the stomach, which develops into shaking legs or hands, which becomes jumpiness, which becomes heavy breathing, which becomes extreme anxiety, which becomes screaming, panic and, finally, running away.

Many movements are common to different emotions The puppet might point when it is laughing, or angry, or accusatory, or just out of interest. It may stamp when it is laughing, or angry, or has cold feet. It may laugh because it is happy, or to be polite; equally, it may laugh sometimes because it is afraid. All these movements are the same in general terms, but what differentiates them is how they do the movement, and how they do the movement is determined by how they are breathing.

CHANGING EMOTIONS

Feelings may last for a long time – for days or even weeks – but the outward appearance of them can change very quickly. They may also vanish in a moment, and return just as quickly. In this exercise you practise changing emotions quickly.

The Exercise

Everyone takes an object and practises alone at first. Afterwards, you can set up an audience and a stage, then show each other and give and receive feedback on how it has worked.

STEP 1: Take an item and bring it to life.
STEP 2: Make the item (the puppet) look at something – say, a spot on the table – and imagine that that thing is what is making it feel the emotion it is feeling. Keep looking at the object and then build the emotion.
STEP 3: Make the puppet begin to breathe in an emotion and build it up with the breath.
STEP 4: Then, make the puppet look up at something else – say, the window – and stop the emotion in its tracks with an in-breath. Express a different emotion.
STEP 5: Next, look back at the spot and make it pick up the first emotion where it left off.
STEP 6: Go back and forth between the two objects, expressing a different emotion when it looks at each one.

Things to Notice

Emotions change in two ways Sometimes, they wear themselves out, as in the first puppeting emotion exercise: after a puppet cries itself to exhaustion, it starts laughing; after shouting and shouting with anger, it sits down, worn out, and becomes depressed; after running away from something in fear, when it is safe, it starts laughing with relief. The emotion runs its course, becomes exhausted and changes into something else. Think of it as climbing up and then going over an emotional 'hill'.
Emotions can change abruptly They may be interrupted by a new event, as in this exercise; perhaps something happens to resolve a problem, or the puppet is just distracted for a moment. For example, if a puppet has been worrying about the outcome of a test, and then it receives the result, the worry will suddenly vanish. Conversely, if the puppet has been happily doing something without a care in the world and then it slips, its mood will change suddenly from carefree happiness to alarm. Such things happen all the time and the puppet's mood and its emotions are constantly changing.

MAKING THE PUPPET THINK

The puppeteer must always be aware of making the puppet think. Every time a puppet moves, the audience reads the movement as the result of a thought it has just had. When it moves a hand, turns its head or walks across the stage, the

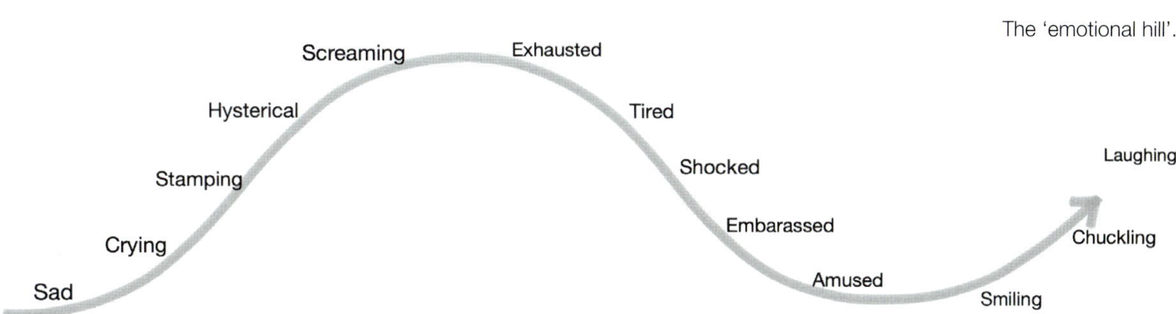

The 'emotional hill'.

audience will assume that it has done so because of something it has thought. Every movement, every word, every breath, is underscored by a series of different thoughts, which happen, one after the other, in a continuous 'inner monologue'.

Puppets, of course, do not have thoughts, so the puppeteer has to have them for them. Whenever you are asked to move the puppet – to make it look at something, to make it go somewhere, to make it say something – you have to make it *think* before it does it.

In this exercise you practise making the puppet think when you move it. You learn how to fill the puppet's movements with thought. You can use this technique when you are improvising with puppets or when you are working with a script.

The Exercise

Take an object and stand in the space. Everyone can work on their own to start with and then work with someone else watching to check what they are doing and see how it works.

STEP 1: Take an object – say, a cup – in your dominant hand. Make it move and, every time it moves, say, 'Thought!'. Make it look to the left: 'Thought!' Make it look right: 'Thought!' Make it take a step ('Thought!'), lean back ('Thought!'), move again ('Thought!'), and again ('Thought') and again ('Thought').

STEP 2: Make the object look right, left, right ('Thought', 'Thought', 'Thought'), then make it

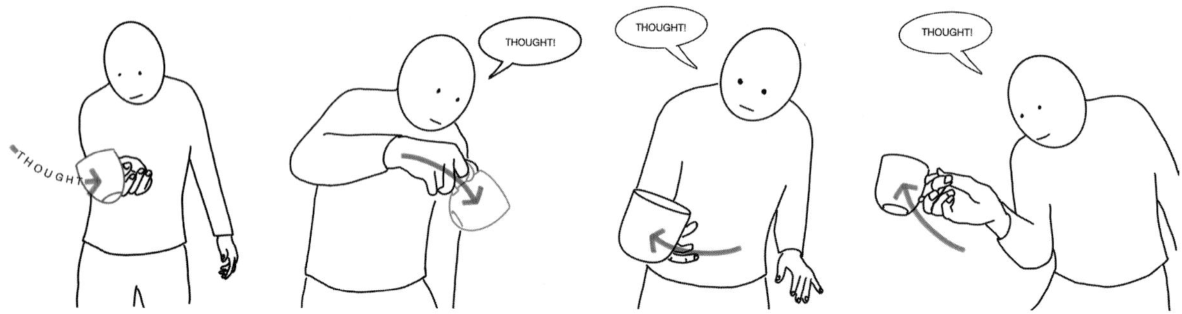

STEP 1: A short movement and a short 'Thought'.

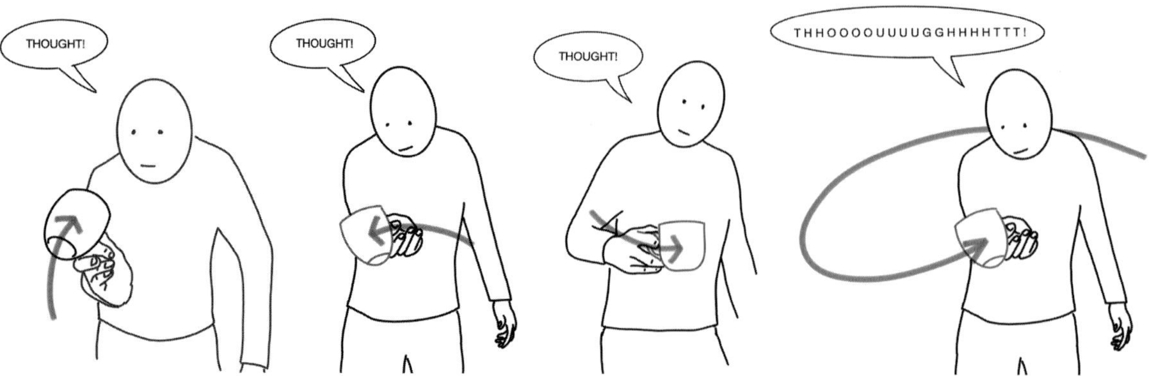

STEP 2: Make three quick movements: 'Thought', 'Thought', 'Thought', and then one long, slow movement: 'T h o o u u u u u g h h t t t'.

sweep all the way around you in a long movement: 'T h o o u u u u u g h h t t t'.
STEP 3: Try varying the movements. Make long moves, short moves, quick moves, slow moves, sharp moves, loud moves, quiet moves. Say 'Thought!' on every move.
STEP 4: Make the way you say 'Thought' match the movement: 'Thought!... Thoooouuuuught... Tho't!, Tho't!... Thhhhought!' Most importantly, every time the object moves, you say 'Thought!'.
STEP 5: Keep going until you feel really relaxed and cannot help saying 'Thought!' every time you move the object, however big or small the movement. Keep varying the way you say the word, so that you can do all the movements you want to make the object do.
STEP 6: Swap around with someone and watch them do the exercise. Look out for the times when they move without saying the word 'Thought', or when they say 'Thought' without moving, and give the appropriate feedback.

Things to Notice

The puppeteer does not need to know what the thoughts are for it to work Even without knowing what the thoughts are, simply saying the word 'Thought' every time you move the puppet changes the way you move the puppet, and begins to join the movements together through a string of related thoughts.
No movement also implies a thought Sometimes, thoughts literally stop the puppet in its tracks. They may even stop it breathing for a bit. The puppet becomes 'lost in thought'. The audience may not know what the puppet is thinking, but they will know that it is thinking something that is important enough to provoke a reaction. When the puppet breathes again, or moves again, they will assume that the moment has passed and the puppet is now thinking something else.
The 'thoughts' start to feel like a story Notice what you feel when you do it, as the 'thoughts' develop into a kind of pattern or rhythm. One 'thought!' leads to another 'thought!' and they start to join up into a kind of story.

MAKING THE PUPPET RESPOND TO CUES

Thoughts occur in reaction to 'cues', so the object needs to be seen to respond to events that happen on stage – which are understood by the audience to have happened. The audience is able to deduce what the puppet is thinking from seeing what cues it responds to and how it responds to them.

In this exercise you make the puppet respond to claps by people in the audience.

The Exercise

Set up the room with a stage area and an audience. One person goes on stage with an object (for example, a cup), and the rest of the group watches.

STEP 1: Hold your puppet – say, a cup – and bring it to life.
STEP 2: Someone in the audience claps their hands. Make your puppet turn and look towards the sound. As you make it turn, you say, 'Thought!'
STEP 3: Someone else claps and the puppet turns again instantly ('Thought!') to look towards the source of the sound.
STEP 4: Another person claps and the puppet turns again: 'Thought!'
STEP 5: The audience members carry on taking turns to clap and the puppet keeps turning to look towards the sound. Each time you make the puppet move, you say, 'Thought'.
STEP 6: Swap around with someone and watch them do it.

If the puppet gets bored and looks away from the person who clapped, say 'Thought'. If the clap makes the puppet jump, say 'THOUGHT!' If the puppet looks at it angrily, or looks away bored, you say, 'Thought!' If the puppet makes any other movement you must say 'Thought'. With every move you make the puppet do, you say 'Thought!'. Do not move the puppet again without saying 'Thought'.

Things to Notice

The audience needs to know how the puppet sensed the cue When the audience sees the puppet move, they will look for a reason – something that happened to cue the puppet's reaction. In the clapping exercise, they know that the puppet heard the clap because they heard it too. In other words, the audience needs to see the puppet sense the cue to understand what it is reacting to.

A lack of event can be a cue too When there is no clap for some time, the puppet relaxes and goes back to whatever it was thinking about before the previous clap happened. The lack of clapping for a certain amount of time makes the puppet have another thought and look away. The audience understands this because they too hear no clap. The lack of clap is a cue.

The reaction to cues develops as the event repeats Each time the clap repeats, the puppet's reaction will be slightly different as its thoughts about the clapping develop. At first it just thinks, 'What was that?', but as the clapping goes on its thoughts about it develop. It may want to find out where the clapping is coming from. Or it may be frightened by it, or irritated. It may want to run away, or make it stop. The repetition of the clapping becomes a narrative which makes the puppet react in different ways.

The puppet's reactions to the clapping, and its subsequent thoughts, will depend on who or what the puppet is. If it is a toddler, it may see the clapping as a game of hide and seek. If the puppet is a dog, the clapping may make it think that there is something to eat. If the puppet is an old soldier with PTSD, the clap may trigger an extreme reaction.

MAKING AN OBJECT BE 'PRESENT'

In this exercise, instead of using claps as cues, as you did in the last exercise, you use ambient noise and things that are visible in your surroundings. The puppet responds to those sights or sounds that are actually going on and that you think will be evident to the audience. As the puppet responds to the room and its vicinity, you start to create a story around what the puppet is doing and thinking.

Remember to make the puppet 'think' every time it responds to a cue. If you fail to do this, the puppet will stop thinking and the audience will see that.

The audience should watch and give feedback afterwards on what they have seen.

The Exercise

Set up the room with a stage area and an audience. Take turns to go up on stage with an object.

STEP 1: Stand the object in a space and bring it to life. Let it see and hear and become aware of where it is and wait for a cue from the real world to react to.

STEP 2: When the puppet hears something, or sees something – for example, a police siren passing in the distance, birdsong, someone in the room coughing or moving a foot, the radiators coming on, people starting to shout outside, a mark on the floor, anything that the audience could possibly see or hear as well – it turns to look at it. As it turns you say, 'Thought'.

STEP 3: Develop the thoughts around the cue to which the puppet has reacted. If the cue repeats, the thoughts will develop around the repetition. If the cue does not happen again, then the thoughts will develop around the mystery of where it has gone, or what it was.

The process is as follows:

- Make the puppet react to the cue: 'Thought!'
- Make it wait for it to happen again: 'Thought!'
- It does not happen again: 'Thought!'
- The puppet looks at the audience: 'Thought!'
- The puppet says to the audience, 'Did you hear that?'
- It looks back to where the sound first came from: 'Thought!'
- And so on.

STEP 4: Let the story become emotional. Let the cues grow in importance. See where it takes you.
STEP 5: Now, instead of saying 'Thought!' aloud, start saying it silently in your head and continue the exercise. See if the audience still 'sees' the thoughts.
STEP 6: Ask the audience to give feedback on what they saw your puppet responding to, and what they saw it think.
STEP 7: Swap around and give someone else a go.

Things to Notice

Thoughts are what the audience see No one can know for sure what the puppet's thoughts are, and the puppet cannot actually tell you. The audience guesses what it is thinking from what they see it do, and you have to guess what the audience is guessing. Watch the puppet when you are doing it, or when someone else is doing it, and ask yourself what it is thinking.

Talking is thinking out loud When the puppet speaks, it is saying what it is thinking. Speaking is thought made audible. That is not to say that it says everything it thinks, or that it means everything it says, but when it is in the act of speaking it is not thinking something else. When the puppet speaks to the audience, they hear its thoughts out loud. When it does not speak, the thoughts continue unheard, and the audience has to deduce them from what the puppet does.

The puppeteer needs to find the right cues When you are given a puppetry direction you will be told what to make the puppet do, but not what it thinks. You need to work out the thoughts that underlie the movements and the cues that trigger them. Look for cues that happen in the play, that the audience can be aware of, and make the puppet move in reaction to them: 'Thought!'

MAKING TWO OBJECTS WORK TOGETHER

In this exercise, two objects are used together to provide a head and a body, and are moved as if they are connected by a joint.

The technique of holding two objects, one in each hand, is the basic building block of puppetry.

Pantalaimon from *His Dark Materials* – a two-handed puppet.

The movement of one object in relation to another, connected by a 'joint', gives an immensely subtle range of expression, body language, movement and performance in the puppet.

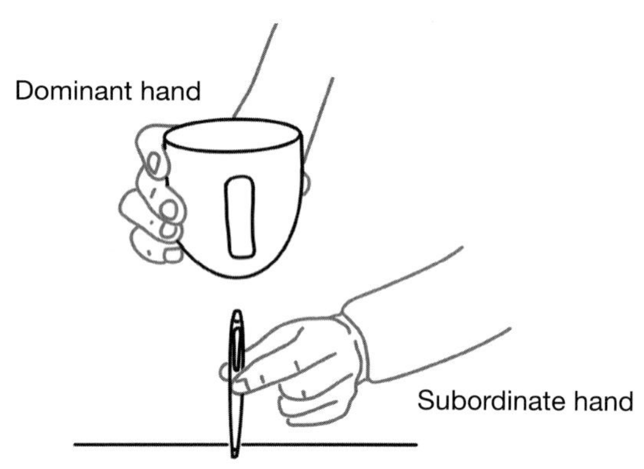

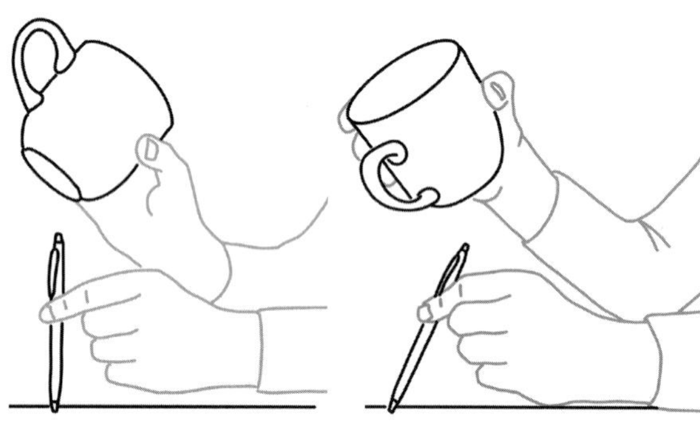

STEP 2: Make the puppet look up.

STEP 2: The puppet pulls back and looks down.

STEP 2: The puppet leans to the left.

STEP 2: The puppet leans to the right.

The Exercise

Begin with everyone working alone and then set up an audience and stage area to share and give feedback.

STEP 1: Take two objects – for example, a cup and a pen – and hold them one above the other to make a two-part puppet. The upper object is the head and the lower object is the body. Joining them is an imaginary neck joint.

Hold the 'head' with your dominant hand and the 'body' with your subordinate hand. Hold the objects with as small a grip as is comfortable and in control, and from behind so that the audience can clearly see both parts.

STEP 2: Stand the puppet on a table top, keep the lower object still and move the upper object, to look around the room. Make it look down at the table and up at the ceiling, and make it lean from side to side. Try lowering the chin and jutting it out, stretching the neck a bit into different positions. How far can you make it go without compromising the illusion of there being a joint there?

STEP 3: Now hold the top object still and move the bottom half of the puppet by 'hingeing' at the neck. It could be a leg stretching out, or an arm pointing.

STEP 4: Make the puppet 'walk': move the feet out from the neck, land, and then pull the head after. You may need to lower the head a bit with each 'step', to keep the neck intact.

STEP 5: Next, keep the top of the head and the feet still, and move the neck joint around. Moving the neck changes the puppet's posture.

STEP 3: The feet swing out to the side while the head stays still.

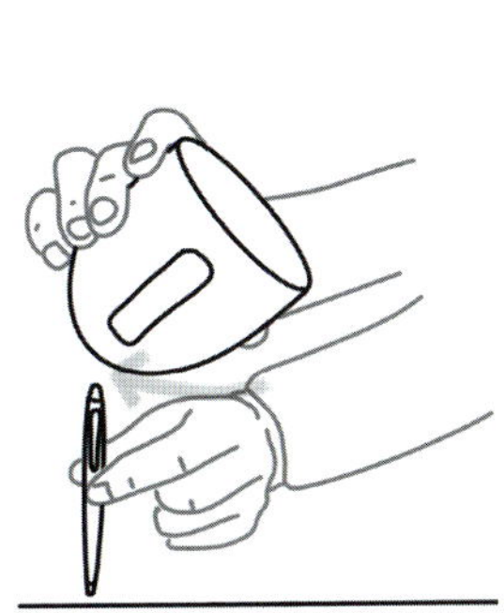

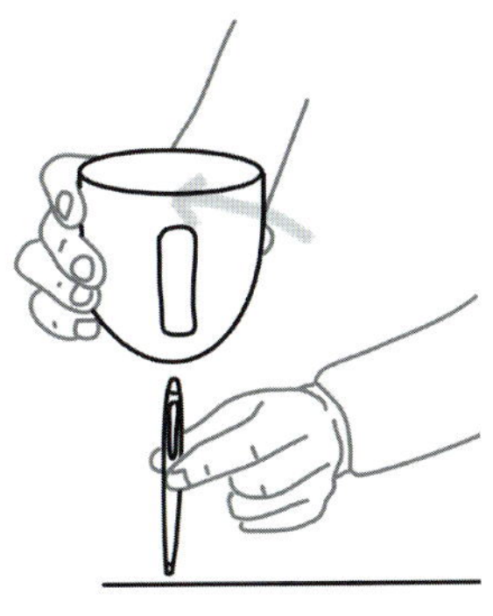

STEP 4: The feet take a step to the side (far left)...

... the body moves upright over the feet pulling the bottom of the head with it (middle left)...

... and the head straightens up on the neck (left).

STEP 6: The puppet bows (below left) and the puppet curtsies (below right).

STEP 6: Now make the puppet bow, curtsey, stare angrily, look taken aback. Try other postures and movements. Make the puppet run, jump, walk like a model, waddle like a duck. Make it sit and crawl and kneel.

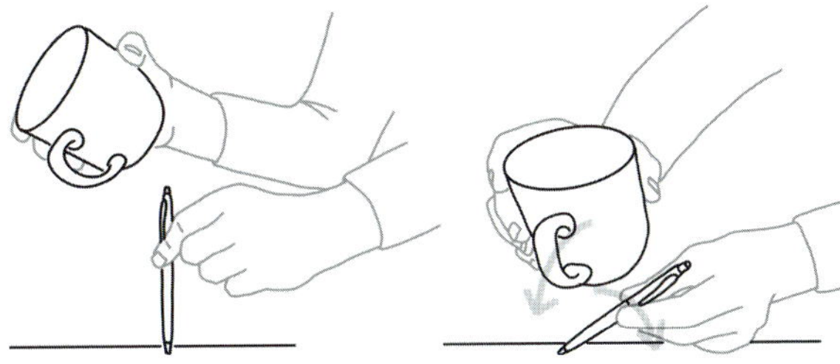

Things to Notice

The joint is best with a little 'air' You do not need to make the two objects touch one another; in fact, it works better with a small gap between them. The audience fills in the neck joint with their imagination and a more expressive range of movement is available. You can stretch the joint to reflect the size of the movement or emotion.

A neck joint is actually two joints It has one joint at the bottom with the body and one at the top with the head. This gives four fixed points around which each part of the puppet can move: what the eyes are looking at, the top of the neck, the bottom of the neck and the feet. This gives the puppet a huge range of movement, posture and expression, although it is made of only two parts.

The neck elongates in surprise.

The puppet peers forwards.

What the audience sees.

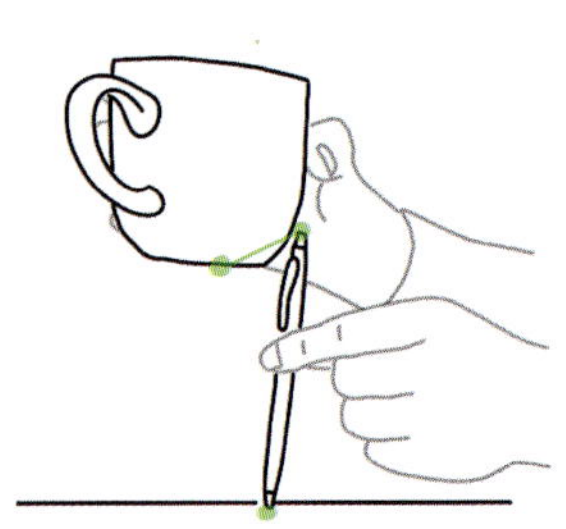

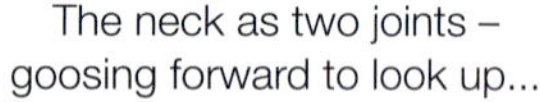

The neck as two joints – goosing forward to look up...

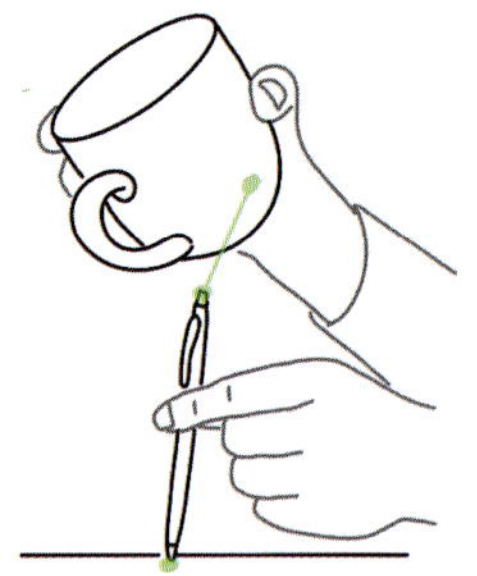

...and pulling back to look down.

The puppet's centre is in the lower object The eyes of the puppet are in the top object (the head) and the centre of the puppet is in the lower object (the body). This means that when you make a movement with one part of the body, the other part of the body has to move to balance that movement so that the puppet does not fall over.

You can lead with different parts of the puppet – the head or the feet or the body For example, the puppet can lead with the head, moving around the visual fixed point, when it is engrossed in looking at something; it can lead with the feet when it is travelling, or from the centre when it jumps.

Other Two-Part Puppets

A puppet made with two objects need not only be a head and a body. It could comprise any number of body parts, connected by any number of joints or other imaginary parts. In this exercise, you try different kinds of two-object puppets, connected by different kinds of 'joints':

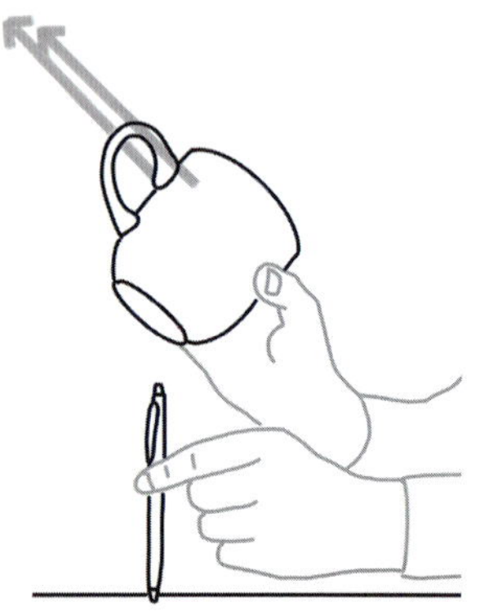

Leading with the eyes – looking at something in the air...

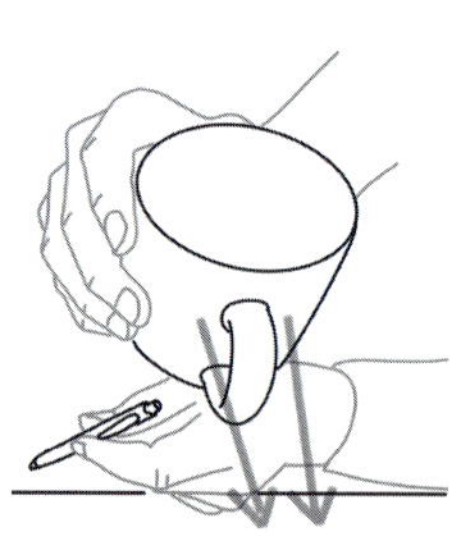

... and looking at a spot on the ground.

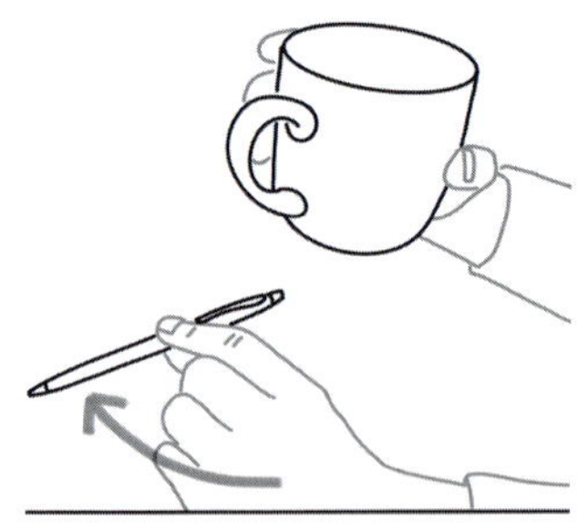

Leading with the feet.

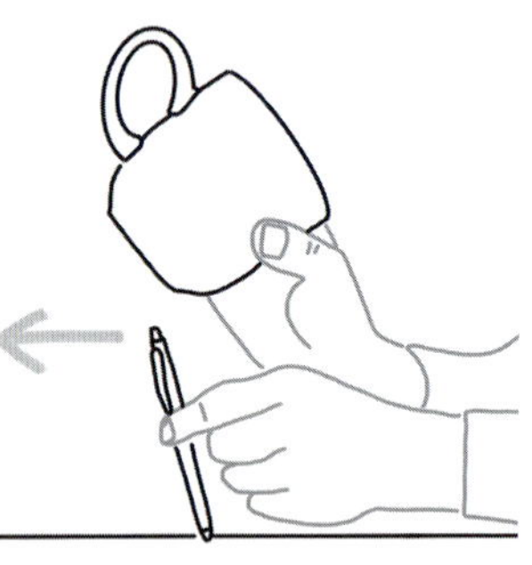

Leading with the chest.

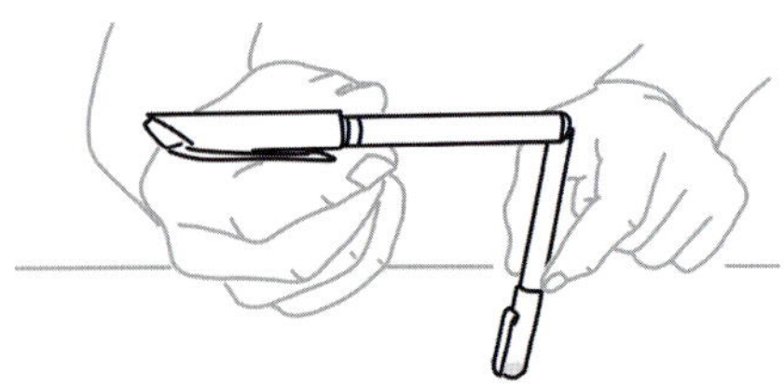

An arm coming out of the table.

- An arm: take two pens and make an arm, with an elbow joint between them. An elbow joint is a hinge that does not extend beyond 180 degrees. Make the dismembered arm pull itself around the table top by the hand. Fix the shoulder at one point as if it is being pushed through a hole in the table by someone below.
- A head and hand: take an object to be a head (for example, a cup), and use your own hand to be the puppet's hand. Visualize the many invisible joints connecting them: wrist, elbow,

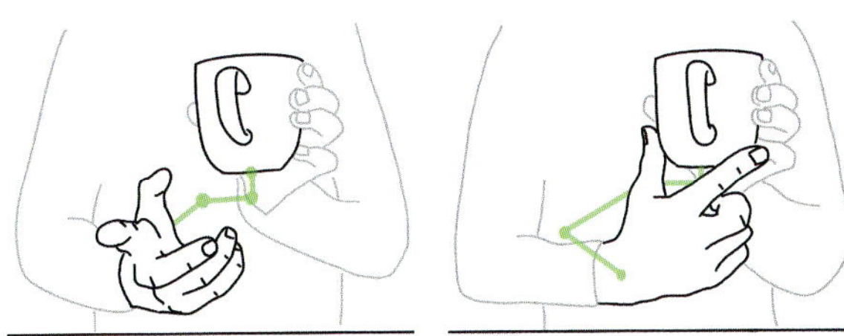

A head and hand puppet - imagine the joints that connect the head and the hand.

shoulder, neck. The audience fills in the rest of the puppet in the space left in between. Remember to move one part and then the other so that you always keep two fixed points, and move the third on them.

- Feet: take two identical objects to be feet. Hold them flat on the table next to each other and picture the invisible legs standing above them, connecting them, and the body above that. Make them shuffle about, then walk on the spot, run and jump. Make them nervous, excited, sad, tired. You could make a whole show out of just two feet.
- A dog or horse: make the head and back of a four-legged animal, and imagine invisible legs supporting the back and carrying it around. At the other end of the animal's back there will be a tail.

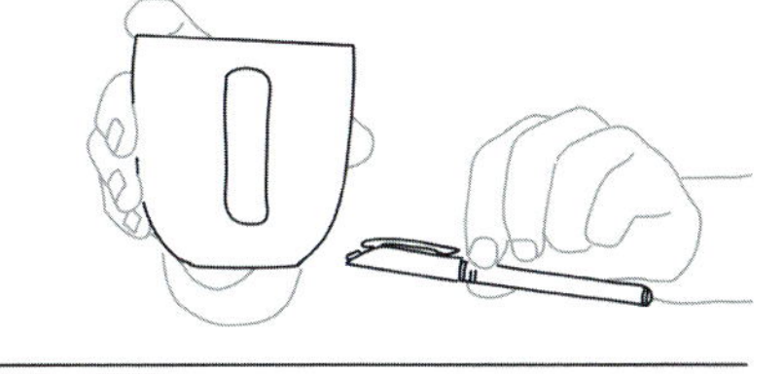

A dog made from two parts.

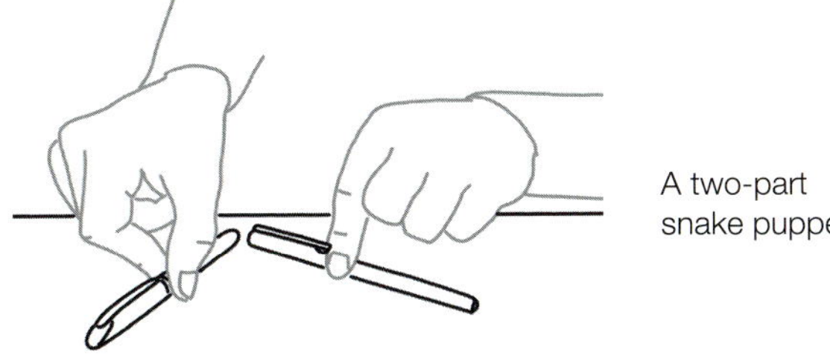

A two-part snake puppet.

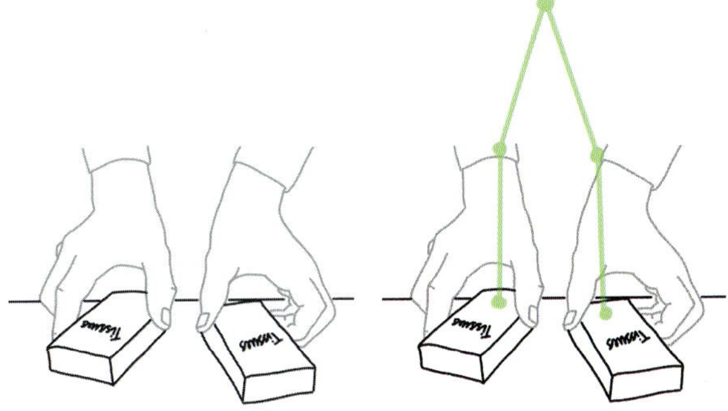

Two tissue packets used to make feet.

Imagine the joints that connect the two feet.

- A snake or fish: join the two objects to make one of these. The 'neck joint' becomes a spine joint, and the objects move around the creature's centre.

MAKING A REAL JOINT

It is not necessary to have a physical join between the objects for the audience to see a joint. However, it is possible to make a real joint, to give you a little more control over the objects. The downside is that it costs you some freedom of movement.

A 'real' joint changes the two objects when it connects them together. Once the joint is made, the two objects no longer function as individual items. They have 'crossed over' to become parts of a puppet.

Connect two pens together with tape to make an actual joint and try a few of the exercises. Consider the advantages and disadvantages compared with implying a joint simply by movement. Join three pens together and try some things, then try with four or five. At what point do you lose control of the puppet with only two hands?

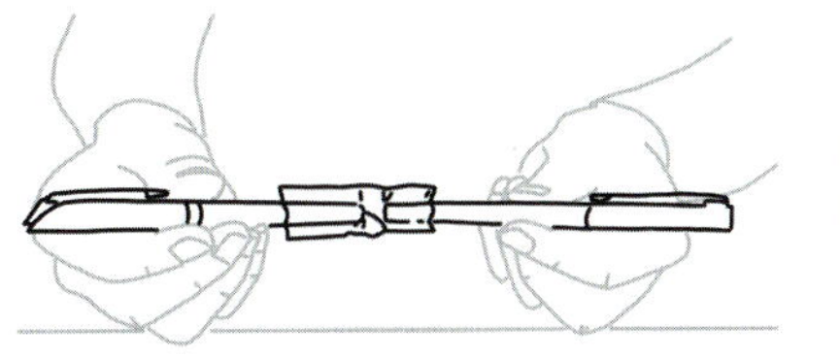

Make a real joint with tape.

2
WORKING WITH RODS, STRINGS AND MECHANISMS

Mechanisms extend the reach of the puppeteer's hands, allowing you to hold the puppet further away from you. They also enable you to control more parts and to control a much bigger or a much smaller puppet.

Direct control is the best way to produce life-like movement, but mechanisms are useful because they allow the puppeteer to hide. The best mechanisms work in tandem with direct control, so that the audience is not able to see where the puppeteer's direct movements end and the mechanism-driven movements begin.

There are basically four types of mechanism used in puppetry: strings, rods, shadows and costume (gloves, and so on).

STRINGS

Strings can be used only to exert a pull on a part of a puppet, so, in order to be effective, they need to be opposed. This is done by gravity, by elastic or by another string. Being almost invisible, string mechanisms can make parts of the puppet appear to move on their own. Strings can be especially successful when used in combination with rods.

String marionettes, operated entirely by strings from above, epitomise puppetry but they are very difficult to control because the only other tool is gravity. Because the strings are more or less invisible, they can be placed in real scenes, but the difficulty of controlling them means that they are always a bit wobbly and not at all suitable for fast, strong movements. Clearly, there are certain advantages and limitations to the use of strings.

OPPOSITE: Death and Rossignol in *Le Rossignol* (Blind Summit).

Advantages

- Strings are very thin. This means that when string puppets pass in front of scenery it is very easy for the audience to erase them from the image. In film and television, they are often used to create special effects. Fishing wire can be made to disappear with lighting or be taken out in post-production.
- Strings are strong and quiet and can pull round corners. They can be threaded over pulleys and through channels to get into complicated corners of a puppet mechanism. Unlike wire, they run quietly and, when attached tightly, they create a very direct control mechanism.
- String marionettes epitomise puppetry. The term 'puppet' generally tends to evoke an image of a string puppet. Commonly used expressions such as 'pulling someone's strings', 'cutting their strings' and 'keeping them dangling' all refer to string puppetry. The image of the string puppet is the metaphor of puppetry.

Limitations

- Strings need to be opposed. Because string can only pull, it needs to be countered by gravity, elastic, a spring or another string to pull it back again. Elastic and springs can tire and break. String puppets are limited by the fact that every movement must be translated into a string pulling up against gravity.

- Marionettes can be 'wobbly'. The long strings to the puppets mean that every move starts a pendulum movement in the limb or puppet. As a result, it is hard to make them do quick, clean movements – they tend to work better with simple, slow, intricate gestures.
- Strings can get stuck, stretch and break. Strings often suffer from friction, which leads to fraying and snapping. They also get jammed in moving parts. Over time, string stretches, leading to loose mechanisms that need to be regularly tightened up.

Examples of Strings in Puppetry Mechanisms

'Citizen Puppet' Mouth Mechanisms

In this mechanism, a string pulls the mouth open and a piece of elastic pulls it shut again. This means that the puppeteer pulls the string to open the mouth, and when they relax the mouth shuts. When they do nothing the mouth is closed. The elastic that pulls it closed directly opposes the string to give the puppeteer the maximum 'feel' for the action. And the mechanism is very 'light' to stop the mouth shutting with a snap.

Fishing Wire Mouth Mechanism for Film

In a film, a fishing wire can be used from the bottom of the mouth, running on the outside of the puppet, to be operated by a hand out of frame. Elastic pulls the mouth closed. The fishing wire can be removed for the non-talking scenes.

Wing Mechanisms

The important thing when making wings is that the action of the puppeteer copies the function of the wing. The wing lifts the bird into the air when it beats downwards: the downbeat of the wing does the work, and the upbeat occurs in relaxation. The best wing mechanisms mimic this, pulling the wings down when the puppeteer pulls, with an elastic mechanism to pull them back up when the puppeteer relaxes.

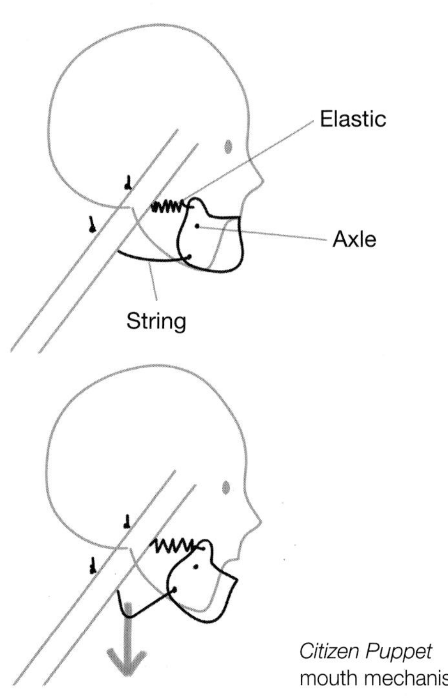

Citizen Puppet mouth mechanism.

The wings are pulled up by elastic in the relaxed position.

The puppeteer pulls the wings down, mimicking the work of the bird flapping them.

Bunraku Hand

In this set-up, two strings, one to the back of the hand and one to the front, run down the arm to a lever mechanism near the elbow of the puppet. When the puppeteer pulls one way, the hand bunches into a fist, and when they pull the other way, the fingers extend to make a flat hand. When the movement in the fingers created by the mechanism is combined with the movement of the arm instigated by the puppeteer, the hands flow through the air in a beautiful dance.

Dog's Paw Mechanism

This is a passive string mechanism. A string in the dog's front leg makes the foot drop in a 'beg' when the paw is lifted; when the leg straightens, the paw extends. The action occurs automatically when the ankle of the dog's front leg is flexed to lift the foot off the ground. The mechanism is very effective in capturing the way that dogs lift their front paws.

Otome Bunraku Head String Mechanism

An Otome Bunraku puppet is designed to be operated by one puppeteer. It is attached to the puppeteer by a hook on their belt, and its arms are operated by the puppeteer's hands. The puppet's

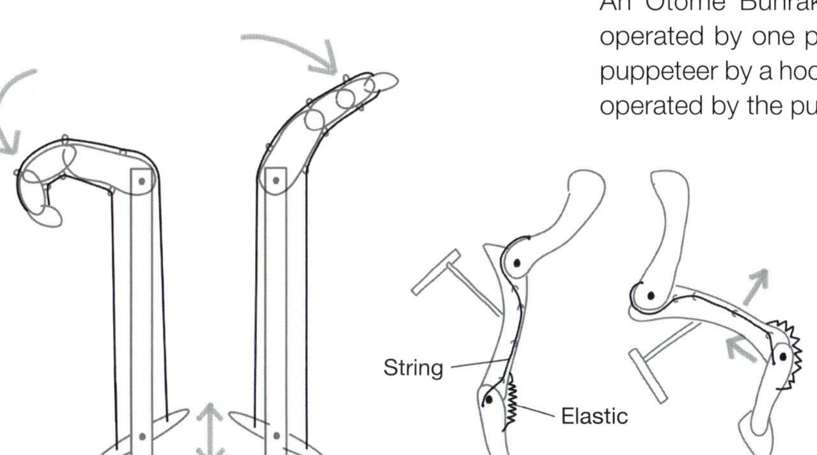

FAR LEFT: Bunraku hand mechanism.

LEFT: Dog's paw mechanism – the string makes the paw 'beg' when the leg is lifted.

BELOW LEFT: Sharik from *A Dog's Heart*.

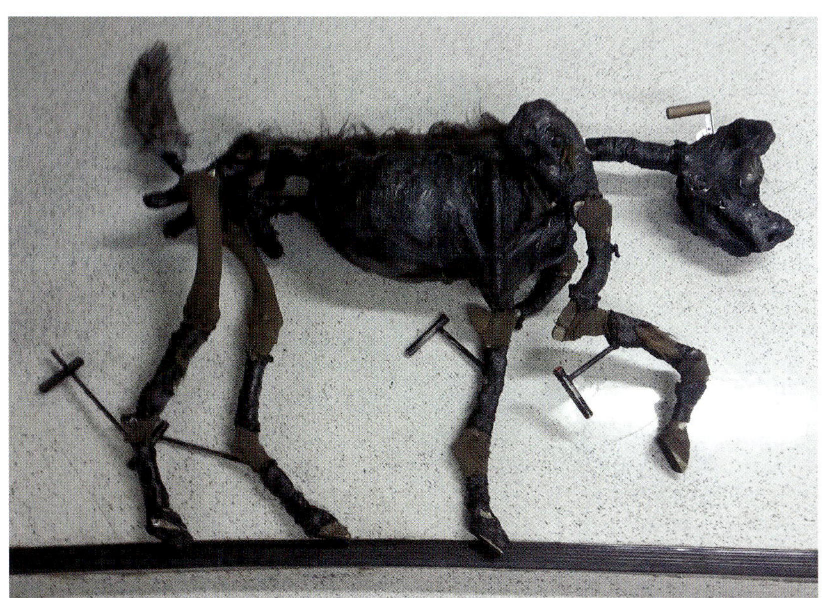

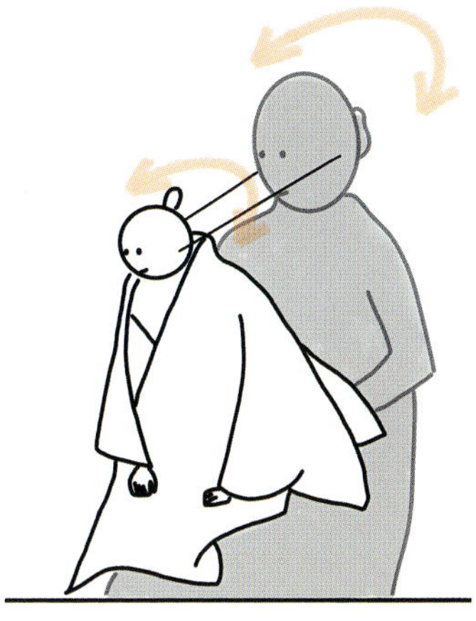

Otome Bunraku mechanism, with strings that make the puppet's head turn left and right in connection with the puppeteer's head.

head is controlled with strings that run from the sides of the puppet's head to the sides of the puppeteer's head. These are attached to a bun in the puppeteer's hair, so that when the puppeteer turns their head it makes the puppet turn theirs. The puppet's head movements mirror the head movements of the puppeteer. The effect is a puppet that is operated by just one person but has an ingenious and wide range of movement.

Ventriloquist Dummy Head Mechanisms

The head handles of Bunraku puppets or ventriloquist dummies have a variety of mechanisms to tilt the head up and down, make the eyes look left and right, raise the eyebrows, and change the expression of the mouth, along with a variety of other tricks. They are controlled by strings running from levers in the head handle up into the head, where they are opposed by springs.

Traditional String Marionettes

The most sophisticated form of string puppet operation is the string marionette. All of its movements are controlled by near-invisible strings from a cradle above it and its companions, who walk around on a stage below the puppeteers. The effect is magical because the puppets can live in a fully realized world, with a stage floor and scenery behind. However, their movement is limited because the parts can be moved in only two directions: up and down against gravity. Examples include the Salzburg Marionette Theatre and *Thunderbirds* on television.

Rod and String Marionette

In the Czech style variation of the marionette, the main string to the head is replaced with a wire so that the puppeteer has more control over the movement of the head. Strings to the arms and knees control the limbs.

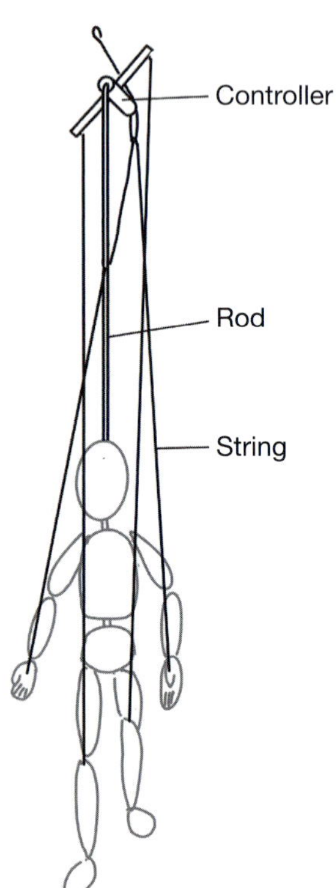

The Czech-style marionette is controlled by a rod to the head and strings to the limbs.

This Hoopoe puppet borrows from the Czech-style marionette: rods are used to move the bird around and strings to make the head turn and the wings flap.

Giant String Puppets

Giant string puppets suspended from cranes or overhead wire systems make a spectacular impression walking down a street or in a stadium. Their movement is limited but the metaphorical impact can be fantastic and emotionally overwhelming. Examples include the creations of Royal de Lux based in Nantes and Voldemort in the Opening Ceremony of the London 2012 Olympics.

A giant string puppet suspended on a travelling crane. Puppeteers control the limbs with ropes and pulleys.

Rod puppets He Liyi and Qiyan from *Mr China's Son* (Blind Summit).

RODS

Rod mechanisms on puppets give most control. They are essentially handles of different lengths that enable the puppeteer(s) to push, pull, turn and twist the puppet. The catch is that the puppeteers usually have to stand quite close behind the puppet, where they are visible in the background to the audience. The further away the puppeteer goes from the puppet, the less control they have.

Advantages

- Very accurate reproduction of movement: the 'direct' control of a rod, or indeed actually holding the puppet directly, makes it possible to have very good control over each part of the puppet. A well-made rod puppet, with the right number of puppeteers, can recreate the most realistic and beautiful movement of any puppets.
- Suitability for interaction with humans: because rod puppets are able to stand on the floor, in the same space as people, they are well suited to stage productions in which they are required to interact with actors, singers or dancers. In recent years they have become the puppet of choice in Western theatre, especially to portray non-speaking roles, such as animals and children.
- Scale: a rod puppet can be as big as the puppeteer can lift, or as small as the audience can see.

Limitations

- Number of puppeteers per puppet: although some rod puppets are made to be operated by one person, on the whole they need several puppeteers to realize the fine movements and realism of which they are capable. On top of this, the puppeteers need time to learn how the puppets work, and to train and rehearse together. Bunraku shows often have as many as 30 puppeteers. (The term 'dead arm problem'

The 'dead arm problem' demonstrated by Moses in *The Table* (Blind Summit).

derives from a situation in which a show is one puppeteer short on a three-person rod puppet, which results in one, un-puppeted arm that hangs loose and appears to be lifeless.)

- The puppeteers are visible to the audience: for most rod puppetry, the puppeteers need to be close to the puppet, often working right behind it, where they are visible to the audience. It can be very beautiful to watch, but needs to be set up by the show for audiences to accept it.

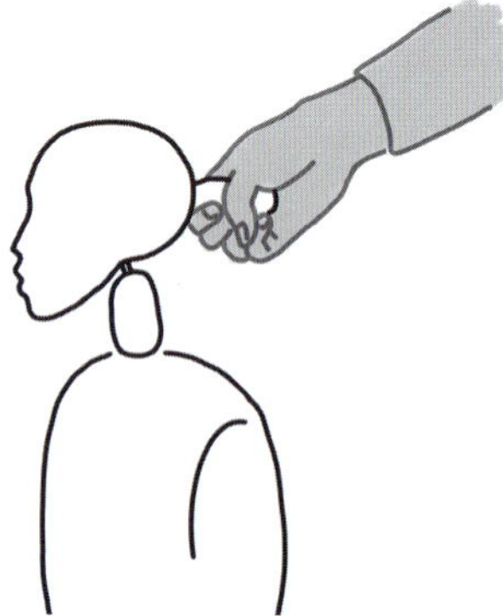

RIGHT: Direct hold head handle.

BELOW: A direct hold head handle on the head of the Sorrow puppet from *Madam Butterfly* (Blind Summit).

Examples of Rods in Puppetry Mechanisms

Head Handle – Direct to the Head

A handle on the back of the head allows the puppeteer to control the head without holding the head of the puppet directly. The head moves independently from the body of the puppet, and two more puppeteers operate the back, arms and legs.

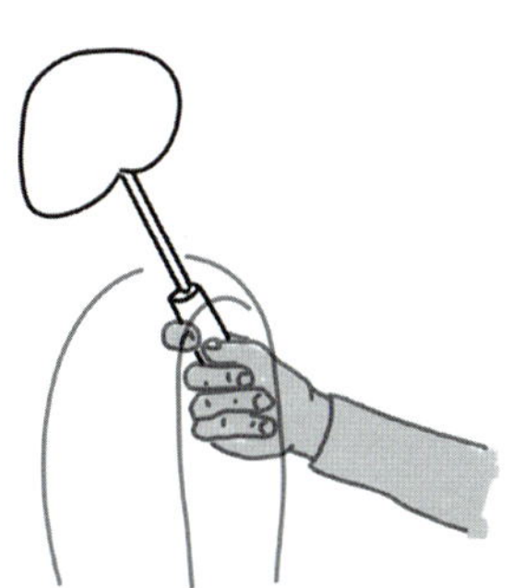

ABOVE: Head handle through the back. Bunraku-style puppet.

RIGHT: Head handle in the body. Indonesian rod puppet.

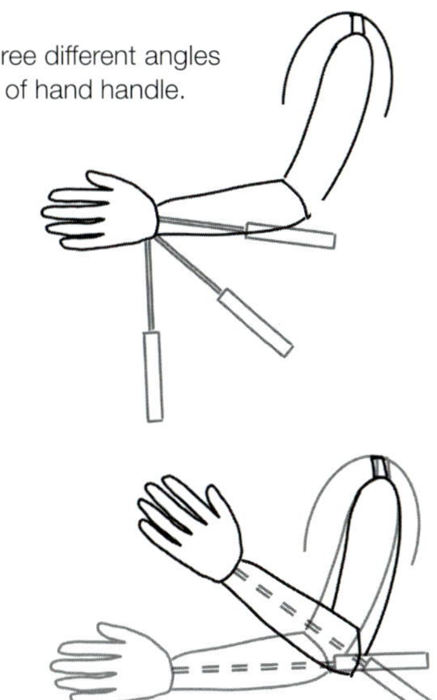

Three different angles of hand handle.

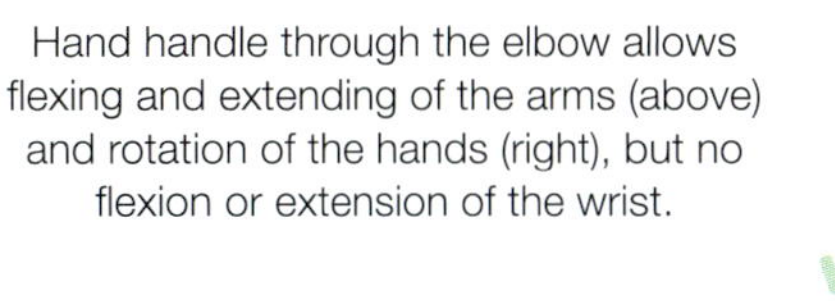

Hand handle through the elbow allows flexing and extending of the arms (above) and rotation of the hands (right), but no flexion or extension of the wrist.

Head Handle – Through the Back

A rod through the shoulders, in the style of the Bunraku puppet or the ventriloquist dummy, acts as a neck and allows the puppeteer to control the head from inside the back. This set-up gives the head puppeteer a lot of control over the body of the puppet, so that it is not necessary to have another puppeteer to do that. Mechanisms in the handle use strings to make the head tilt, move the eyes and mouth, and create other special effects. Visually, although the puppeteer is still behind the puppet, the fact that their hand does not touch the head directly means that it seems to move on its own.

Head Handle – From Below

The typical Indonesian-style rod puppet has a head rod that runs up through its shoulders from inside the puppet's body, and two rods to the arms. It is typically operated by one puppeteer, who holds the head rod in one hand and the two arm rods in the other hand. The puppeteer can make the head turn and the arms perform gestures from out of sight below the puppet.

Arm Rods – Direct to the Hands

What you can do with rods attached directly to the hands very much depends on the angle at which they are attached. Rods attached at 90 degrees to the arm allow you to operate them directly from below, out of sight. Examples include the Muppets' arms or the Indonesian rod puppets (*see* above). You can do the two arms with one hand, or have a second puppeteer control them separately.
Rods attached at a 45-degree angle allow you to operate from behind the puppet. You will need two puppeteers to do both arms.

Arm Rods – Through the Elbows

Rods that run through the elbows allow the puppeteer to control the whole lower arm and make the hand rotate at the wrist. You can also add a simple mechanism to make the hand flex and extend, resulting in a full range of hand movement (like the Bunraku hand mechanism). The effect can be quite magical, although the range of movement is restricted by the extent to which you can reach with your hand to operate it.

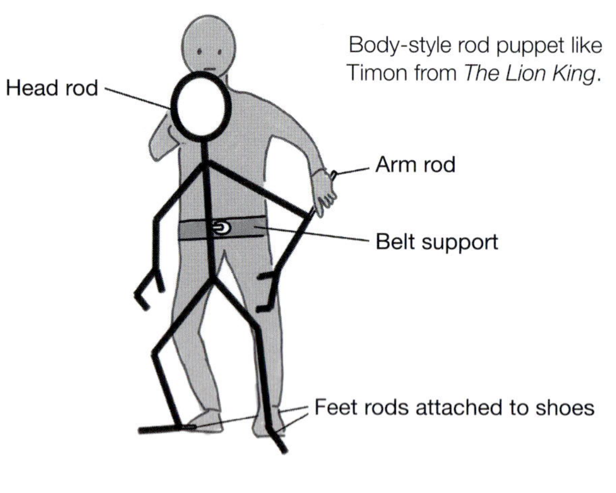

Body-style rod puppet like Timon from *The Lion King*.

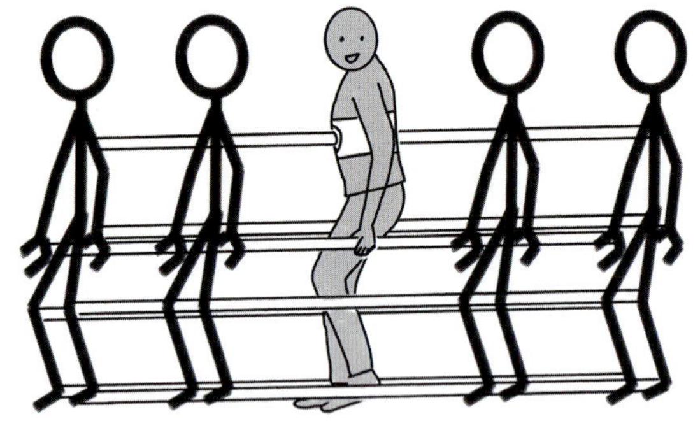

Multiple body puppets all move together.

Rods Attached to the Puppeteer's Feet

The feet of the puppet can be attached to the puppeteer's shoes so that they mirror whatever the puppeteer does with their feet. The walk is slightly flat-footed, but it gives working feet without the need for more than one puppeteer. Several life-sized puppets may be attached together, using rods to hands and feet, in front and behind, to make a line of people who move together.

Leg Rods

A handle on the back of the puppet's calves, with a mechanism to flex and extend the ankle, means that the puppeteer does not have to reach all the way to the ground and the feet move free from hands. But the legs cannot bend completely into a kneel because the handles will be in the way.

Foot Rods

Rods attached directly to the feet of the puppet allow the puppeteer to control them directly, and increase the range that the puppeteer can reach with their arms. The challenge with feet rods is finding the angle that works for your puppet: a handle in line with the sole of the foot will be flat

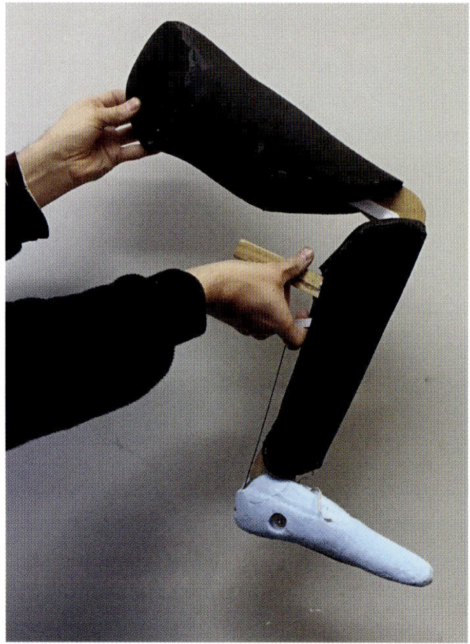

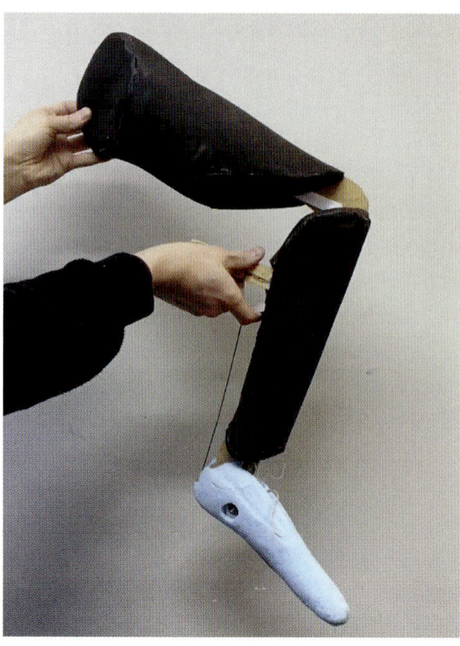

A mechanism in the calf makes the foot flex and extend.

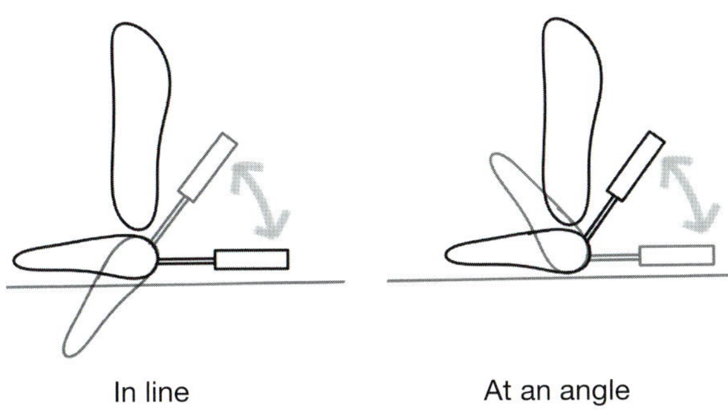

A direct handle on the foot is restricted by contact with the floor.

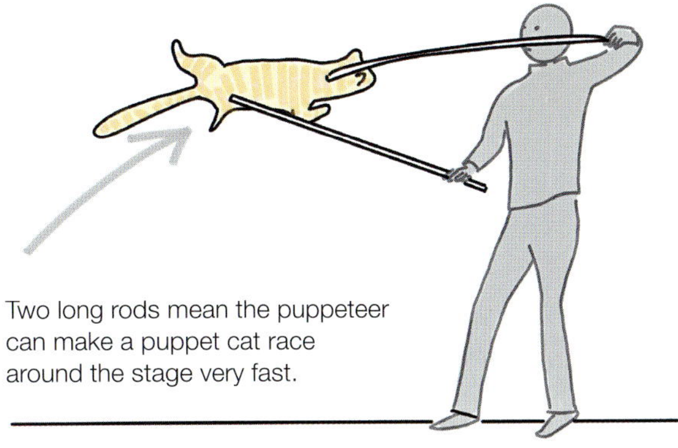

Two long rods mean the puppeteer can make a puppet cat race around the stage very fast.

on the floor and not allow any more flexion, and a handle that is at an angle to the floor will limit the range of foot extension.

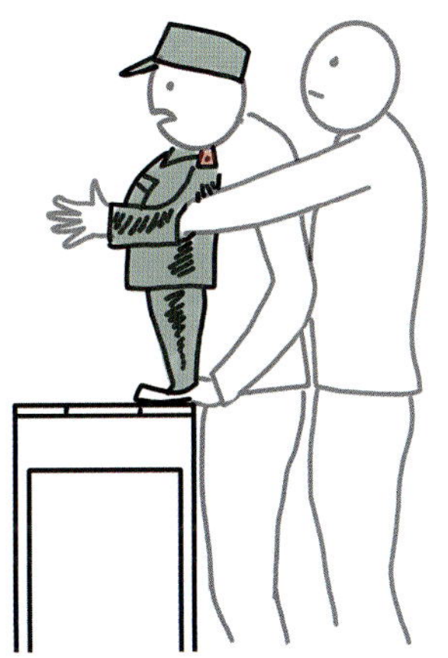

LEFT: A humanette puppet with two puppeteers. The front puppeteer does the head and feet, and the back puppeteer the hands.

BELOW: A humanette puppet with one puppeteer.

Long Rods

Long rods are excellent for puppeting flying birds, a rat or a cat running round a room, or any puppet that needs to move fast through the air, but under control. The rods allow the puppeteer to throw the puppet quickly across the stage from point to point.

Different Types of Rod Puppets

Rod Marionettes

Traditional 'Czech-style' puppets have a rod to the middle of the head and strings to the arms and legs. The rod gives the puppeteer direct control to the head for moving the puppet around. It cannot be made to look up or down, however, without bringing the cradle into view. There is also a Sicilian tradition of rod and string marionettes.

Humanette Puppets

A humanette puppet has a body that hangs around the neck of the puppeteer and stands on a table to make a miniature person with the puppeteer's head. The puppeteer controls the legs from behind. A second puppeteer standing behind them can control the arms or even use their own hands to be the puppet's hands.

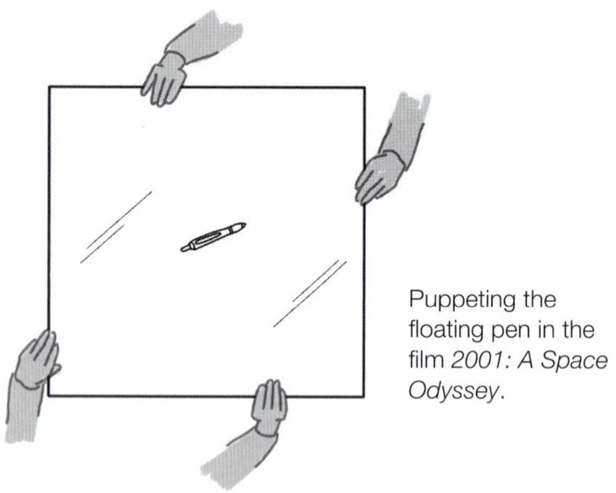

Puppeting the floating pen in the film *2001: A Space Odyssey*.

Gigantic Pageantry Puppets

Giant puppets held above the puppeteers' heads and controlled by rods are part of traditional carnivals and religious parades. The puppet company Bread and Puppet make gigantic cardboard totem-like puppets, with arms made of cloth operated by hundreds of people to surround a whole field. usually with a political theme.

Using a Pane of Glass

In the film *2001: A Space Odyssey*, a pen was made to look like it was floating in the foreground of a scene by attaching it to a large sheet of glass, which was puppeted by puppeteers just off camera.

SHADOWS

Shadow puppets are cool, cinematic and mysterious. Suspended on beams of light, they appear and disappear at the flick of a switch, change scale rapidly or transform from one thing into another magically in front of the eyes of the audience. They are beautiful, magical and steeped in tradition. Maybe making shadows around a fire was one of the very first forms of theatrical storytelling. Their charm is their apparent simplicity, but they are in fact very technical, and can involve complicated stage set-ups.

Advantages

- Sharp, clean images: a shadow puppet does not have to look good in real life because the light will 'clean it up'. It can be as simple as an old cereal packet stuck together with tape; when it is put in the light, it is only the edge – the outline – that matters. This contrast can be used to great dramatic effect.
- Scale: a shadow puppet can be as massive as the light can project. A small puppet can make a shadow as big as a building if the light is focused and strong enough.

Shadow puppets create simple, sharp images.

Shadow puppetry allows the director to play tricks with scale.

Shadows can create multiple identical images.

- Transformations and illusions, doubles and repetitions: by hiding inside each other's shadows, you can create the illusion of things disappearing into other things, magical changes of scale, objects changing shape in front of you. One puppet can break into many. A shadow puppet can fold flat and disappear, or multiply in front of your eyes. A big figure can swallow a little figure.
- The drama of monochrome: shadow puppetry has a cool black and white quality that can offer a refreshing change of pace in a live production. It is often used for transformation montages and ghostly scenes. Shadows can be a witty way to represent an operation, a murder or a birth.

Limitations

- Lack of connection with the audience: while shadow puppets have great charm, they are also quite cold and the audience only has the outline of the figure to relate to. The puppeteers are trapped behind a screen, in the dark, so it is more difficult for the audience to connect with them. Many traditional forms get around this by also having a storyteller and musicians in front of the screen.
- The puppeteer is locked into position by the light beam: light travels in a straight line and, once the light beam is in place, the puppeteer is bound by it. Anything that intrudes on the beam will be projected on to the screen. It is a challenge to get the puppets into the light, while keeping yourself out of it.
- The need for lots of puppets: shadow puppetry tells stories through a continuous parade of new images. Each image requires new puppets, so you get through puppets very quickly and you use a lot. It is vital to work out how to organize your puppets so that you can reach the right ones quickly, and to plan beforehand where you will put them down when you have finished with them.

Examples of Using Shadows

Flat Shadow Puppets Up Against a Screen

In the classic shadow puppetry set-up, there is a screen on a table with a light behind. The puppeteer brings the puppets from behind the light and puts them against the screen, where they can be manipulated using rods. The rods are visible in the shadow but are out of focus as they go backwards towards the light. Everything behind the light is unseen and the puppeteer has a lot of freedom backstage to move about and arrange their puppets.

The puppets are usually flat with articulated parts. Some shadow puppets have details cut out of the bodies of the puppets and glazing to introduce colour.

Many light sources will work for this way of doing shadows, including a torch, a candle or the sun. A frosted bulb will diffuse the light well and give it less of a 'hot spot'.

RIGHT: Classic shadow puppetry set-up with a light behind a screen. The puppets are held up against the screen with a rod and the puppeteer stands behind the light.

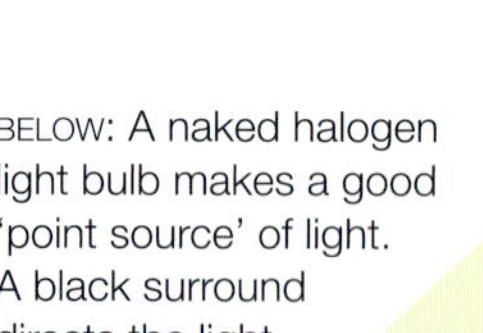

BELOW: A naked halogen light bulb makes a good 'point source' of light. A black surround directs the light.

Using a 'Point Source'

If you want to move your puppets around in the light, or use three-dimensional puppets, then you need to use a 'point source' so that they will stay in focus. A point source is a light that comes from only one point. You need the smallest bulb you can get, with no reflectors. A 12V, 50W naked halogen bulb is good. To direct the light, you can shutter it in with a black surround. (*See* Chapter 9, for more on screens and light sources.)

Performing Tricks with Scale

When you move the puppets closer to the light they get bigger, and when you move them further away they get smaller, allowing you to achieve special effects and perform tricks. As well as moving the puppet in the light, you can also move the light source to baffle the audience further about what is moving and what is still.

Shadows in Front of the Screen

Having the light source in front of the screen means that the audience can watch the puppeteer make the shadows. This can give you more opportunity to engage with the audience as a storyteller.

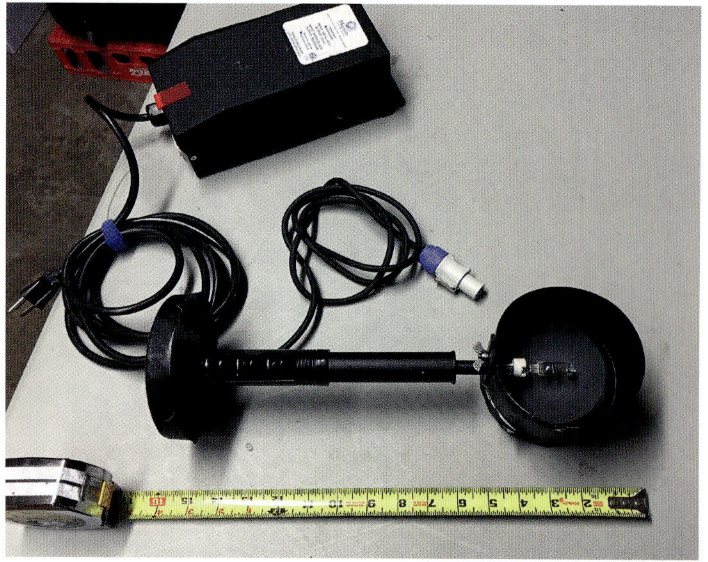

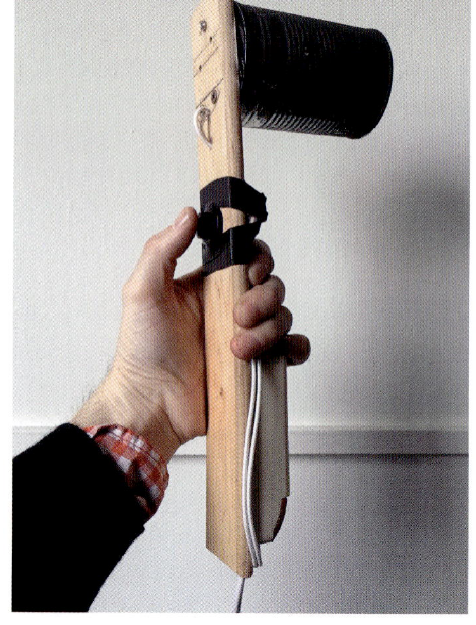

A portable point source with pressure 'On–Off' button.

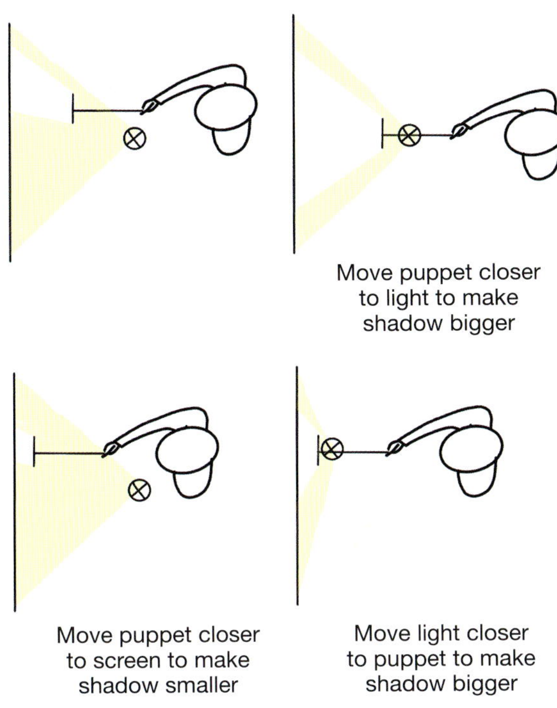

The shadow changes when the puppet and the light are moved closer or further away from the screen and each other.

Using an Overhead Projector

An overhead projector produces a focused square of light and has the huge advantage that the light source is a flat screen where you can lie puppets down. You can put down layers of shadow puppets, use scrolling images, and bring in materials such as water, sand or mud on the screen to create special effects. You can also put shadow puppets directly into the beam of the light. However, you need to be aware that the light is polarized, which gives it a slightly strange quality.

Hand Shadows

Most people will have made shadow puppets with their hands as a child. There are many ways to set this up. With a point source they will always be in focus. In a projector light or a focused theatre profile, however, they will go in and out of focus depending on where you put them in the beam.

Adapted Costumes and the Human Body

Augmenting the human outline with simple cardboard add-ons and costume allows you to make

The costume (far left)…

… and the shadow (left).

bamboozling illusions. It is thrilling to see the mixture of flat images and three dimensions working together. When a big shadow puppet turns sideways to the light, it disappears.

Using Sunlight

Sunlight is a fantastically powerful light source for shadows; because it is so far away, the beams are parallel, so the shadows it casts are always in focus. The challenges are that it moves during the day and disappears at night. And sometimes it rains!

Combining Shadows with a Camera

You can film shadow puppetry and achieve another level of control over the manipulation and viewing of the shadows. This can be combined with live projection in the theatre, or made into an edited film.

GLOVES

Glove puppets are *always* fun, *often* naughty and *sometimes* violent. A glove puppet goes over the hand, like a glove, and the puppeteer controls it with their fingers from inside. It usually appears over the top of a wall, which hides the puppeteer. The top edge of the wall, known as the 'playboard', forms the glove puppets' stage.

Glove puppets are cheap to make, easy to use, and fantastically successful. They are probably the best-known type of puppet, since they include Punch and Judy, *The Muppets*, *Spitting Image*, Chinese fighting puppets, and the Guignol tradition in France. They work very well on television and can be sufficiently sophisticated to play a major character in a movie.

Although they are probably the type of puppet that is most often seen, they may also be the least appreciated.

Advantages

- Talking to the audience: glove puppets are fundamentally naïve, with a limited range of movements. Their main power is talking, which can be very realistic. They can address the audience directly, and talk to each other, either by waggling the head to indicate who is speaking, or by using a moving mouth. They interact well with audiences, using pantomime routines such as, 'It's behind you' and 'Oh yes, I did, oh no you didn't', or addressing the audience directly like a television presenter. Glove puppets have become almost ubiquitous on television.
- Anarchic comedy: glove puppets can portray extreme emotions and perform outrageous actions. They can be rough, violent and funny. They chase and shout at each other, hit each other, bite, eat, slap, scare, cheat and steal. They are brash, funny, scatological and sentimental. Scenes often conclude with a puppet dying or exploding. They are anarchic and violent. The puppets are often made of wood, so the audience can even hear them hitting one another.

A glove puppet.

- One puppeteer can do a whole show: one of the great conveniences of the traditional glove puppet is that it can be operated with just one hand, meaning that one puppeteer can perform a whole show on their own in a series of two-hander scenes. The magic of the illusion comes from the fact that the audience knows that all the scenes are being made by the same two hands.
- Chases and fights: glove puppets are very good at chasing and fighting each other. The thrill for the observers is that the puppets really look like they are engaging in conflict, although they know full well that underneath the gloves it is just the puppeteer's two hands.
- Suitable and easy for children to use: glove puppetry is very popular with children. The simplicity of the illusion is easy to follow and it is something they can recreate at home.
- Capacity for satire: glove puppets are excellent for satire because they can be made to be talkative and even violent to an extreme degree. Even just making a glove puppet of someone brings them down a peg or two.

Limitations

- Size: glove puppets are restricted by what can be held and controlled with one hand. For this reason, they tend to be small. Puppet-makers often give them big features or make them in bright colours, to make them easier to see. A big nose helps the observer know where the puppet is looking.
- Range of movement: a glove puppet can only go where the puppeteer is able to reach with their arm. If you want a glove puppet to be on the floor, you need to make space for the puppeteer underneath and cut a hole for them to put their arm through.

One puppeteer can create operate two puppets.

Examples of Using Gloves

'Classic' Children's Glove Puppet

The classic children's glove puppet is made of cloth and goes over the puppeteer's hand like a mitten. The puppeteer uses their index finger to control the head, their thumb to do one arm, and their middle finger to do the other arm. Some puppeteers use two fingers for the head and the arm. The puppet communicates by waggling the head, and can carry things with its arms. These puppets are easy to make and can be bought cheaply in toy shops and online. Famous examples include Sooty and

LEFT: Simple cloth glove puppet.

BELOW: Two-finger method and one-finger method.

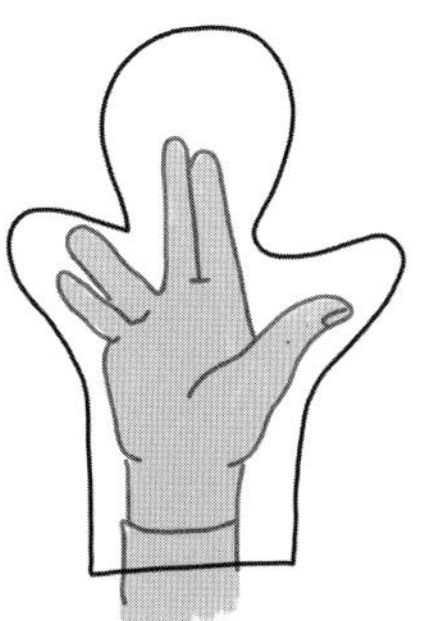

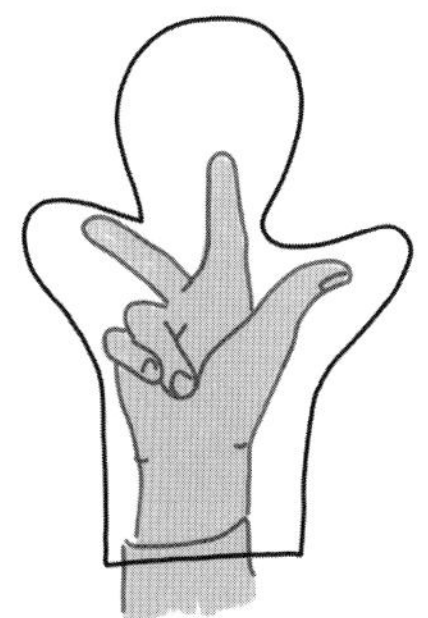

Sweep and Gordon the Gopher, who appeared on BBC Children's television on the 1980s.

Glove Puppet with a Cloth Body and Sculpted Head and Hands

Some puppets have a cloth body and a head and hands sculpted out of wood, papier mâché, latex or plastic. They tend to have a detailed character-ful face and work in the same way as the classic version, with a hole in the head for one or two fingers and holes in the hands for the thumb and other fingers. They may have legs that hang on the front of the puppet and can be thrown over the play board to look like the puppet is sitting down. Examples include Punch and Judy, Chinese fighting puppets, French Guignol, Jan Klassen, and countless other traditional cultural figures.

Sock Puppet

Sock puppets are probably the simplest kind of puppet you can make. A sock goes over the puppeteer's hand and the sole of the sock is pushed in between the thumb and the fingers to make a working mouth. You can decorate with buttons for eyes, put in a mouth lining or a tongue, and add any other features you can think of. The working mouth means that the puppet can talk using lip-sync.

Sock Puppet with a Sculpted Head

This is a more sophisticated version of the sock puppet, where the head is made of wood and the body is cloth. It works in the same way as the sock but the wooden sculpture extends the action of the fingers considerably making its action more dramatic. An example is the crocodile in Punch and Judy.

Muppet-Style Glove Puppets

These puppets are a further development of the sock-type glove puppet, made from fleece with a sculpted foam skeleton. Developed specifically for television, they have eyes that focus on the lens and their big working mouths allow them to lip-sync perfectly to camera. Examples include the Muppets, Zippy from *Rainbow*, Basil Brush and the characters in *Avenue Q*.

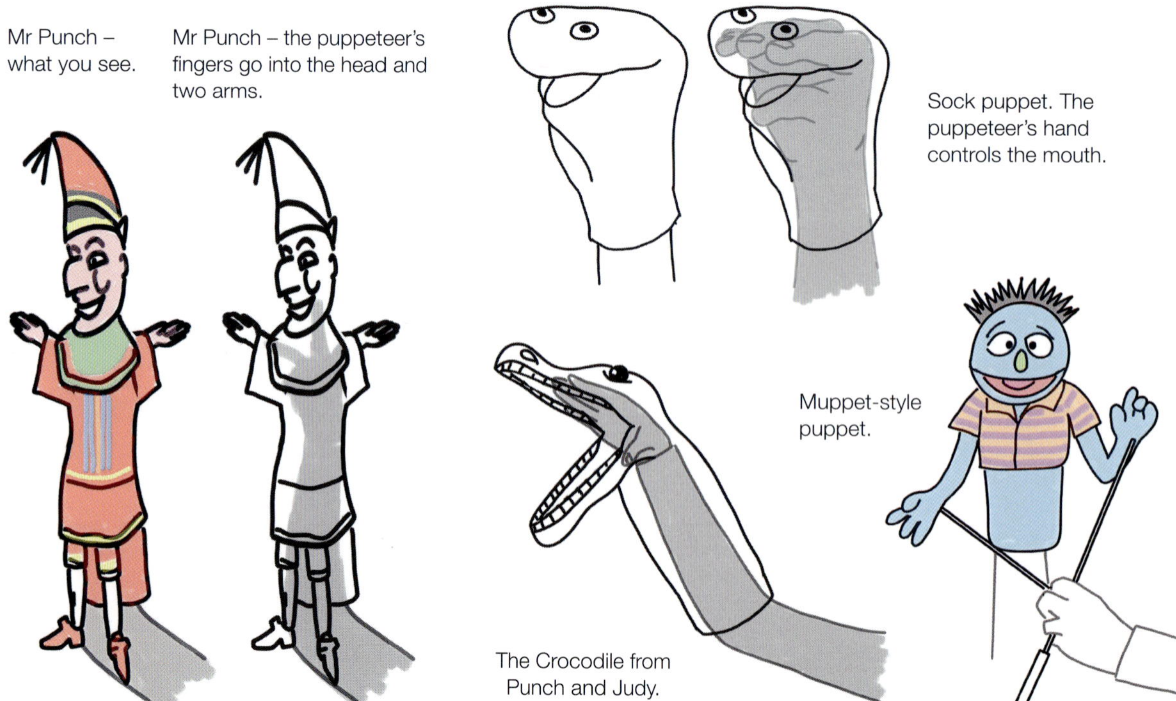

Mr Punch – what you see.

Mr Punch – the puppeteer's fingers go into the head and two arms.

Sock puppet. The puppeteer's hand controls the mouth.

The Crocodile from Punch and Judy.

Muppet-style puppet.

Head and Hand Glove Puppets

Some glove puppets have glove-operated hands as well as glove-operated heads. The head puppeteer puts their other hand into the glove hand of the puppet. If the puppet has two hands, then a second puppeteer operates the other hand, or may do both hands. Examples include Fozzy Bear and the Trekkie Monster in *Avenue Q*.

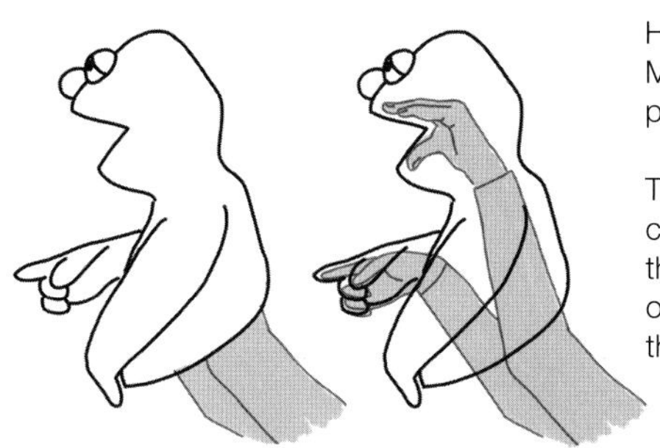

Hand in glove Muppet-style puppet.

The puppeteer can operate the head and one hand of the puppet.

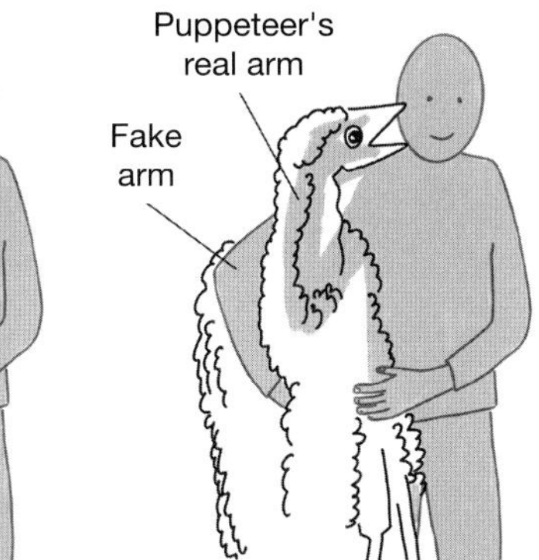

ABOVE: Rod Hull's Emu. The puppeteer's real arm operates the puppet (right).

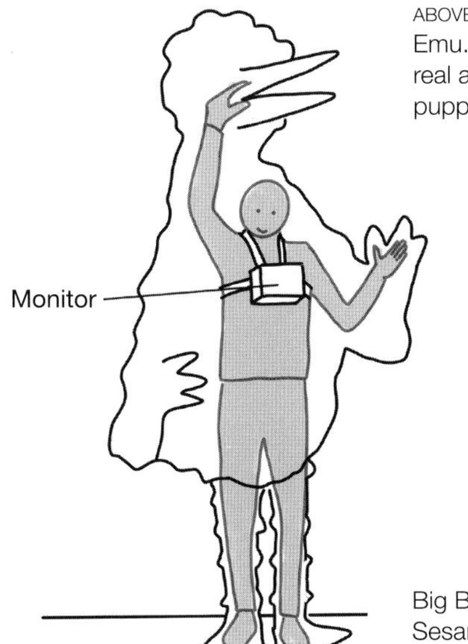

Big Bird from Sesame Street.

Latex Glove Puppets

Glove puppets made of latex can be extremely realistic, especially on camera. Modelled in clay, cast out of latex rubber, painted and set in position, they can be used for special effects and made to seem completely real or at least very life-like. Examples include the alien in *Alien*, Yoda in *Star Wars*, and the characters in *Spitting Image*.

Costume Glove Puppet with a False Arm

The puppeteer appears to be carrying a puppet under their arm but in fact it is a false arm and their real arm is inside the puppet's head, operating it. The puppeteer is able to carry the puppet anywhere and give it fantastically life-like movement. Probably the best-known example from British television is Rod Hull's Emu.

Costume Glove Puppet Worn by the Puppeteer

This kind of puppet is worn by the puppeteer and operated by them from inside. The puppeteer's legs become the legs of the puppet, and they operate the arms with one hand and the head with the other hand. This means that the puppet is completely mobile and able to go anywhere. Examples of this kind of puppet include Big Bird on *Sesame Street* and the velociraptors from *Walking with Dinosaurs*.

Finger Puppets

These very simple puppets are designed to go on each finger, so one puppeteer can do ten puppets at the same time, to give the effect of a crowd.

Hand Creatures

With just two fingers, it is possible to make a person walking on a table; with four, you can create a four-legged creature. You can also put on a glove and adapt it with attachments, as the puppeteer did in *Fingerbobs* on British children's television.

3
PUPPETING THE HEAD

All puppets have a head. Even when you use your hand to be a puppet, the first things the audience will look for are the head and the eyes. If you puppet an object, the audience will find its eyes and decide which part is the head. Specially made puppets come in many shapes and sizes, with and without legs, with arms and without, but they are never without a head.

As always in puppetry, the question for the puppeteer doing the head is how to move it, and why. The two main reasons the head moves are to look at things and to talk. The head is also the area where the puppet listens, smells, touches, tastes, eats and thinks, but a lot of these it can do without moving. This chapter has exercises to help you understand when, how and why the head moves.

Most of the exercises here refer to the workshop puppet but you can use any kind of puppet, or a random object to be a head. For more information about the workshop puppet, *see* Chapter 8.

MAKING THE HEAD LOOK AT THINGS

The main task you perform as a head puppeteer is to make the puppet look at things. In this exercise you practise making the head look quickly and accurately so that the audience can see immediately what it is looking at. The more accurate you are, the more subtle you can be with the puppet's focus. The audience reads changes in focus as changes in thought.

The Exercise

Take a workshop puppet, hold it by the head and feet, and stand it on a table.

STEP1: Focus on the puppet's head, and make the puppet look at a specific object in the room, say, the back of a chair.
STEP 2: Move the puppet around on the table top, keeping its eyes fixed on the back of the chair. Keep your focus on the puppet's head, and the puppet's focus on the chair. Move the puppet off the table and come closer to the chair, then further

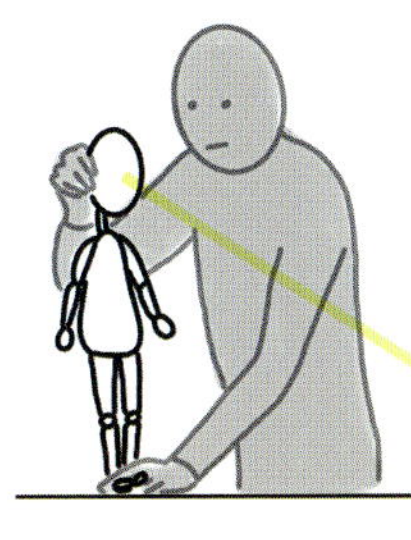

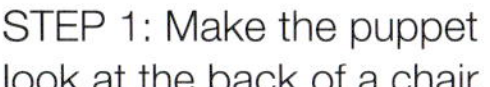

OPPOSITE: A head from *The Heads* (Blind Summit).

STEP 1: Make the puppet look at the back of a chair.

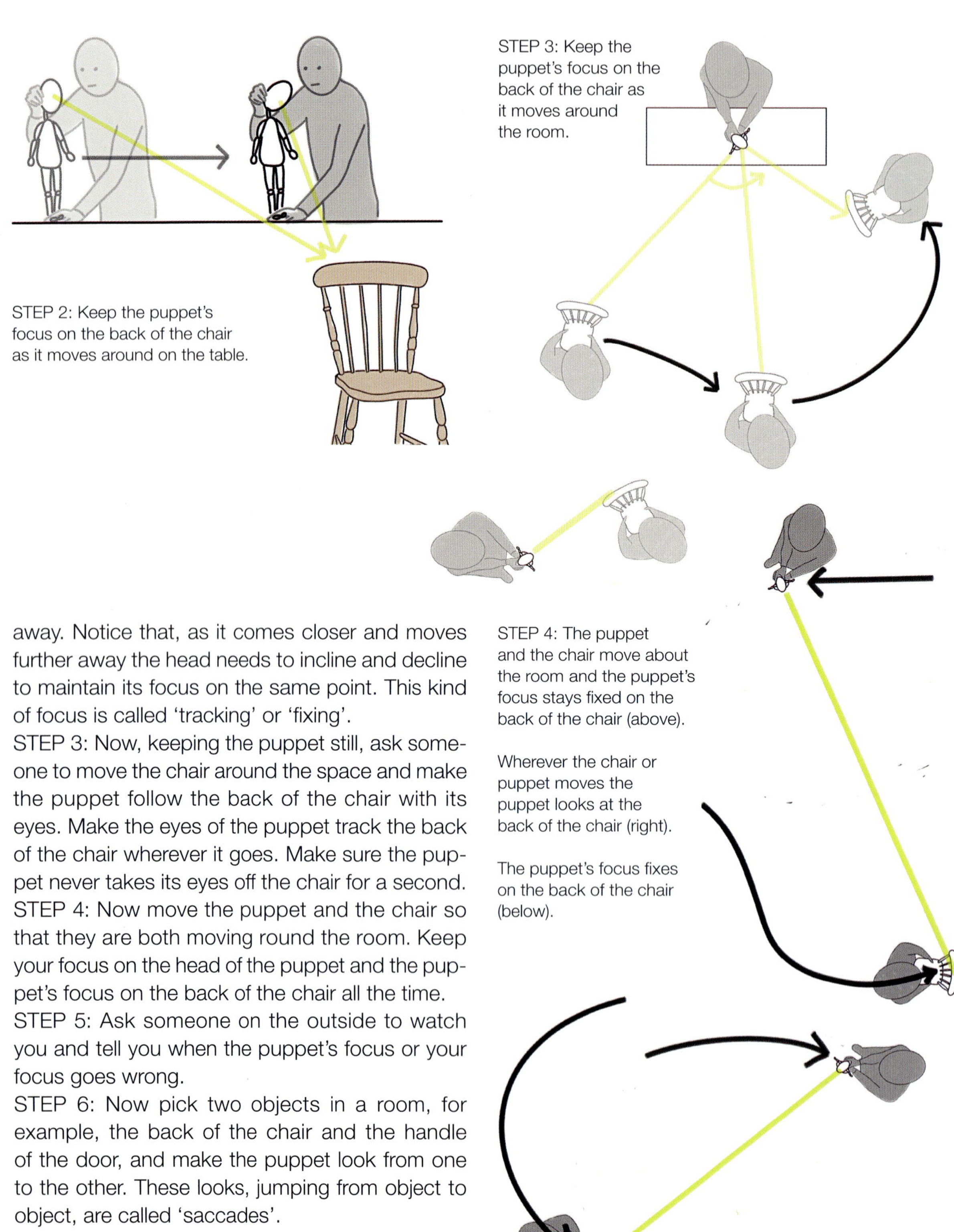

away. Notice that, as it comes closer and moves further away the head needs to incline and decline to maintain its focus on the same point. This kind of focus is called 'tracking' or 'fixing'.

STEP 3: Now, keeping the puppet still, ask someone to move the chair around the space and make the puppet follow the back of the chair with its eyes. Make the eyes of the puppet track the back of the chair wherever it goes. Make sure the puppet never takes its eyes off the chair for a second.

STEP 4: Now move the puppet and the chair so that they are both moving round the room. Keep your focus on the head of the puppet and the puppet's focus on the back of the chair all the time.

STEP 5: Ask someone on the outside to watch you and tell you when the puppet's focus or your focus goes wrong.

STEP 6: Now pick two objects in a room, for example, the back of the chair and the handle of the door, and make the puppet look from one to the other. These looks, jumping from object to object, are called 'saccades'.

Ask someone watching to say what they think the puppet is looking at and see if you are getting it right. Keep adjusting until you can do it 100 per cent accurately 100 per cent of the time, without taking your focus off the puppet.

STEP 7: Now make the puppet look mainly at the door handle, and look only occasionally and quickly at the back of the chair and back at the door handle. Make the door handle the major point of the puppet's focus, and the back of the chair a minor point of focus. The look back at the chair is a 'check look'.

STEP 8: Now see if you can make the puppet look at the back of the chair in different ways. Can you make it look at it shyly up through its fringe or condescendingly down its nose? Can you make it look at it out of the corner of its eyes, or inquisitively, or kindly, aggressively or directly? Ask someone to watch you and say what they are seeing. Can you make them see the puppet look quizzical, in love, or angry, just by the way it looks at the back of the chair?

STEP 9: Now make the puppet break its focus for a moment. Begin with the puppet looking at the back of the chair, which is now still in the space, then make the puppet turn away, turn all the way around the back of you. Make it look at the back of the chair again as soon as it is able to see round the other side of you.

Things to Notice

Looking at things makes the head move The head can also do many things without moving – hear, taste, smell and think – so it is not always possible for the audience to see it doing these things. However, when it looks at something, it moves its

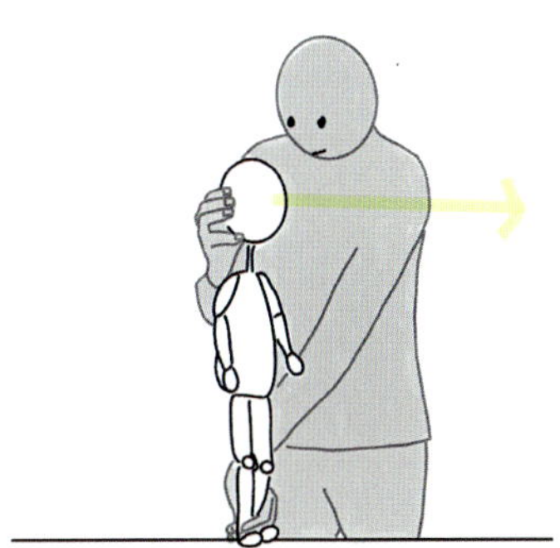

STEP 7: The puppet looks at the door handle. This is the major point of focus.

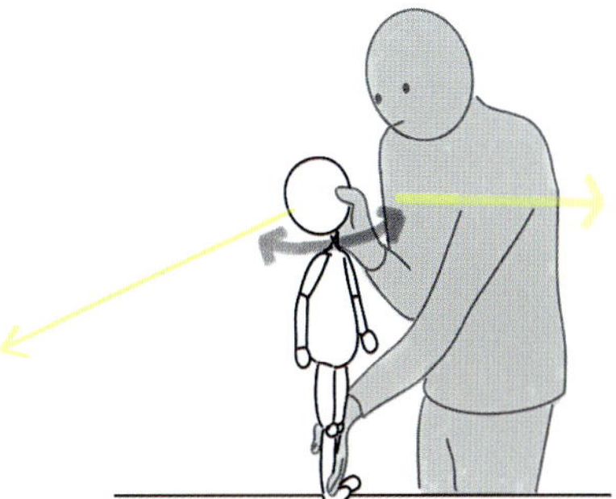

STEP 7: The puppet looks briefly at the chair (minor point of focus) and then back at the door handle (major point of focus).

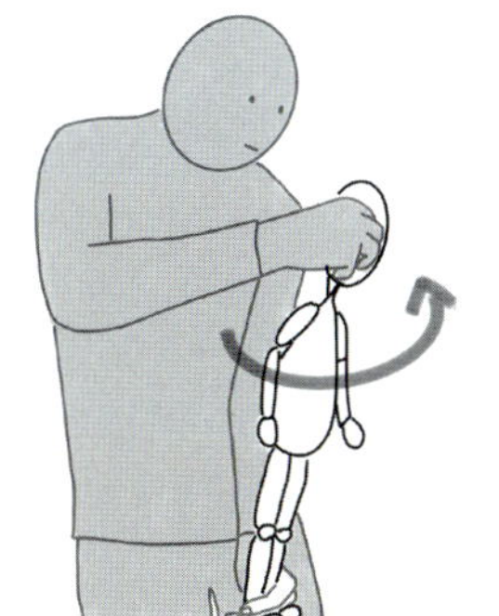

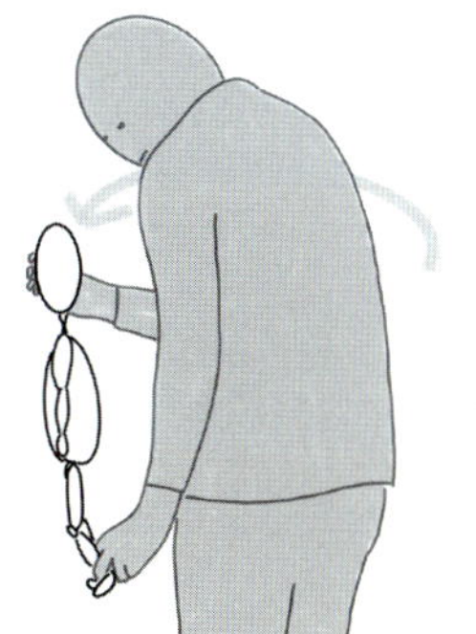

STEP 9: The puppet looks all the way round behind the puppeteer (left) and then at the chair again (right).

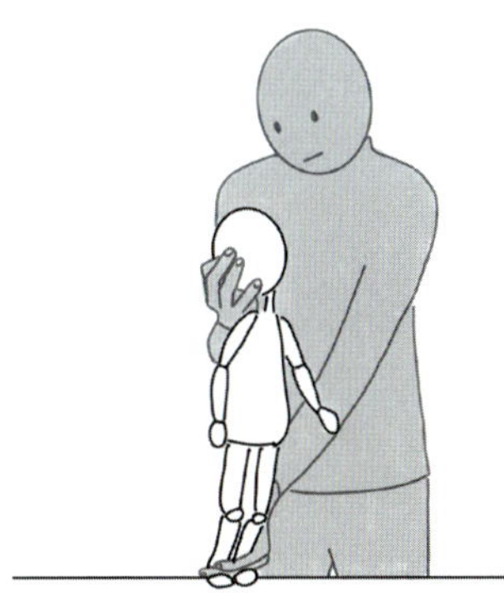

The puppet looks at something on the ceiling or in the sky.

head to point its eyes towards it. The audience can always see what the head is looking at.

What the head looks at tells a story If the puppet looks at the chair, then it is interested in the chair; if it looks at the door handle, then it is interested in the door handle; and when it looks from one to the other, then it is trying to make some sort of choice between them. When the puppet looks from the door handle to the chair, and from the chair back to the door handle, the audience will try to piece together a story: is the puppet expecting someone to come through the door, and take the chair?

You can make the audience see different kinds of look Even with simple workshop puppets that have no eyes, the audience is able to see when the puppet is looking out of the corner of its eye, down its nose, up through its fringe, staring with anger, looking with love. If you get the look right, the audience will see it.

Looking away is just as important as looking at The head may look away from something that the puppet does not like, that embarrasses it, or that scares it. It may pretend to look at one thing, in order not to look at something else, which is the thing that really interests it. The puppet may be fully focused on something it is not looking at. Focus and looking can be different.

LEADING WITH THE HEAD

The head is mostly concerned with looking at things, and generally it can do that from wherever it is. It does not need to move the rest of its body in order to look at things. But in extremes – when the puppet needs to stretch to see something, or when it goes to kiss someone, or it wants to touch something with its cheek – the head can lead movement.

In this exercise you practise leading the three-person workshop puppet with the head.

The Exercise

Have three people on a workshop puppet and stand the puppet on a table. (For more about three people on the workshop puppet, see Chapter 8.)

STEP 1: Make the head look at the back of the chair. Do not do anything else – just stare at the back of the chair and wait. Eventually, one of the other puppeteers will make the puppet walk closer to it, or back away from it, or walk sideways around it. If you keep the head's focus on the same thing, the head will appear to be leading the movement.

STEP 2: Now make the puppet listen to a noise. Turn its head and point its ear to the noise. Hold this position. The puppet may lift a hand to its ear, or move closer to the noise. Again, by keeping the ear's focus on the sound, the head appears to lead the movement.

STEP 3: Now make the puppet look at the back of the chair again, and this time pull the head back, keeping the eyes fixed on the chair, as if the

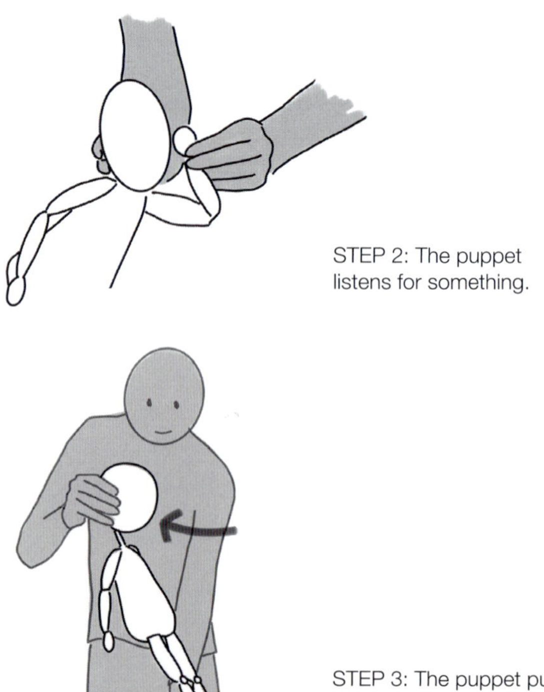

STEP 2: The puppet listens for something.

STEP 3: The puppet pulls back from something it doesn't like.

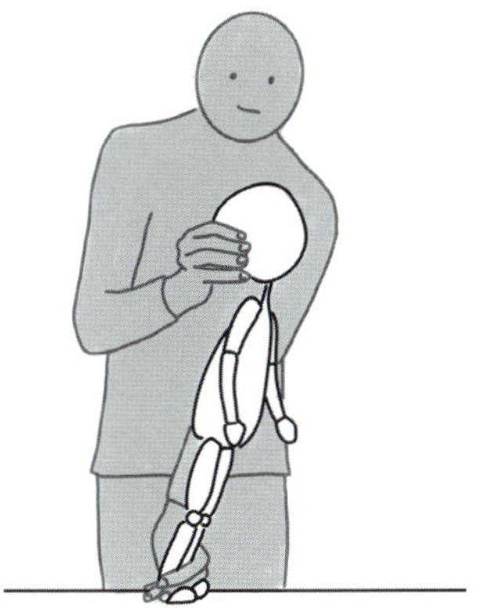

STEP 6: The puppet reaches for a kiss.

STEP 7: Looking completely behind (180 degrees) makes the body turn 90 degrees.

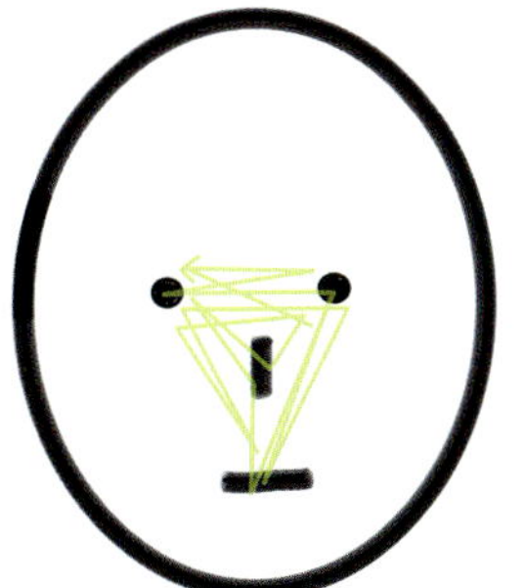

People have a particular way of looking at the faces of others.

puppet does not like what it sees. In this position you can actually pull the puppet backwards, while still looking completely natural.

STEP 4: Make the puppet look up at something on the ceiling and turn left and right trying to see it. The body and the feet will follow.

STEP 5: Make the puppet put the top of its head down to touch something. Make it push out its cheek to feel something. Make it pout its lips to kiss something. As long as it is clear what the puppet wants to touch, the rest of the puppet should be able to follow.

STEP 6: Make the head sniff the air as if it can smell something and is trying to detect where it is coming from. Once the rest of the puppeteers realize that the puppet is searching for the source of the smell, you can literally lead it by the nose.

STEP 7: Make the head turn so that the puppet looks round behind itself. After turning through 90 degrees, the body must follow it to look further. The feet do not need to turn, but they probably will do if the puppet keeps looking behind it.

Tips for Doing It Well

When looking at something for a long time, look 'actively' Think about making the puppet look for details in the object. For example, if the puppet is looking at someone's face, make it look at all the features of the face. Look from eye to eye, at the nose, at the lips. Think of trying to 'read' the face. Inspect the shape of the nose, watch the mouth, notice the hairs on their skin, the cells, their emotions. This is what a person does in real life.

Looking away and back again builds focus If you want to show that the puppet is particularly interested in something, make it look away for a moment, and then turn back. This builds the idea of the puppet's interest in the thing. You can even make it walk away and then look back.

Things to Notice

The head often leads with stillness One of the most powerful tools for leading with the head is simply to look at something and wait. The longer the puppet looks at the object, the more interesting it becomes. Eventually, any movement by the rest of the body will add to the drama of the stare.

Keeping the head still makes space for the rest of the puppet to understand what is happening and work out how to participate. If, on the other hand, you keep moving the head, it is impossible for the rest of the puppet to follow.

Leading means owning whatever happens When you make the head stare at something and wait for the other puppeteers to do something, it does not matter what they do: if the puppet walks closer to it, then it wants to look closer at it; if it backs away from it, it wants to look at it from further away. Accept whatever happens. Own it. Sometimes, leading just means pretending to lead.

FOLLOWING WITH THE HEAD

The head relies completely on the rest of the body to carry it around and mostly this means that the head is following where the rest of the body leads it. Being a good follower is a key skill of the head puppeteer. In this exercise, you look at how the head follows the rest of the puppet.

Exercise

Take a puppet with three people and stand it on a table.

STEP 1: Let the feet puppeteer make the puppet walk around on the table top, leading with the feet. They can make the puppet do anything they want: run and slide, take giant steps, hop on one leg, and so on. All the time the head puppeteer follows, keeping the head on the shoulders, and the shoulders over the feet. Make sure that you always know what the head is looking at.
STEP 2: Now let the back puppeteer lead the puppet. Make it kneel down and stand up, make it bend over forwards, backwards and to the sides, make it jump up and down, make it lie down and get up. Follow with the head by keeping it over the shoulders and always looking at something.
STEP 3: Finally make the head talk by following the hands and the feet. Move the hands and then make the puppet say something. Move the feet and then make the head say something. Make what the puppet says follow the end of the movement of the hands and feet.

Something to Notice

The head can look wherever it wants The head follows the body because it is attached by the neck; it does not need to look where it is going. The head looks at what interests it. The head can be looking behind it while walking across a room. It is always looking at something, however, and it will need to check where it is going occasionally, in order to be safe.

MAKING THE HEAD TALK

Puppets do not talk. It is an illusion. Someone talks for them, and the puppet mimes along. For the illusion – that the puppet is talking – to work, the audience must be looking at the puppet before it speaks. If they are not already looking at it when the words are spoken, they will look to where the words have come from, towards the person who actually spoke.

In this exercise, you practise moving the puppet before it speaks, to direct the line it speaks to someone or something.

The Exercise

Take a workshop puppet and hold its head in your dominant hand and its feet with your subordinate hand. Have an audience watch you and give you feedback, to let you know if it is working.
STEP 1: Focus on the puppet's head, and make it look at something, for example, a mark on the floor.
STEP 2: Now turn the head to look at someone in the audience, and say something: 'Do you see that?'
STEP 3: Then look back at the mark on the floor.
STEP 4: Turn the head to look at another person in the audience, and say something else: 'That mark on the floor?'

Daz from *Citizen Puppet* (Blind Summit).

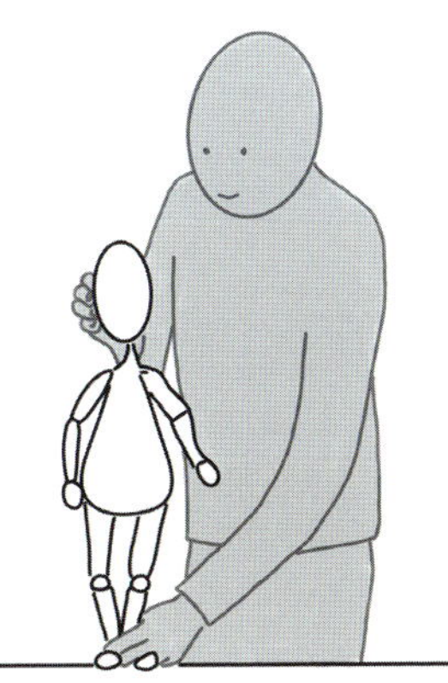

Hold the head with your dominant hand and the feet with your subordinate hand.

STEP 5: Make it look back to the mark, then to the audience, and then say something: 'I don't like it…'

STEP 6: Try making the puppet deliver its lines to different places, always looking back at the mark on the floor in between the lines. Make it say the line to someone on stage, to another puppet, to the floor, or to a piece of furniture. Can you make the puppet say the line into the middle distance? Can you make it say the line to a ghost? What happens if the puppet says the line to you?

Tip for Doing It Well

Connect the turn of the puppet's head and the delivery of the line The turn of the head and the delivery of the line should be connected, but separate, so that they happen one after the other. The turn of the head will trigger the delivery of the line. It will look as if the puppet is delivering the line to the person to whom it turned.

Things to Notice

The movement is realistic It does not represent the physical movement that produces speech. Instead, it shows where the puppet looks when it speaks, and what or who is the receiver of the line. We always speak to someone or something, even if it is the floor! We look at them for inspiration, or reassurance, to feel safe, or to see if we are getting through. **Puppets usually deliver lines out to the audience** When the puppet delivers a line to the audience it appears to speak aloud, but when it speaks to something on stage it appears to be speaking to itself. When puppets look at things on stage, they appear to the audience to be listening, not speaking.

PHRASING THE SPEECH WITH THE BREATH

Speaking involves blowing air out of the lungs and through the vocal cords in the throat, to create a voice. The mouth is then used to turn the voice into words. In order to be able to blow air out, you have to breathe in first. In this exercise, you connect the movement of the puppet's breathing to its speaking, so that you make it not just say its lines, but also perform them like an actor.

The Exercise

Take a workshop puppet and set it up in front of an audience.

STEP 1: This time, before you make the puppet speak, first make it take a breath in. To make it look like it breathes in, pull the head of the puppet back slightly as you take a noisy breath in through your teeth.

The puppet talking to itself, and talking to the audience or someone else.

STEP 1: Pull the head back to make the puppet breathe in (above).

STEP 2: Push the mouth forwards to speak (right).

STEP 2: Now push the head forward and say the line. Make the puppet's head start to move forward just before you speak, so that the movement of the head leads and its words follow. This makes it look like the words come from the movement of the puppet's head – that the puppet spoke them – and not that the movement of the puppet's head comes from the words.
STEP 3: After the puppet says the line, breathe out the rest of your air before you make it breathe in again.
STEP 4: Repeat. Breathe in and pull back the head, then push the head forward and speak.
STEP 5: Combine this 'breathing movement' with the 'directing movement' from the previous exercise. To do this, make the puppet breathe in as it turns its head to look at someone in the audience, then push the head forward towards that person as it says the line.
STEP 6: Finally, as the puppet speaks, imitate the movement of the mouth by 'waggling' the front of the face up and down and side to side. The waggling mainly follows the pronunciation of consonants: imagine the puppet's mouth being 'bumped' by the words as they pass out of the mouth. Try to move only the mouth part of the head and match the movements to the rhythm of the words the puppet is saying. Keep the puppet always focused on who they are talking to.

Something to Notice

The in-breath gets people's attention When the puppet breathes in, if the action is audible and visible, it makes the audience look at the puppet. They turn expectantly to hear what it is about to say. Taking an in-breath indicates that the puppet is about to speak.

MOVING MOUTHS AND LIP-SYNC

If you have a puppet with a moving mouth such as a Muppet or a ventriloquist dummy, you can make the mouth open and close as it speaks, representing the movements of a real mouth talking. This technique, commonly used by television puppets, is called 'lip-sync'.

This exercise breaks down the basic sequence of lip-sync.

The Exercise

You can do this exercise in front of an audience or using a mirror. You can also film it and watch it back. You can use a puppet with a moving mouth or a sock, or you can use your hand.

STEP 1: Take your hand and make a 'frog' face with it.

STEP 6: Waggle the mouth up and down and sideways on consonants.

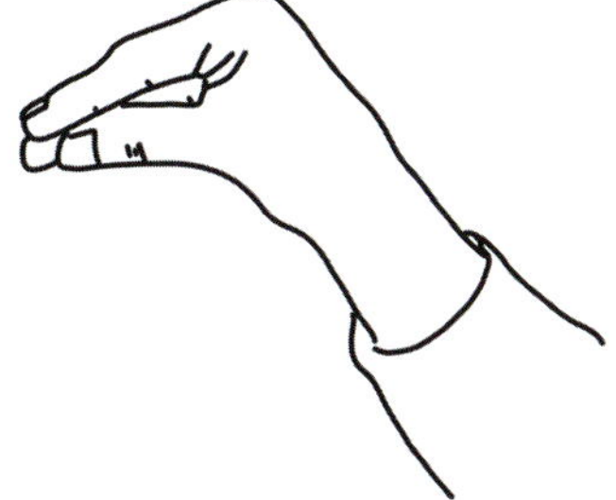

STEP 1: Make a 'frog' with your hand.

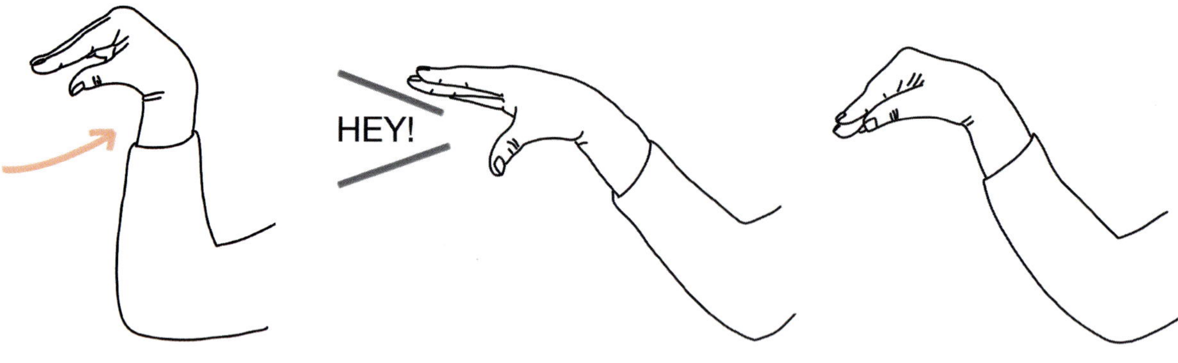

STEP 2: Pull back the head and open the mouth to breathe in.

STEP 3: Push forwards, open the mouth and speak.

STEP 4: Close the mouth after each syllable.

STEP 2: Now make the frog breathe in by pulling the head back as you make the appropriate sound.
STEP 3: Push the frog forward, opening the mouth at the same time and make it speak a one-syllable word. Something like 'Hey!' will do. Make the mouth open first and the word follow after.
STEP 4: Finally, as the word finishes, close the mouth and pull the head back to its starting position.
To recap: the head pulls back and breathes in, thrusts forward and opens the mouth, speaks a one-syllable word, closes and pulls back to the middle, starting position.
STEP 5: Now make the frog say a phrase: 'Hey! I'm a frog!' Breathe in at the beginning, then open the mouth for every syllable that the puppet speaks, and close it between every syllable. This phrase has four syllables, so the frog's mouth opens and closes four times.

Make sure you lead the speaking with the movement by opening the mouth a fraction before the syllable.
STEP 6: Film your hand speaking, with you out of the frame, and watch it back.
STEP 7: Keep practising until it is instinctive to open and close the mouth along with the syllables.

Tips for Doing Lip-Sync Well

Open and close the bottom jaw Try to operate the puppet so that you are moving the bottom jaw, in this case the thumb, and keeping the top jaw

Keep the puppet focused on the person it is addressing.

If you open the top jaw, the puppet looks at the ceiling and the audience looks down its throat.

still. This is what we actually do when we speak. If you open the top jaw, you point the puppet's eyes to the ceiling every time it opens its mouth. To help you keep the top jaw still, think of keeping the puppet's focus fixed on the person to whom it is talking, and delivering the words to them.

Move the mouth before you speak It is very easy to get into a habit of following the words you are saying with the movement of the mouth, but it is much better if the mouth movement leads the words. To do this, open the mouth first, and then say the syllable fractionally after. This will make it look as if it is the action of the puppet opening its mouth that produces the words.

Add an extra syllable at the end of a phrase Instead of making the puppet say, 'Hey! I'm a frog', with four syllables – and four openings and closings of the mouth – add an extra syllable to the last word. As a result, 'frog' will become a two syllable word – 'fro-geh' – and the mouth will open and close twice for that word. The phrase will become a five-syllable one: 'Hey! I'm a fro-geh.' The extra syllables are not there in the written sentences, but they do seem to be there when a person speaks. This technique will make the puppet seem to be more in control of the speaking, give it good diction and add a sense of realism.

Things to Notice

You need to do all the movements Notice that doing lip-sync with the moving mouth does not replace the need for the other movements. It is still necessary to direct the words at someone or something, to breathe, and phrase the lines.

Lip-sync has many variations Some puppeteers are slavish about lip-sync being as accurate as possible, and other puppeteers prefer it to be less accurate. It is up to you to decide what your puppets and production need.

WHERE THE WORDS COME FROM

Since the puppet does not actually say the lines, there is no absolute rule about where the text should come from or how it should be done. The words can come from anywhere and be done by anyone.

So far in these talking exercises the words have been spoken by the puppeteer doing the head. This exercise tries out different ways of delivering the text.

The Exercise

Take a workshop puppet, three puppeteers, an actor, and try these different set-ups. See how they work differently and think about what you like about them and what you do not like.

SET UP 1: Have the actor stand beside the puppeteers and deliver the lines. Use the breath to control when the actor says the line. The puppet and the actor take an in-breath together, then the puppet pushes its head forward to speak and the actor says the line. The puppet waggles as the actor speaks.

SET UP 2: Give the actor the role of the body puppeteer. Get them to breathe with the puppet so

The head puppeteer speaks the text.

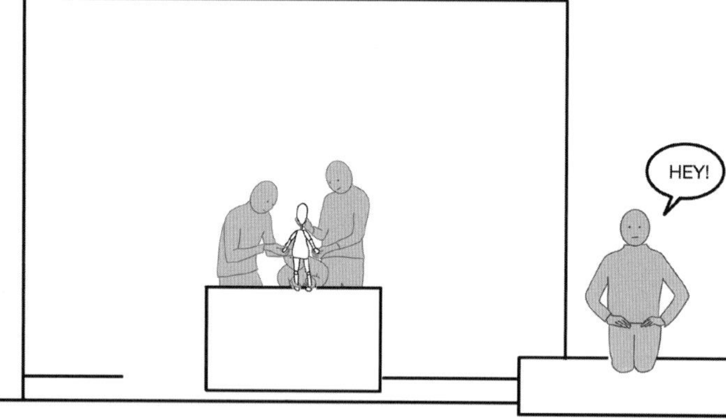

ABOVE LEFT: SET UP 1: An actor speaks the text beside the puppet.

ABOVE RIGHT: SET UP 2: The body puppeteer speaks the text.

LEFT: SET UP 3: A narrator at the side of the stage speaks the text.

BELOW LEFT: SET UP 4: The text is pre-recorded.

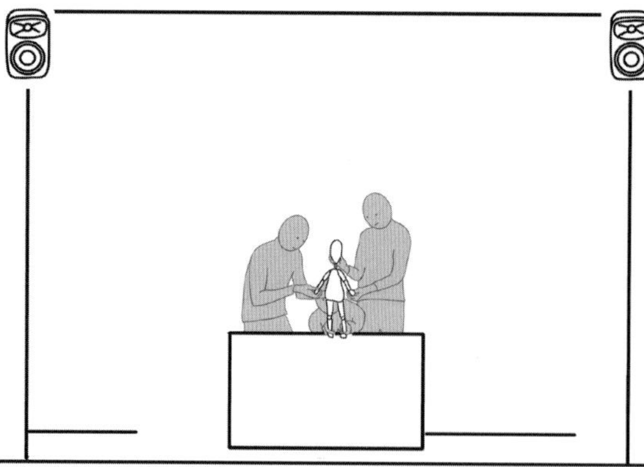

that the speaker and the puppeteer synchronise their speaking with the movements of the puppet. SET UP 3: Move the actor to the side of the stage and have them speak the puppet's lines from there. Is it possible to co-ordinate the movement and the voice when they are this far apart?

SET UP 4: Try recording the text and playing it back on a tape. Can you make it clear to the audience that the puppet is talking? Or does it look like it is a voice in their head?

Things to Notice

It is easier to improvise when the head puppeteer speaks the lines The specific advantage of the head puppeteer saying the lines is that it creates a special connection between the movement and the voice, and the puppet can improvise in the moment. But it also means the head puppeteer needs to be an actor, an improvisor and a puppeteer.

A performer at the side of the stage creates a pleasing formality The effect of separating the voice and the puppet creates a very interesting deconstructed and collaborative performance. The great advantage of this set-up is that you can have a specialist actor or singer performing the words and a specialist puppeteer operating the puppet.

A recording means you can have anyone do the voices The advantage of recording is that the voice actors can work on their performances separately and you can mix a soundtrack in a studio. A recording may lack charm in the live setting, but in a setting where voices are amplified and the puppeteers are not visible, such as filming, who would be able to tell the difference?

GESTURING AND TALKING

A three-person puppet has arms and legs that can move while the puppet is speaking. This can make things very confusing, but when it is done right it focuses the speaking and make the puppetry wonderfully real. In this exercise, you make the puppet speak after it moves its hands or feet. When the puppet leads with the body and follows with speech, the scene takes on a life of its own. The effect is counter-intuitive but magical.

The Exercise

This exercise is done with a workshop puppet with two or three puppeteers. Practise alone but then share your improvising with an audience for feedback.

STEP 1: Place the workshop puppet on a table and bring it to life.
STEP 2: The performers on the feet and body make the puppet perform a single movement: a step, or a jump or a gesture of the hands. They can also do a step with a gesture of the hands at the same time, as long as it is a single gesture.
STEP 3: As soon as the movement by the feet and hands finishes, the head puppeteer follows by making the puppet say something. They make it speak one line.
STEP 4: The feet or hands move again, and the head follows by speaking.
STEP 5: You continue to repeat this sequence until it flows easily and comfortably: Hands/Feet – Speak. Hands/Feet – Speak.
STEP 6: Swap with someone in the audience and watch them do it.

Tips for Doing It Well

Say the first thing that comes into your head If you are on the head and you are worried about what to say, do not think too much about it. If you are not sure, you can always make the puppet say, 'I don't know what to say…' Or say what you see the puppet doing: if it points its hand at something, say, 'What is that?' Something will follow. Keep to single phrases, and let the hands and body lead you.

Save up your lines Resist the urge to say more than one line after each gesture. If you have more to say, save it and wait for the next gesture. You can say half a line, or a phrase, or maybe even only a word, but try not to say two lines at a time. Avoid making a speech. Wait for the next gesture to come and then continue with what you want to say. If you say too much, the puppet's body will stop moving and it will just be talking. It may feel odd to wait for the puppet to move before speaking, but the audience will tell you the puppet looks very alive. In addition, by saving up lines you will never run out of things to say.

You can pause after speaking, but not before The puppet can pause between STEP 3 and STEP 4 (after speaking), but not between STEP 2 and STEP 3 (after gesturing). The speaking must follow the movement closely so that they seem connected: 'Movement – speak – pause – movement – speak – pause' is correct, while 'Movement – pause – speak – movement – pause – speak' is wrong!

4
PUPPETING THE BODY AND LIMBS

When you use two hands to control a puppet, you can make the body move separately from the head. This allows you to create conflict in the puppet. Conflict is interesting: the head wants to go one way, and the heart wants to go the other; the puppet thinks one thing, but feels another. The body puppeteer holds the physical centre of gravity and controls the breathing of the puppet. Puppeting the body is about centring the puppet in action and stoking the furnace of the emotions with the breathing.

Hands are an extension of the body. Puppet hands are operated in a number of ways: with rods, with strings, and directly with the fingers and thumbs of the puppeteer. Hands are not just for scratching; they are specialized, multifunctional tools. They point at things, grab for things, pass objects to people, move objects from here to there, operate machinery, play instruments, draw and write. And they do puppetry. As interesting as all these actions are, however, they are only worth doing if they advance the story.

Many puppets do not have feet or legs, and they get along perfectly well without them. Glove puppets, for example, are seen only from the waist up. In puppets that do have feet and legs, such as string puppets and three-person-operated table-top puppets, they add new dimensions to the character of your puppet. Although feet have a function as the transport system for the puppet, they are actually more interesting when they reveal what the puppet is thinking and feeling. Puppet feet are made for thinking.

This chapter has a series of practical exercises for exploring how to puppet the body and limbs of puppets. Most of the exercises refer to the workshop puppet; for more about this, *see* Chapter 8.

OPPOSITE: Bud in *Low Life* (Blind Summit).

HOW THE BODY MOVES

The body connects all the parts of the puppet together and contains the centre of the puppet. This means that, whenever it moves, lots of other parts move with it. The art of the body puppeteer therefore is knowing when to move, and when to be still.

The Exercise

You can do this exercise on your own and then share with each other to see what you have learned.

STEP 1: Take a workshop puppet and hold its head in one hand (your writing hand) and its rear end in the other hand, and stand it on a table top. Focus on the midline of the body.
STEP 2: Move the body in all the ways a person can move. Make it bend at the waist, forwards and backwards, and lean right and left. Keep the hips as the fixed point of the bend and keep the feet on the ground. When leaning to the side you will find that the weight transfers to one leg and the other leg comes off the ground.

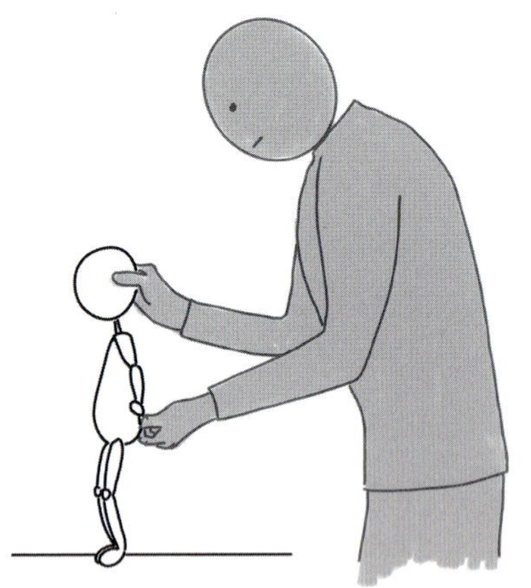

STEP 1: Hold the head with your dominant hand and the bottom with your subordinate hand.

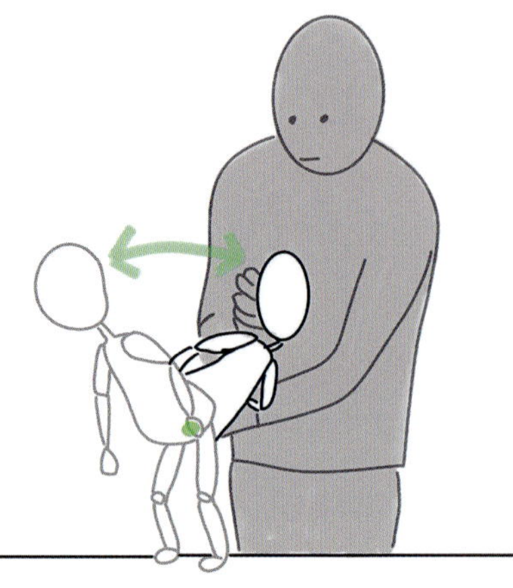

STEP 2: Make the puppet bend forwards and backwards at the waist.

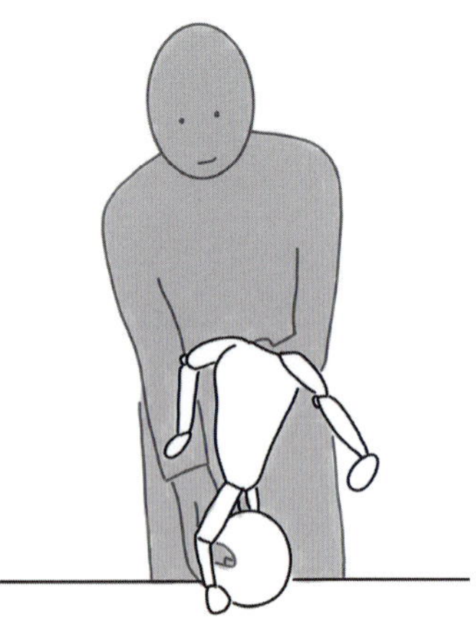

STEP 5: Hold the rear end up and the head down to make the puppet stand on its head.

STEP 3: Rotate the hips, keeping the feet and the shoulders still as fixed points. Then make the puppet twist to look behind it, turning the body with the bottom hand and with the head hand, and trying to keep the feet still, facing forwards.

STEP 4: Make the body go up and down so that the puppet kneels, sits, lies down and gets up.

STEP 5: Make it jump. Try making it walk and run. Make it stand on its head – of course, this will make the limbs flop about, but there is no need to worry about that right now.

STEP 6: Make the puppet breathe by moving the chest up and down gently in sync with your own breath. Keep the head still while the body moves. Make it breathe quickly and slowly, lightly and then more deeply. Using breath, make the puppet laugh, cry, cough, and hold its breath. Notice when the movement of the chest breathing starts to make the rest of the puppet move as well.

Things to Notice

The body moves around two fixed points – the shoulders and the hips When you move the top half of the body, you need to hold the waist still to move around. Conversely, when you make the waist move, you need to hold the shoulders still to balance the movement.

The body contains the lungs The breathing of the puppet is visible in the movement of the chest. When the puppet becomes emotional, the breathing becomes heavier, and the movement of the chest gets bigger. The body puppeteer holds the emotional centre of the puppet.

The body contains the centre Puppeteering the body is all about controlling the centre of the puppet – the point around which everything moves. The body puppeteer holds the centre of the puppet and makes sure that the puppet remains balanced. When the puppet moves around the stage, the body puppeteer guides where it goes.

LEADING WITH THE BODY

As the body puppeteer, you are in the middle of the puppet, connected to all its other parts. The main method of leading with the body is by working with the puppet's breathing to develop the emotional story. The body puppeteer also works the legs, in collaboration with the feet puppeteer, to make the puppet stand up, sit down and jump.

The Exercise

Have three people on a workshop puppet. It is good to have someone watch you doing this exercise and give feedback.

STEP 1: Stand the puppet on a table, make it breathe, and try leading it with the breath. Make the puppet's breathing heavier and make the body move up and down with the breath. Keep developing the sound of the breath and the movement of the chest, and see what you can lead the head or the feet to do. Perhaps the feet may start to step anxiously around, or the head will start looking left and right in fear, or the puppet may start laughing or crying or shouting. Join in and keep the chest breathing.

STEP 2: As the breathing gets bigger, make the body go up and down with it. Start to make the knees bend, and push the head up. Make the puppet jump up and down on the spot. Make sure that you give enough time for the head and the feet to follow you.

STEP 3: Make the puppet stop still, fall on to its knees, and then sit back on its feet. Then see if you can make it sit down and lie down.

STEP 4: From lying down, pull the bottom up into the air so that the puppet is on its hands and knees. Lift the bottom further until it is on its feet and hands, then wait for the head to come up too.

STEP 5: Swap around and watch someone else have a go.

Something to Notice

Puppeting the body is shared In the workshop puppet the movements of the shoulders and the top half of the body are not actually done by the body puppeteer, but by the puppeteer doing the head. As the body puppeteer, you cannot make the puppet bend at the waist or lean left and right. You can only provide the fixed point of the waist for the head puppeteer to move around.

Similarly, when you move the body of the puppet up and down to make it stand, or sit or jump, you are actually puppeting the legs, and the feet puppeteer is making fixed points for you to move around.

The precise sharing of these functions between the head, body and feet puppeteers will vary in different puppets, but the principles are the same. Because the body is the middle of the puppet, everything the body does will be shared with other parts.

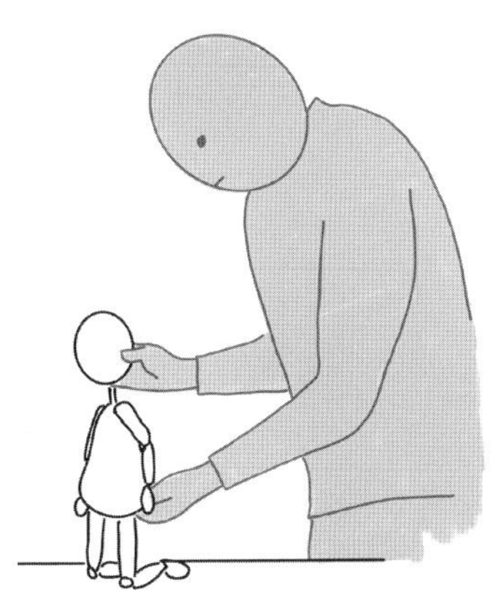

STEP 3: Lower the rear end to make the puppet kneel.

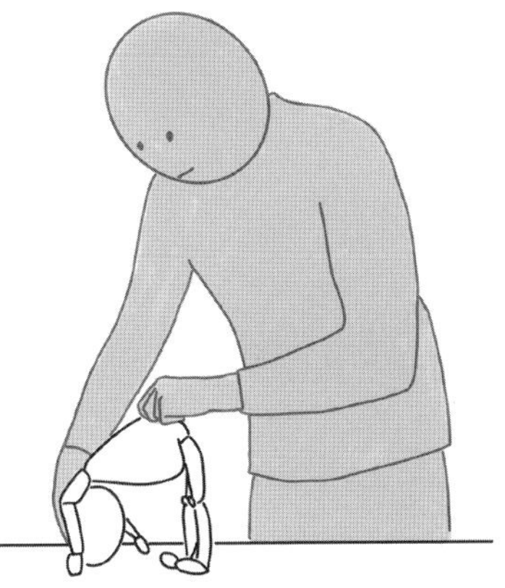

STEP 4: Lift the rear end up to bring the puppet on to its feet.

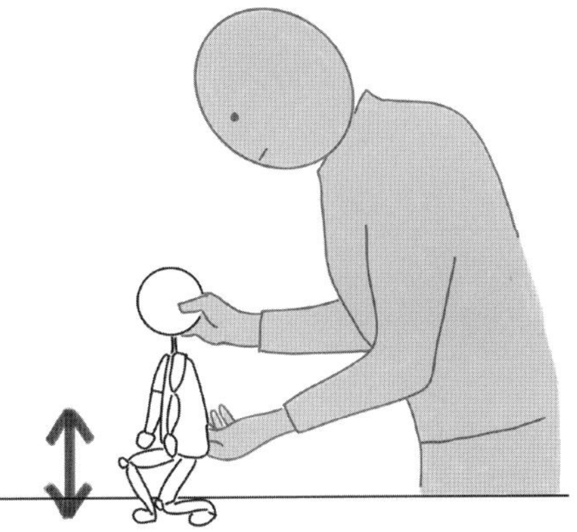

Moving the body up and down bends and straightens the legs.

FOLLOWING WITH THE BODY

As with so many elements of puppetry, the technique of following with the body is often paradoxical. It means moving the body to look as if it is actually being moved by its arms or legs. Sometimes, following with the body means not moving it, but making it a fixed point for other parts to move around.

In this exercise you explore when you need to puppet the body and practise being a good centre for the puppet.

The Exercise

Have three people on a workshop puppet and someone to watch and give feedback on what works and what does not work.

STEP 1: As the body puppeteer, let go of the puppet's rear end and allow the puppet to move around without holding it. Keep your hand close by all the time so that you are ready to take hold of it when you need to.

For much of the time, when the puppet is walking around upright, there is no need to hold the bottom at all when the body is not leading. It will follow the puppet naturally, suspended between the feet and the head. You will need to take hold of it again when it needs to be a fixed point for the rest of the puppet to move around.

STEP 2: Take hold of the bottom when you anticipate the puppet needing it. Think about actions that the puppet does that will require you to hold its rear end. If the puppet wants to bend over at the waist, or reach down to pick something up from the table, you will need to hold its bottom so that it does not collapse. If the puppet jumps in the air, you will need to control the flight of the centre of the puppet. If the puppet crawls, sits down or lies down, you will need to keep it still as a fixed point.

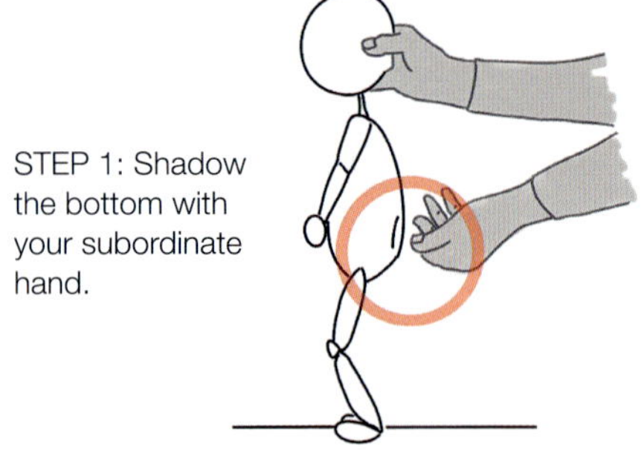

STEP 1: Shadow the bottom with your subordinate hand.

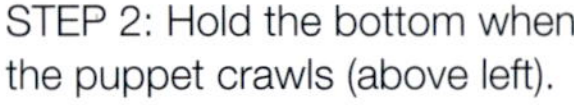

STEP 2: Hold the bottom when the puppet crawls (above left).

Make the body go down and up to cause the puppet to jump (above right).

Hold the bottom still to make the puppet sit (left).

Hold the puppet's bottom still to lie down (right).

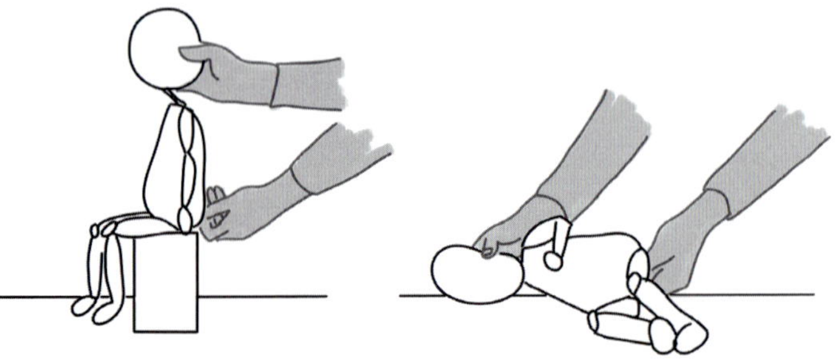

Things to Notice

Aligning the head with the body changes the story When you are not holding it, the body of the puppet will mostly align with the feet. This is its most natural position. However, when puppeting the body, people often feel compelled to align with the head. This is actually less natural. Think before you make the body follow where the head looks, as this will change the story. Turning the head makes the puppet look at something; turning the body makes the puppet face it.

The body is all about fixed points It is always tempting in puppetry to focus only on the part that is moving, but it is very important to control the fixed points as well. To make the shoulders bend forwards, you need to hold the rear end fixed still over the legs at the same time. To push the pelvis forwards, you need to hold the shoulders back in position.

The body puppeteer guards the centre of gravity As the puppet bends over, its centre of gravity moves forwards. It would naturally fall over. It does not, because as it leans forwards the bottom moves backwards very slightly, in counterbalance. This occurs because the puppet moves around its centre, not around the hip joints that are making it bend forwards.

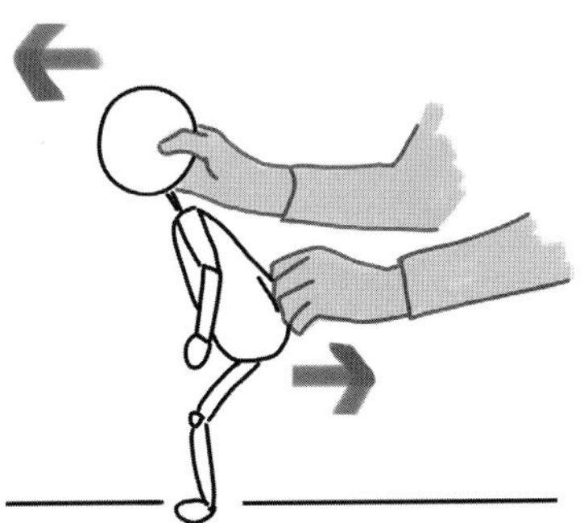

The rear end goes back slightly to balance the head leaning forwards.

THE HANDS ARE PART OF THE BODY

When you puppet a hand, you are actually puppeting one end of the arm, in collaboration with the body puppeteer, who is puppeting the other end. The hands and arms are part of the body and mostly move with the body. In this exercise, you practise making the hands follow the movement of the rest of the puppet. The hand puppeteer keeps the integrity of the shoulder and upper arms.

The Exercise

Have three puppeteers take the workshop puppet and stand it on a table. The head puppeteer takes one hand and the body puppeteer takes the other hand. Hold the hands at the wrist from behind, with your thumb on the outside and your fingers pointing down to the table top.

STEP 1: Test the range of movement of the hand without changing your grip. With this grip you can move the hand to every position it needs to get to without changing.

Holding the hands of the puppet: the fingers point down with the palm facing forwards (left)…

… take hold of the hand (right).

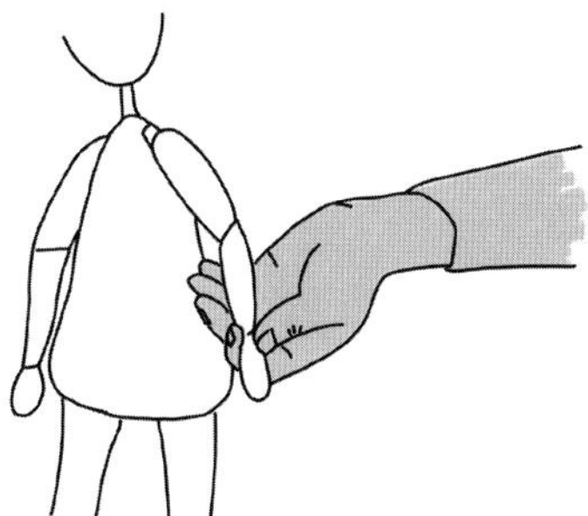

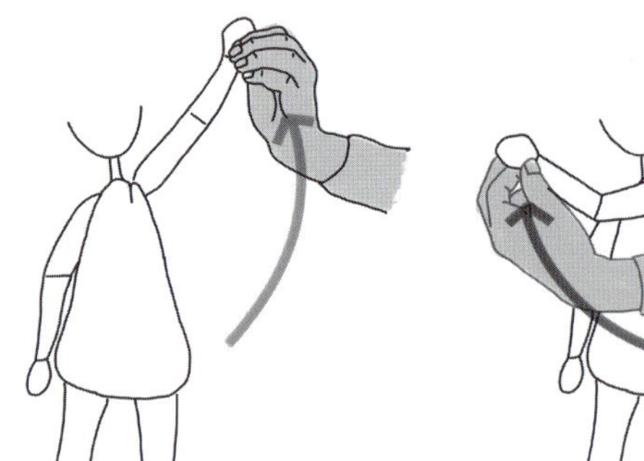

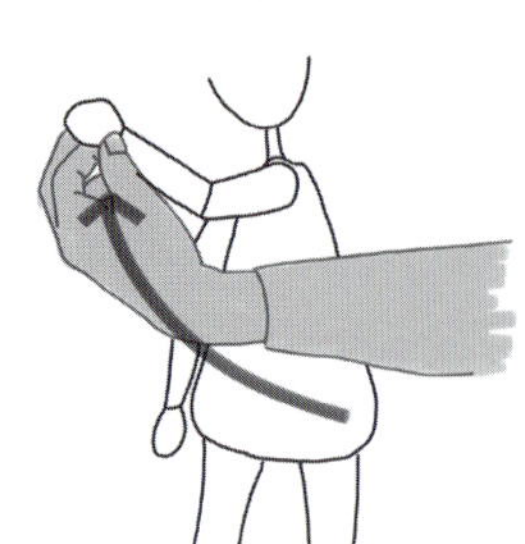

STEP 1: You can reach a full range of movement without changing your grip.

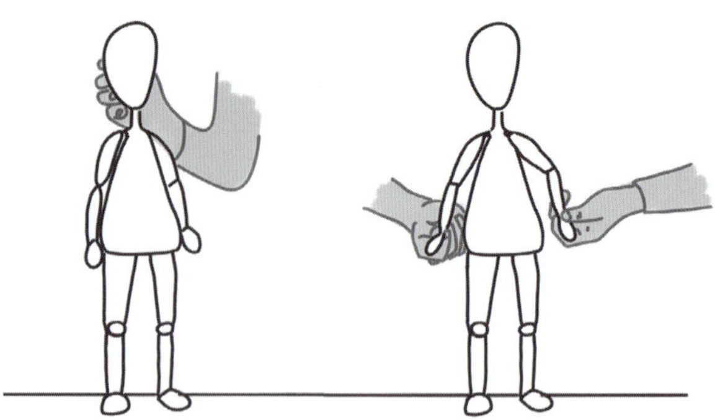

STEP 2: Hands hanging too close to the sides of the body look 'dead'.

STEP 2: Hands hanging with a little space under the arms seem more alive.

DI Clive from *Citizen Puppet* (Blind Summit).

STEP 2: Hold the hands slightly away from the body at the sides, making a bit of space under the armpits so that the arms look muscular. Make sure both sides are the same.
STEP 3: Let the puppet walk around on the table, and keep the arms in the same place in relation to the body all the time. Make them turn with the body, and travel with the body, so that the shoulders look like they are holding the arms.
STEP 4: Now make the arms react to the movement of the rest of the puppet by making them swing as it walks. Make the puppet run on the spot and swing the arms as it does. Make it go into a skid and stop. How do the arms react?
STEP 5: Make the puppet squat and stand up; as you do so, make the arms come up and out, then back. Make the puppet lean forwards and backwards, and move the hands in the opposite way to balance the movement. Make it look left and right and make the hands cross the body to exaggerate the looks, as if in a cartoon. Make the puppet bend over and lower the hands to touch its toes. Make it fall on to its knees and let the hands go up from the sides to balance the fall. Make it step back and raise its hands in a defensive posture.
STEP 6: Try other movements with the puppet, where the puppet moves first and the arms follow.

STEP 5: The arms balance the movement of the body forwards and backwards.

Tip for Doing the Hands Well

Focus on the midline, not the hand You are puppeting a hand, but in your other hand you are holding either the head or the body of the puppet. This means you have to choose which of your own hands to focus on. This should be the one that is holding the body or the head. It is easy to get carried away doing things with the hand and forget that you are also puppeting the body and head. The most important thing for a hand puppeteer is to make the hand look like it is connected to the puppet's arm. Focusing on the midline of the puppet helps keep the integrity of the arm.

Things to Notice

The hand hold 'feels like' the hand Holding the hand from behind with your palm facing forwards not only gives you the full range of movement that you need to make the hand do everything, but also gives you the feeling of where the hand is, and what it is doing.
When you puppet the hand, you are also working an elbow joint The elbow can be very expressive: putting a hand on the hips, leaning on an elbow, or sticking the elbows out, for example. Make the most of working the elbow when you are on the hand.

LEADING WITH THE HANDS

As the hand puppeteer, you control one end of the arm, and the other end is controlled by the body puppeteer – who may or may not be you as well. Hands reach for things, carry things, and handle things (of course). They also grab hand-holds to pull and push the body around. One of the main roles of the hand is as a moveable, useable fixed point around which to move the body.

The Exercise

Have three people on a workshop puppet and explore leading with the arms. What can they make the puppet do?

STEP 1: Make the puppet reach for something, then pick it up. The hand goes out towards whatever it wants and 'pulls' the shoulder of the puppet after it.

STEP 2: Now take the thing the puppet has picked up and give it to someone. The hand leads the puppet by reaching with the object towards the person and again 'pulling' the rest of the puppet along after it.

STEP 3: Make the puppet go to shake someone's hand in the same way: the puppet puts out their hand and pulls the rest of the puppet after it. Then make the puppet wave to the person, in which case it will stay where it is. Make the puppet point, make emphatic gestures, and draw things in the air.

STEP 4: Make the puppet swing its arms back in preparation for a jump action. The body will follow the lead, with the puppet bending its legs. Then, throw the arms forwards, 'pulling' the body after them into the air. After it leaves the ground, the centre of gravity will take over in flight, and the arms will follow to balance it.

STEP 5: Now make the puppet reach for the ground with one hand, then rest on the hand, then lower

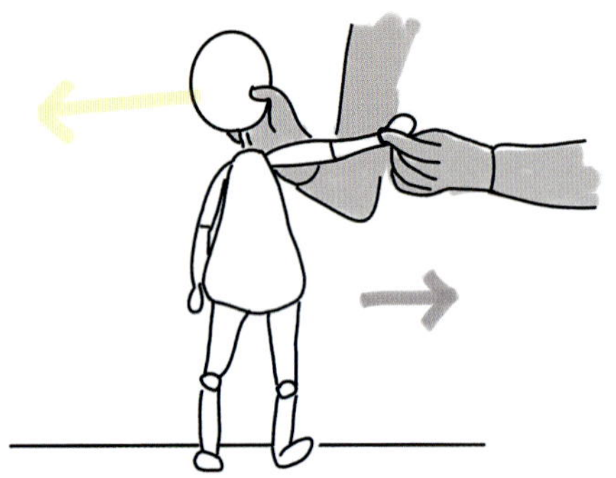

STEP 1: The hand reaches for something and leads the puppet that way.

STEP 3: The hand reaches to shake hands and leads the puppet.

STEP 3: The puppet waves.

STEP 4: Arms swing back and then forwards, in combination with bending the knees, to lead into a jump.

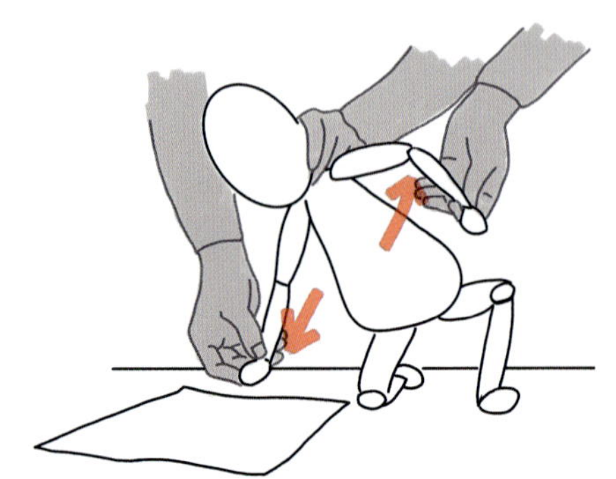

STEP 5: The 'back' hand balances the leading hand.

itself into a kneel, then sit, and then lie down. Use the hands as fixed points to manoeuvre the body into a comfortable position. Make it stretch an arm out and pull the rest of the puppet along on the floor. Use the hands to help it sit up and stand up again.
STEP 6: Make the puppet climb on to a table. To do this, it needs to reach up with one hand, then the other hand, and hold the edge of the table. It then pulls itself up, over its hands, which act as fixed points, to rest its middle on the edge of the table. It swings one knee up on to the table, then the other knee, and then it pushes up its bottom. Up until this stage in the proceedings, the hands make fixed points on the edge of the table. The final action occurs when it stands up and releases them.
STEP 7: Make the puppet climb a wall, looking for hand-holds to be fixed points, and pulling itself up by them.

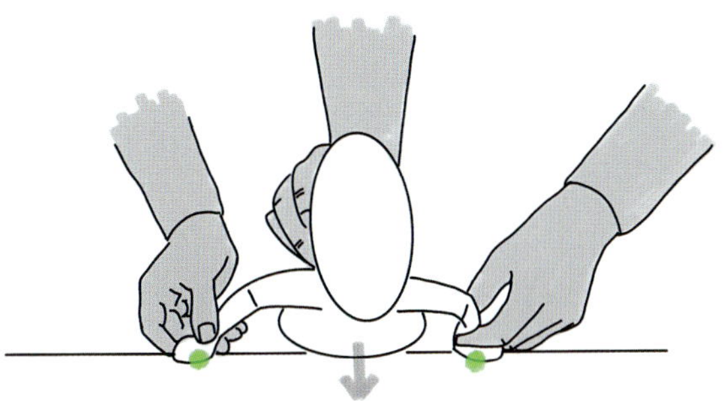

STEP 6: The hands stay on the edge of the table and the puppet pulls itself over them.

Tips for Doing Hands Well

Reach for things with the nearest hand When you make the puppet reach for something, use the nearest hand: for something on its right, use the right hand, and for something on its left, use the left hand. If you use the opposite hand, you will turn the puppet's body sideways to the audience, and they will see your arm crossing in front of it. If the puppet reaches with the near hand, the audience can watch the whole puppet carrying out the action.
Try not to get trapped in technicalities Because hands are functional, it is very easy to get distracted by all sorts of details and technicalities about how they work, and forget that you are, essentially, telling a story. When the puppet's hands are reaching for something, or picking something up, think about *how* it would perform that action. With what sort of attitude? *Why* is it picking the thing up? How long should it take? If, for example, the character in the story would be likely to pick something up without looking at it, or without even thinking about it, then you should not make the puppet labour over it just because it is a puppet.
Use your own hands to make the puppet hold things When you need the puppet hand to do something, you can do it with your own hand. Hold the puppet's hand with finger and thumb, and pick up the other items with your other three fingers. Remember, the technical details are not important; only the story matters.

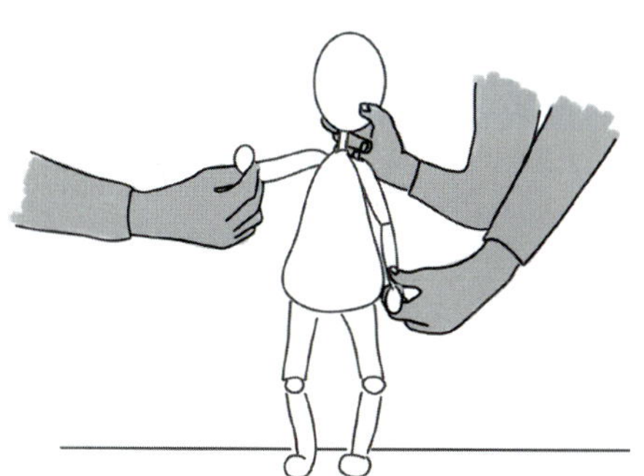

Reaching with the nearest hand keeps the body visible to the audience.

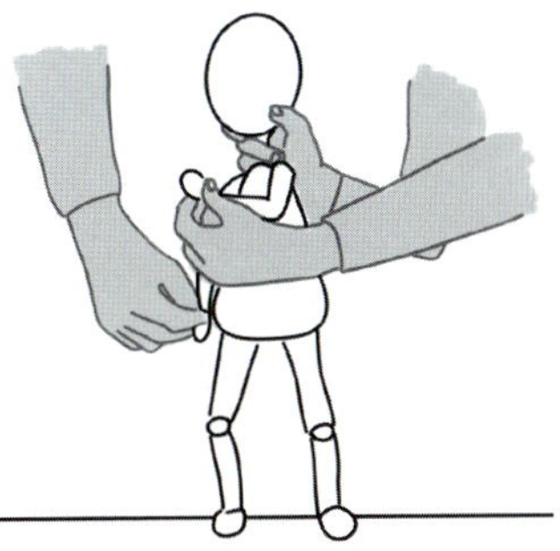

Reaching across the puppet obscures it.

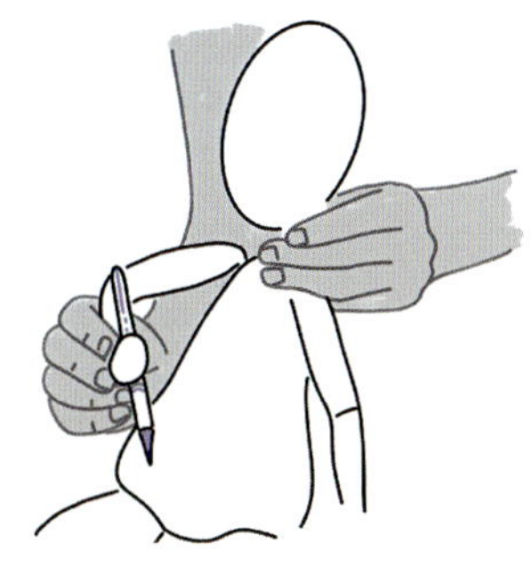

The puppeteer's hand holds objects in the puppet's hand for it.

Think of the hand as moving from the spine When leading with the hand, keep your focus on the midline of the puppet when you are operating the hand, and think of the arm starting from there. When you are puppeting the hand, you are operating a two-handed puppet that is either a head and arm puppet, or a body and arm puppet.

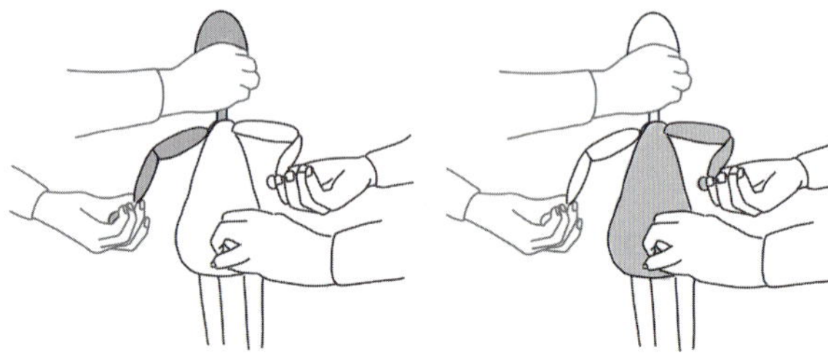

A right-handed head puppeteer does the left hand.

The body puppeteer (working with a right-handed head puppeteer) does the right hand.

Something to Notice

The hands are anchor points In order to use the arms to move the body around, the puppeteer creates fixed points with the hands either by using weight or by grabbing hold of something. Creating these anchor points makes the puppet look as if it is using its arms to manoeuvre it about.

LEADING FEET GO UP AND DOWN

When you are the feet puppeteer, travelling is your 'moment'. Whenever the puppet goes somewhere, these are your 'lines'. Your job is not just to get the

Feet leading on the workshop puppet.

puppet from one place to the other, but also to show the audience *how* it gets there. The way in which you execute the movement of the feet should tell the audience what the puppet is thinking, what it wants, and why it is going. You should tell a story.

When you want to lead with the feet to make the puppet travel you make them go up and down. Making the feet go up and down connects you with the upper parts of the puppet so that they know to follow.

The Exercise

Take a workshop puppet with three people, stand it on a table and practise walking around on the table top.

STEP 1: Start by making the feet go up and down on the spot and then, once they are 'going', start to move the puppet where you want it to go. Three steps on the spot is usually enough to get the puppet ready to go.
STEP 2: When the puppet arrives where it is going, you can make it stop by causing the feet to go up and down again on the spot. After a few steps on the spot, you can come to a standstill. When you want to make it move again, start making the feet go up and down on the spot, and off you go.
STEP 3: Now try making the puppet run on the spot. Then make it run around the table top.
STEP 4: Make the puppet take a big step sideways. To do this, push the weight down on one foot and lift the other foot through the air, bringing it to land where it was stepping. Then change the weight on to the foot that just landed and bring the other foot through the air to join it.
STEP 5: Now pick up one of the feet and turn it over to initiate kneeling. Seeing this, the body puppeteer should respond by lowering the puppet. You then guide the knee on to the ground next to the other foot. Then, making this knee a fixed point on the ground, turn over the other foot and move the second knee to complete the kneel. Practise with the body puppeteer a few times, to get the timing right.

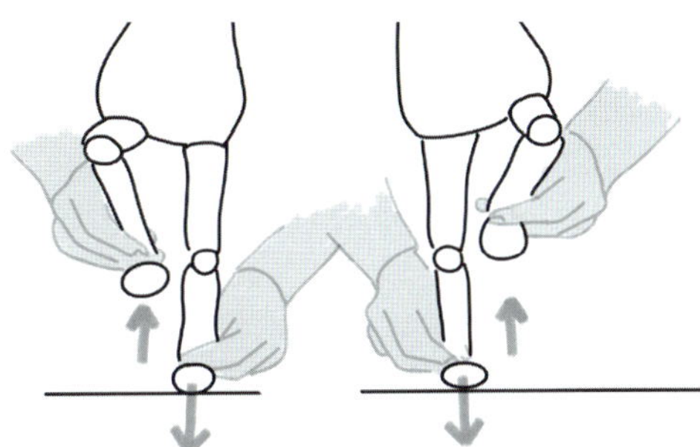

STEP 1: Make the feet go up and down to walk.

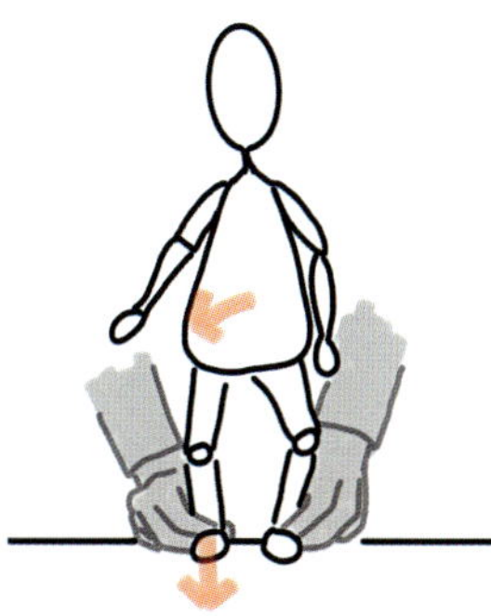

STEP 4: Transfer the puppet's weight on to the back foot...

... lift the puppet's weightless leading foot...

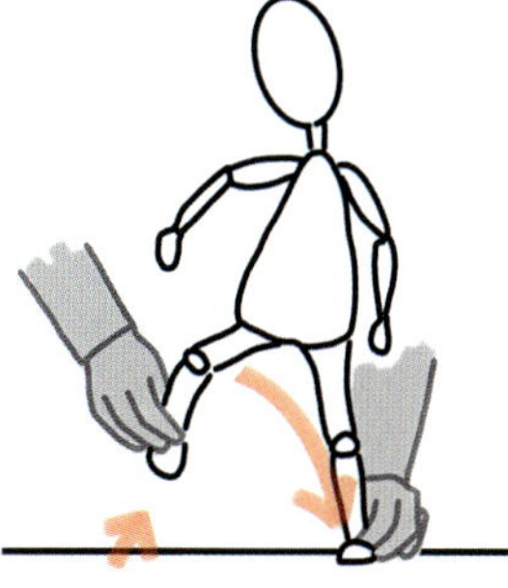

... transfer the weight on to the leading foot...

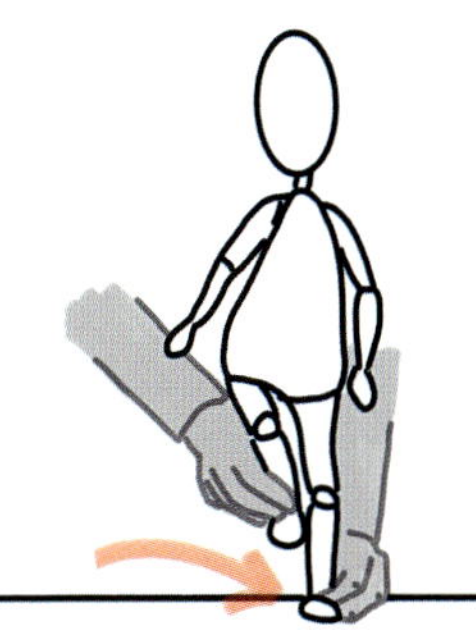

... then make the back foot follow to stand next to the leading foot.

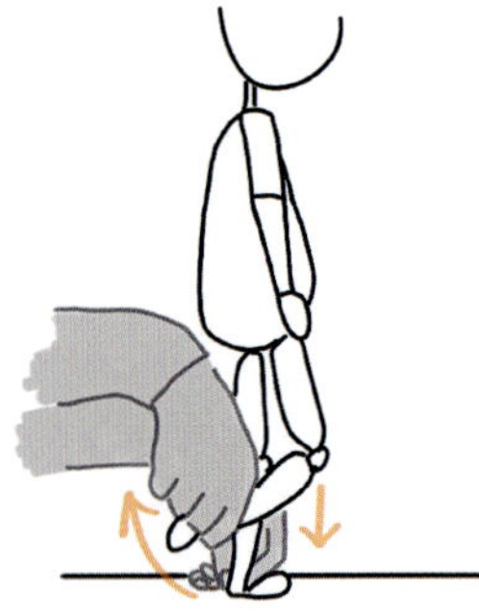

STEP 5: Turn over one foot to lead the puppet kneeling…

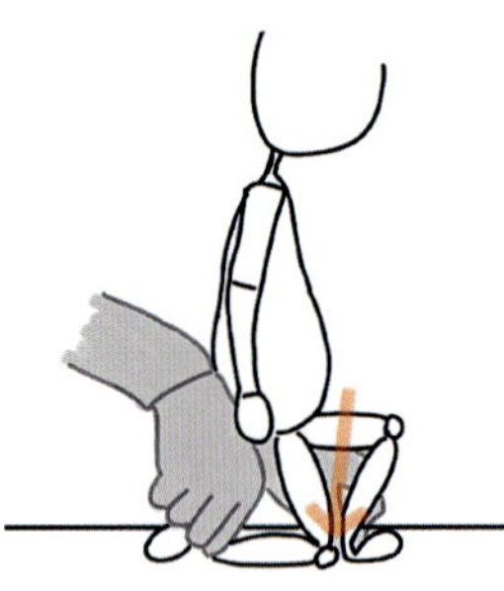

… then the body puppeteer follows to make the puppet kneel.

STEP 6: Try to make the puppet dance by tapping a foot and then wait to see what else the puppet does. Wait for the back puppeteer to join in with the hips and the arms before you get more involved with the feet.

STEP 7: Make the feet go completely still and see what the effect on the rest of the puppet is. Feet are not still very often so stillness should have an impact.

STEP 8: Explore what emotions you can initiate from the legs. Fear and agitation begin with restless legs. Legs shiver and shake when they are nervous. You step from from foot to foot when you are anxious or need to go to the toilet.

STEP 9: See what else you can make the puppet do. Try making it walk like it is drunk. Make it slip or trip over; make it skate or jump into a surfing position.

All the time, remember you are trying to do things that make the other two puppeteers and the rest of the puppet follow you.

Tips for Leading with the Feet

Don't wait for permission Feet are irrepressible. They naturally want to be active. They only stop when they are stopped by the rest of the puppet. Be like feet. Try things and see what effect you can have. You will get things wrong a lot, but then you will get things right.

Keep your focus on the feet You might be tempted to look up to see what the rest of the puppet is doing, but you don't need to. If you look up to see what the body or the head is doing, you have to look away from the feet. The puppeteers above you doing the head and the body can see the whole puppet and the feet without moving their focus off their own part of the puppet. It is their job to follow you.

Do not get too close If you are too close to the puppet, it is very difficult to see what you are doing. You need to be able to see both feet all the time. Stand well back so you can keep your focus on both the feet and think about how they work together to move the centre of gravity between them.

Think about 'legs' Think of the feet as a joined-up system: the two feet are connected by the legs and that system is connected to the centre of the puppet. By moving the two legs, it is possible to have quite a lot of control of the centre of the puppet. If

Focus on the feet.

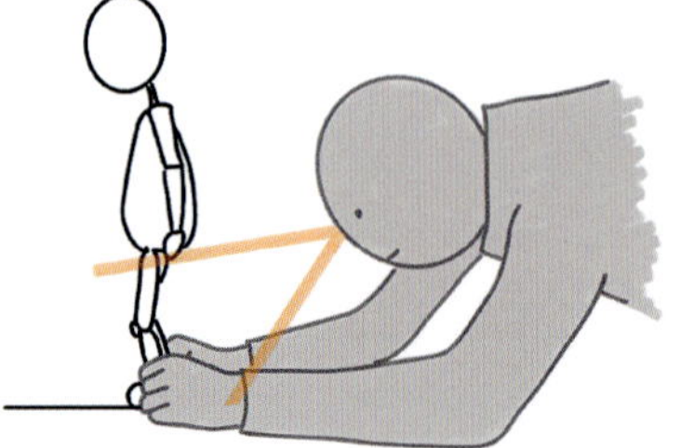

Being too close to the feet restricts your view.

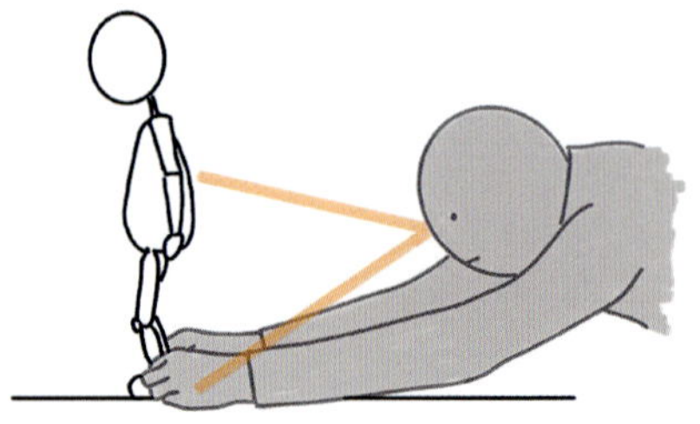

Standing further back lets you see much more.

When the puppet does the splits the feet puppeteer has complete control of it.

Think about how the legs connect to each other through the centre of the puppet.

you make the puppet do the splits you can actually control entirely what it does. Rather than thinking about where the feet are going, think about *how* they are taking the puppet to its destination.

Put the weight down on one foot before lifting the other one up Before lifting a foot to go somewhere, put the weight on to the other foot first. In a way, the puppet steps back in order to go forwards.

Sometimes – for example, when you are trying to make it run – the puppet can look ungrounded, as if it is bicycling in the air rather than running. When you see this problem, think about making the back foot push down as well as making the front foot pull up. Say to yourself as you do it: 'down down down', rather than 'up up up'.

Follow the journey of the feet When you are making the feet lead the puppet, make them lead you as well. Follow the puppet through its full journey and, when they stop, line yourself up behind where they are pointing. If the puppet feet are standing

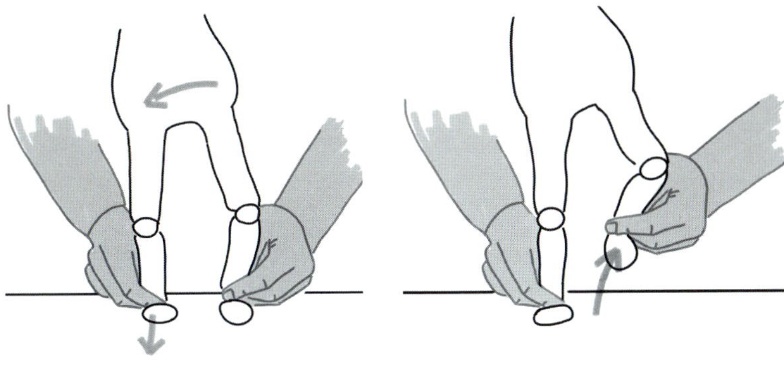

Transfer the puppet's weight on to the back foot first (far left)…

… before lifting the other leg to walk (left). Think about moving backwards to go forwards.

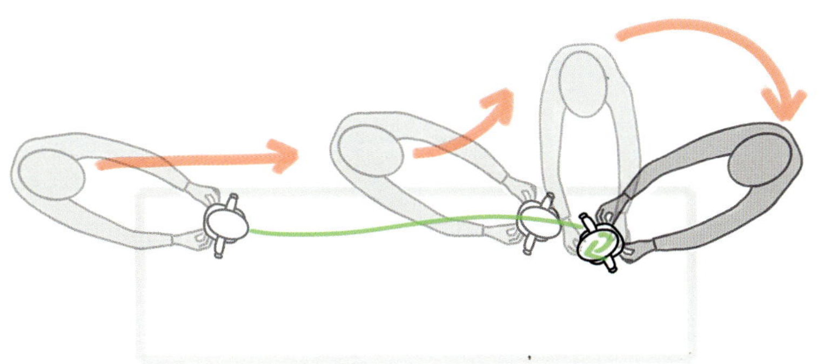

Follow the puppet through its full journey.

sideways on to the audience, make sure you are behind them, also standing sideways, and not upstage of them. When the puppet turns, follow in its footsteps, as if you are being pulled like a trailer. You will experience the puppet's journey in your own body, and tune in to its performance. If you cut corners you will get confused about what the puppet is doing.

Things to Notice

The puppet is an upside-down version of reality In reality, the feet hold a person up, but a foot puppeteer holds the feet *down*. Their task is to make the puppet look as if it is standing on its own feet, even though it is being supported from above by the puppeteer(s).

Still feet are unusual and will attract the attention of the audience When the puppet is paying attention to something, its feet will be stilled. It is an unnatural state for this part of the body; if the feet stop moving, the audience will wonder why. The stillness tells the audience that the puppet is listening to or looking at something, or trying to work something out.

Go up and down with the feet on the spot The 'up and down' movement engages the rest of the puppet and prepares the other two puppeteers to follow you. If you just step off with the leading foot, you will take them by surprise. Your leg will pull the puppet, and you will all be in for a bumpy ride.

FOLLOWING FEET MOVE SIDEWAYS

Even when the puppet is standing still, the feet are nearly always moving. Feet are a classic 'tell'. Everything that the puppet feels or thinks leaks out in clues through their movement. To do following feet you need to think like the puppet, and make the feet do what the feet of someone thinking those things would do. The audience should be able to tell what the puppet is thinking and feeling just from watching what the feet are doing.

The Exercise

Place the workshop puppet on the table. Let the other parts of the puppet lead and follow with the feet.

STEP 1: Make the puppet look at things, listen to things, touch things, think, feel, talk, and let the feet 'follow' these leading actions. This means allowing them to respond to what the puppet is thinking.

To make the feet look as though they are 'thinking', move them sideways on the floor, rather than up and down. Transfer the weight from foot to foot in a rhythm and pattern that follows the thoughts and feelings of the puppet.

STEP 2: Breathe with the puppet, and with the other two puppeteers, so that you can develop the

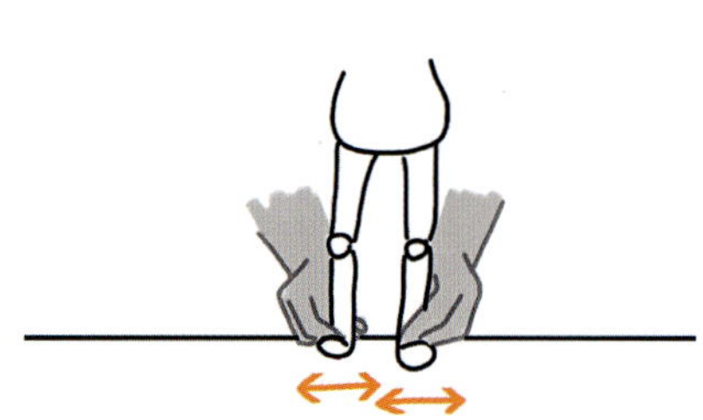

STEP 1: Following feet move sideways.

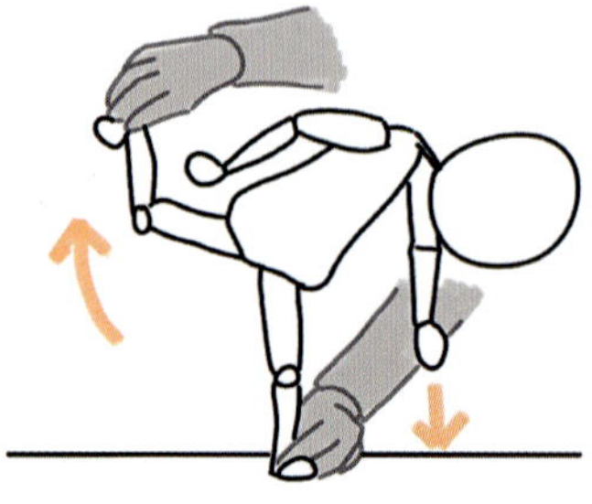

STEP 4: The back leg balances the puppet as it leans over to pick something up.

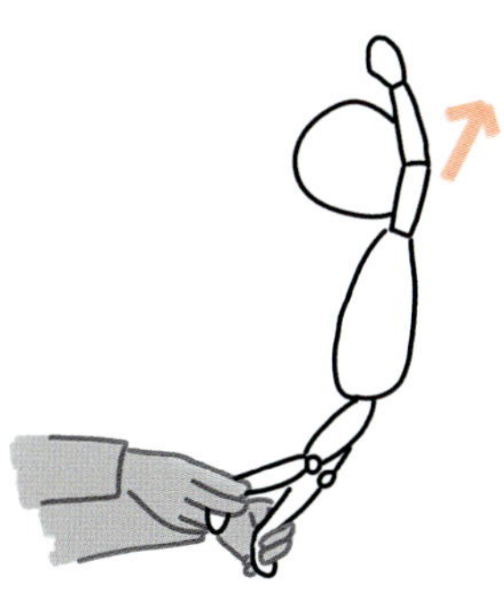
STEP 5: The feet follow into a jump.

STEP 5: The feet tuck up under the body at the apex of the jump.

STEP 5: The feet lead the puppet into the landing.

puppet's emotional state. Let the feet become agitated by the breath as the emotion grows. Make the feet move with happy jerks when the puppet gets excited, step from one to another when it becomes worried, turn inwards when it is sad, or try to run away when scared. Try doing bored feet and tired feet. The feet move in different ways because of what the puppet is feeling and what it is trying to hide.

STEP 3: At a certain pitch of emotion, the feet will change from sideways feet to up and down feet. The puppet will lift them high and they will engage with the body and start to lead: stamping, jumping and taking the puppet towards an emotional climax.

STEP 4: Now try other things that make the feet follow. Make the puppet lean over to pick something up, putting all the weight on to one leg, lifting the other leg off the ground to balance. Make it do a handstand.

STEP 5: Make the puppet jump. To jump, the puppet swings the arms, bends the knees (this is done by the body puppeteer), then throws the body into the air. The feet are pulled after it. They catch up with the body in the suspension at the apex of the jump and then lead into the landing.

Tips for Doing Following Feet

Get the story right first If you are struggling to get the movement of the feet right, try working out the story vocally first. This might involve a pattern of breathing or thinking, or mumbling under the breath. Make it into a concrete thought that you can say out loud: 'I feel ner…vous….' Then say it as you do the feet and let the feet do whatever they do. You might feel like they are a mess to begin with, but, if you have the story right, they will correct themselves with repetition.

Study real feet Become a feet expert. Look at people's feet in the rehearsal room, outside on the street, at home. Block out the rest of the body with your hand and just watch the feet. What can you find out from looking only at the feet? Can you deduce what the person is thinking and doing? Can you tell what they are saying?

Things to Notice

Feet are always moving They are constantly adjusting and re-adjusting their position to ease pressure, tiredness or pain. Everything makes them move. They move because they are nervous, and they move because they are not nervous. They

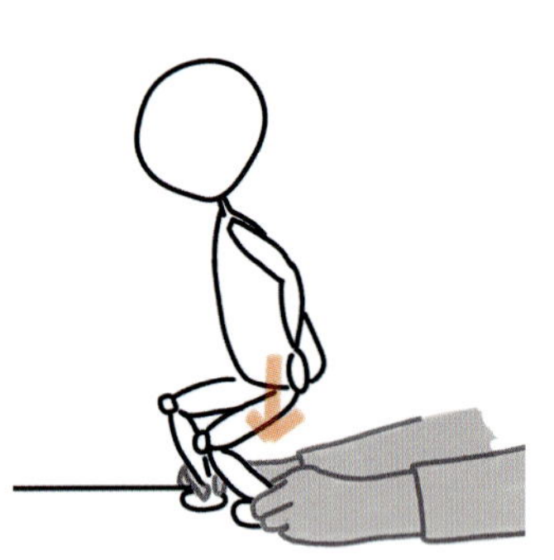

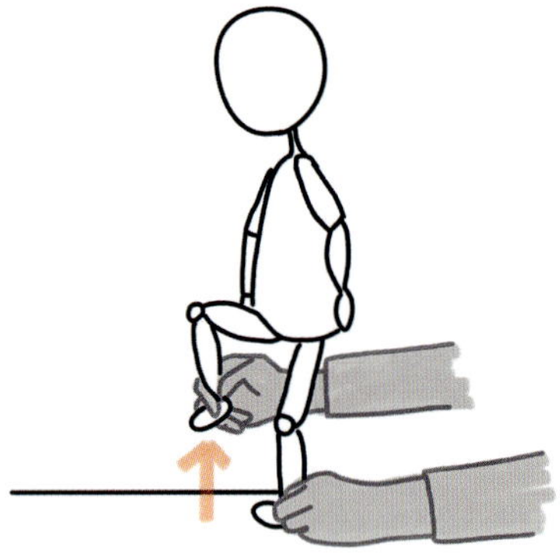

FAR LEFT: The body puppeteer bends and straightens the knees to make the puppet squat.

LEFT: The feet puppeteer makes the puppet pick up a foot.

may be active because they are happy or unhappy, excited or bored. They are almost never absolutely still. As a result, they give away what the puppet is feeling, as well as what the puppet is trying to hide. That is why audiences love feet.

'Following feet' are all about weight transfer The weight of the puppet can be fully on one foot or the other, evenly shared between the two feet, or unevenly shared between the two feet. The weight is constantly changing in response to what the puppet is thinking. As the feet puppeteer, you need always to know where the puppet's weight is, so that you know which foot it can pick up when the puppet goes to move.

Puppeting the legs is shared between the body and the feet puppeteers It is not always the feet puppeteer who makes the legs bend. The back puppeteer bends the knees to make the puppet squat, kneel, jump or hop. The feet puppeteer bends the knees to lift the feet to make the puppet walk, run, think and feel.

CHANGING BETWEEN LEADING AND FOLLOWING FEET

Following feet move sideways. They communicate to the audience what the puppet is thinking. You can also think of them as 'listening' feet. Leading feet go up and down to take the puppet somewhere, either geographically or emotionally. By going up and down, they affect the rest of the puppet, and communicate with the other puppeteers, so that they can make the puppet do something. In this exercise you practise changing between the two states.

The Exercise

Place the workshop puppet on the table with three puppeteers and practise going from leading up-and-down feet, to following sideways feet, and back again.

STEP 1: Begin with following feet, stepping side to side, without making the puppet move anywhere.
STEP 2: Without discussing what you are doing, change the feet to leading feet, by making them start to go up and down on the spot. Take three leading steps on the spot and then, on the fourth step, make the puppet start to travel.
STEP 3: When the puppet arrives where it was going, make it do three 'leading' up-and-down steps on the spot, to stop the puppet, and then change back into 'following' sideways steps.
Practise changing following feet into leading feet and back again until you and the puppeteers above are able to move and stop the puppet smoothly and confidently without having to plan or make signals.

Tips for Doing It Well

Start moving the feet before they have to walk Feet are always ready to go. Unless the puppet's legs are exhausted, they seem to know that the puppet is going to go somewhere almost before it does and start getting ready to move before they are allowed to. Practise changing from sideways feet into up-and-down feet before the puppet needs to walk, so that you are ready to go before you get your cue.

When the puppet arrives at its destination, the feet slow down into the stop, and then change from up-and-down feet back into sideways 'thinking' feet.

Know where you are going before you go there Decide, before you start changing the feet, where the puppet is going to go. The audience can see from the way the puppet starts walking how far it intends to go. Every journey has a beginning, a middle and an end. The journey may be interrupted, or the puppet may change its mind and go further, but the audience will see that too. This is your language – the language of the feet.

PART II – TRAINING

5
BREATHING AND CENTRING

This chapter is focused on making your hands 'breathe' and move around an imaginary 'puppet centre'.

Puppets don't breathe so the puppeteer has to do it for them. Connecting your breathing to the movement of your hands is a fundamental technique of puppetry. You need to be able to use your breathing to change the movement of your hands, and use the movement of your hands to change your breathing. You need to understand the effect that breathing will have on the movements of the puppet, and transmit that effect through your hands to the puppet.

There are many centres of gravity in puppetry: the real centres of gravity of the puppeteers, the real centres of gravity of each part of the puppet, and the imaginary centres of gravity of the puppet character. The most important one to make the puppet come alive is the imaginary centre of the puppet character. You need to understand how these different centres of gravity interact with each other to create the imaginary centre of the puppet character, and move around it.

This chapter has exercises to practise moving your hands around the centre and the breathing of the puppet. They are good for practising fundamental skills, and for warm ups before rehearsals and performances.

OPPOSITE: Shadow puppets from *Little Match Girl* (Blind Summit/Improbable).

THE 'TAI CHI' BREATHING EXERCISE

This exercise is inspired by a Tai Chi activity, in which participants breathe in a group and synchronise their hand movements with their breathing. It is a really good way to warm up the body and tune in with the other people.

The Exercise

You can do this exercise on your own or in a group. If you are in a group, one person leads and the others follow so that you all breathe together.

STEP 1: Make a circle. Stand with your feet parallel and shoulder width apart. Your knees should be soft.

STEP 2: Imagine that your head is suspended from the ceiling by a string. The string holds you up. From your head hangs your neck, and from your neck your shoulders and spine. From your shoulders your arms. Hanging from your spine are your chest and abdomen, and, at the bottom, your pelvis. From your pelvis hang your legs and at the bottom of your legs hang your feet.

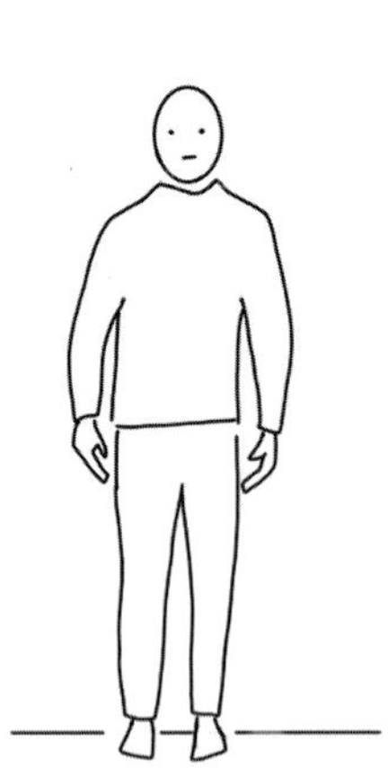
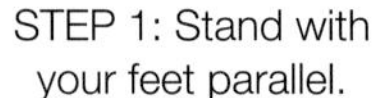

STEP 1: Stand with your feet parallel.

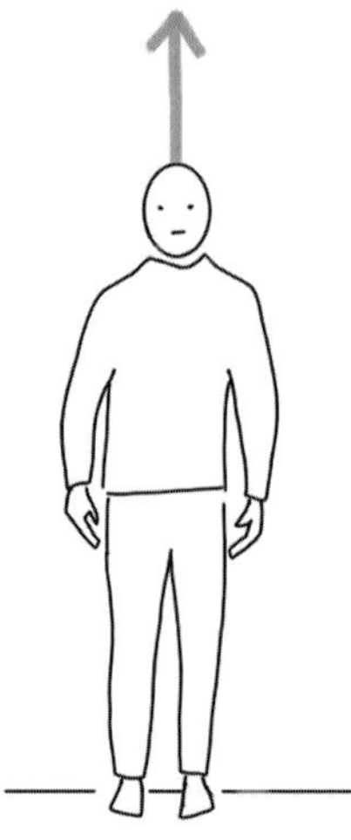

STEP 2: Imagine a string holding up your head.

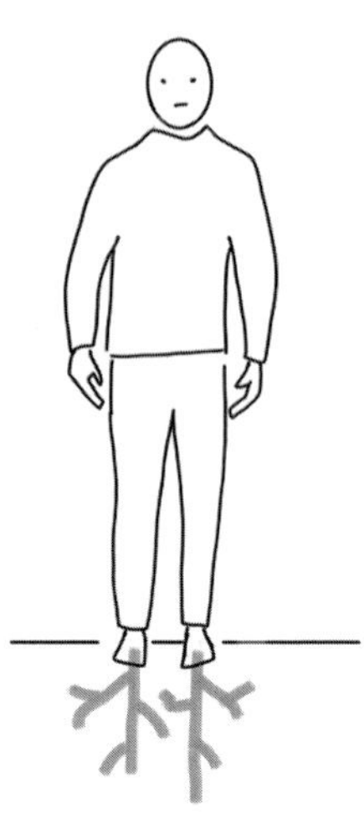

STEP 3: Imagine roots holding your feet down.

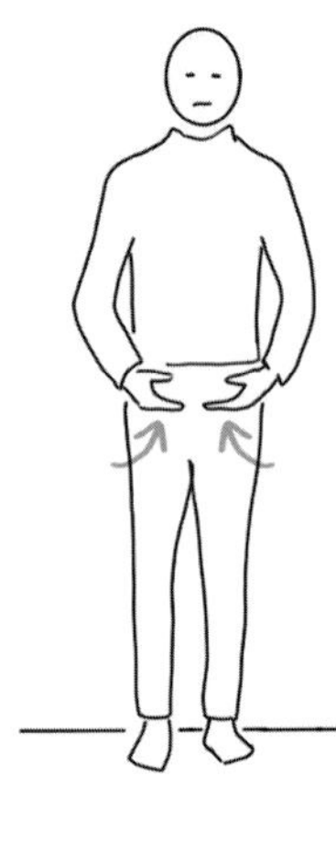

STEP 4: Bring your hands together in front of you, palms facing up.

STEP 3: Imagine roots growing from your feet into the ground. They hold your feet down, and the string to your head pulls you up. Every part of your body is hanging on the string, like a puppet. You can feel yourself being pulled upwards by the string and held down by the roots. Your body straightens out in between.

STEP 4: Now bring your hands together in front of you, so that the fingertips nearly touch, palms facing upwards.

STEP 5: Take a deep breath in. As you do so, raise your hands up to your mouth, as if they are being sucked upwards by your breath.

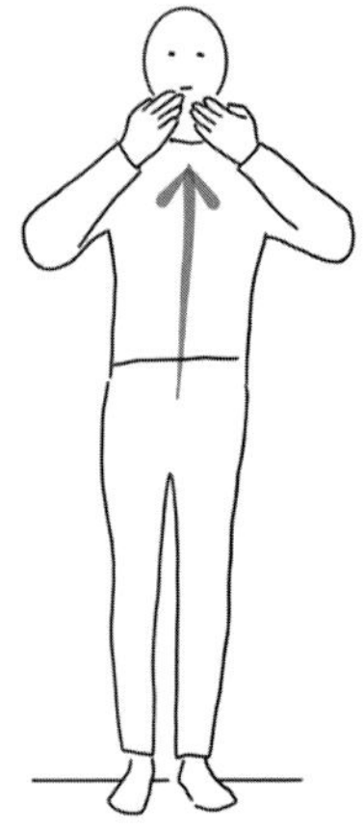

STEP 5: Breathe in and pull your hands up to your mouth.

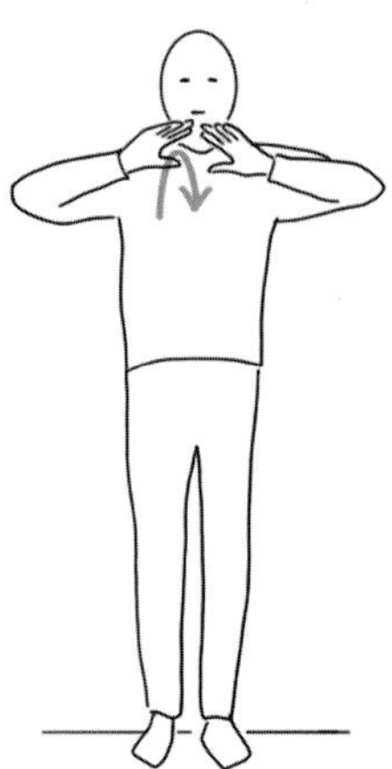

STEP 6: Turn your hands over in the suspension between breaths.

STEP 7: Breathe out and push your hands down.

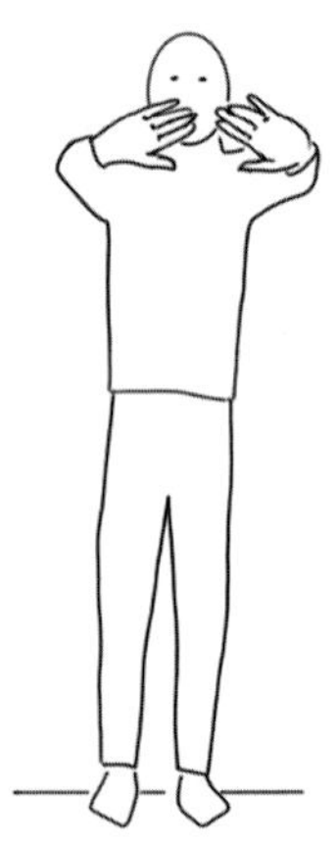

STEP 10: Breathe out and push your hands forwards away from your mouth.

STEP 6: As you finish your in-breath, your hands arrive close to your mouth and your breath suspends. You are full of air. You can barely take in any more. You might be able to squeeze in a bit more, but you don't need to. Pause your breathing and, in the suspension, turn your hands slowly in front of your mouth so that your palms face downwards.
STEP 7. Breathe out and, as you do so, push your hands downwards.
STEP 8: At the bottom of the out-breath, your breath rests and your hands turn slowly.
STEP 9: Breathe in again, drawing your hands up to your mouth, then suspend your breath again and turn your hands.
STEP 10: Breathe out again, but this time push your hands straight out in front of you.
STEP 11: Rest, turn, and breathe in, bringing your hands in towards your mouth again, then suspend your breath and turn your hands so that the palms face upwards.
STEP 12: Complete the pattern by breathing out and pushing your hands upwards over your head then out to your sides, describing two big arcs, until they are back where you first started, fingertip to fingertip in front of you (Step 4).
STEP 13: Repeat the sequence a few times.
STEP 14: After repeating the cycle a few times, try changing how long each part takes. Breathe in quickly, and slowly, hold the suspensions between the breaths for different lengths of time, then breathe out quickly, and slowly. Try different combinations of in-breaths and out-breaths and suspensions. Try breathing with more 'attack' or making the out-breath last longer. See if you can take an extra in-breath when you seem to be full of air, or an extra out-breath when you are empty. If working in a group, make sure that you are all breathing together.

Tips for Doing It Better

Don't hyperventilate! Practise taking big breaths, rather than deep breaths. If you actually breathe deeply you will hyperventilate and become light-headed. This is not the aim. Think of it as a performative breath – you are *pretending* to breathe deeply. In the Tai Chi exercise you are practising breathing for yourself, but in the puppetry exercise you are practising breathing in order to connect your breath with the movement of your hands.

STEP 11: Turn your hands over in the suspension to point the palms up.

STEP 12: Breathe out and push your hands up…

… out and down, back to the starting position.

Make your breathing audible Hearing your breathing really helps you connect the movement of your hand to the breath. Breathe in through your teeth. And as you breathe out, use your tongue and your top teeth to make a 'shhhhhh' sound. Learn to 'play' with the sound and the rhythm of your breathing.

Things to Notice

Your hands are in suspension between breaths When the breathing suspends, at the end of a breath in or out, the hands also suspend. They are no longer going anywhere – there is nowhere to go – but at the same time they are not completely still. They don't freeze. In suspension, they continue to move very slowly, turning gradually, in anticipation of moving on the next breath.

Breathing is a cycle of tension and relaxation When your lungs are full of air, at the end of an in-breath, your body is tense and upright. Your body is lifted by the air you have taken in. Your chest is fully inflated, your spine is straighter, your arms are pushed slightly away from your body, your head tilts slightly up, your eyes are slightly more open, your leg muscles tighten, your knees straighten, and your feet are tense, with your toes curling up off the floor.

At this point, you are alert and ready to do something; you are 'inspired' – literally 'full of air' – and you feel full of possibility. Your brain is quick, your eyes are sharp, you are only just balanced, you are ready for action. If something happened suddenly right now, you would jump, or attack, react fast.

Conversely, when you breathe out, your body relaxes: your chest collapses, your spine bends, your hands hang by your side, your head drops a little, your knees soften, and your feet flatten into the floor. You feel calm, comfortable and grounded. Your feet connect to the floor and you are balanced, relaxed.

In this state, you are less ready to do something. You will react slowly. You are not ready for action. If something happened to frighten you now, you would need to breathe in first before being able to react to it.

Breathing has a 'shape' The in-breath and out-breath both have a beginning, a middle and an end. At the beginning of the breath the air accelerates, in the middle it goes at a constant speed, and at the end it decelerates, until it stops. Think about moving your hands in the same way. Make them accelerate at the beginning of the breath, then move with constant speed like the air in the middle of the breath, and then slow down at the end of the breath.

The cycle of breath goes on all day This cycle – in, suspend, out, rest – is continuous, with all the tensing of the body and relaxing that goes along

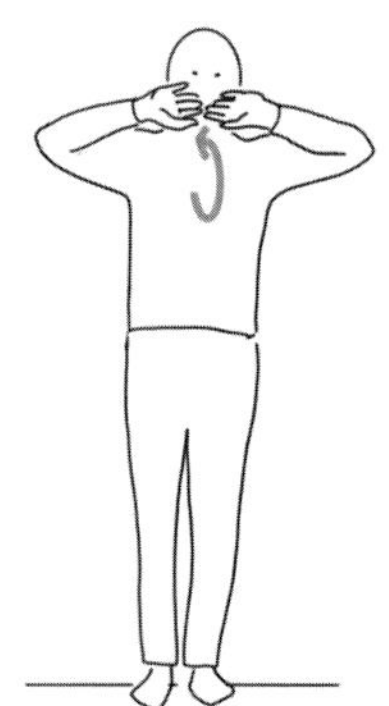

The hands turn slowly in the suspensions – they do not freeze.

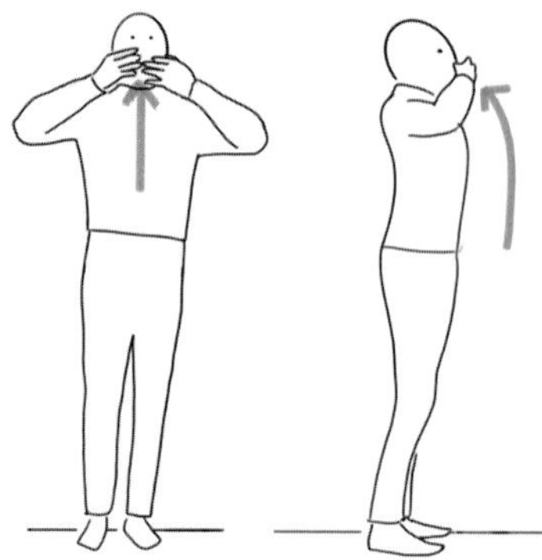

Inspired, full of air, tall, tense, edgy, quick to react, 'ready'.

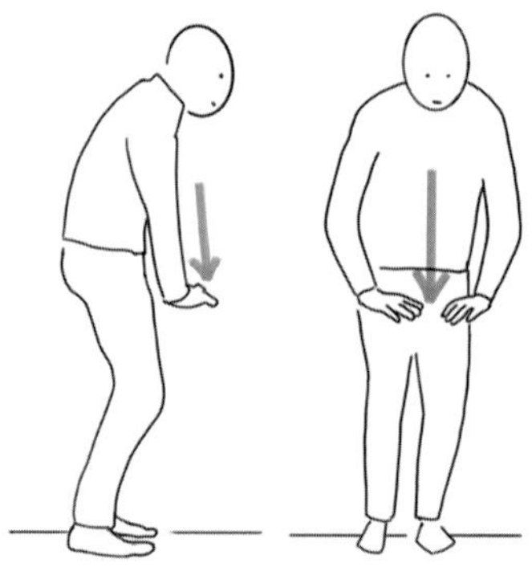

Deflated, empty of air, relaxed, receptive, friendly, slow to react.

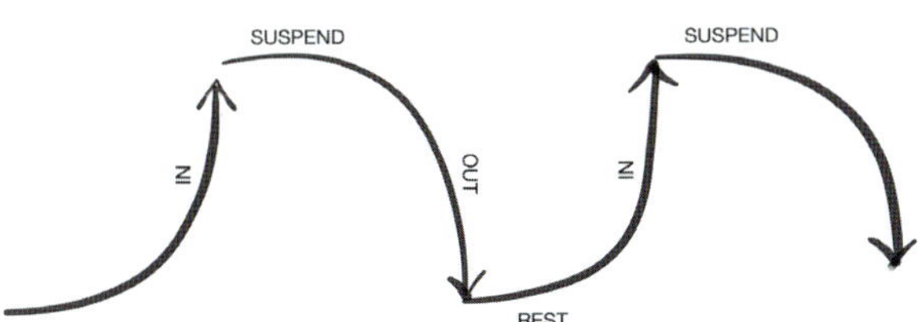

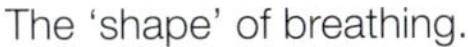
The 'shape' of breathing.

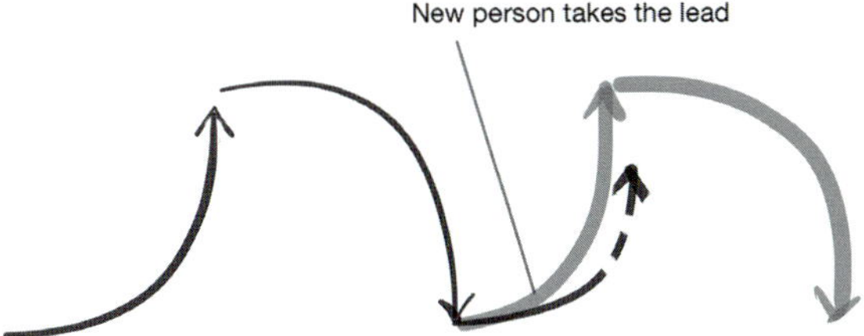

STEP 2: To take the leadership, come in just before the rest of the group is about to breathe in.

with it. Most people breathe in and out about 12 to 16 times a minute. As a result, 12 to 16 times a minute you are more tense and more ready to do something, and 12 to 16 times a minute you are flat-footed, relaxed and off guard. The breathing speeds up when you are tense or exercising, and slows down when you are resting or asleep.

It is all connected When you change one part of the cycle of breathing, the other parts of the cycle change in response. Let yourself be led by what feels natural.

TAKING LEADERSHIP WITH THE BREATH

In this exercise, you change who is leading the breath. You keep the sequence of the hand movements the same, but vary the rhythm of the breathing. Your aim is to keep breathing together as a group as you change leader from person to person, and let the rhythm of the breathing change organically between you.

The Exercise

The group stands in a circle facing each other.

STEP 1: Start by breathing together, making the same 'Tai Chi' pattern with your hands, following one person's lead.

STEP 2: Once you are all breathing together, someone else takes over the leadership of the breath. To do this, they come in at the end of a suspension or rest, just before the group is about to take the next breath. They breathe loudly to make sure that everyone hears them take the lead and can follow them. The group now follows that leader until the next person takes the leadership.

STEP 3: Someone else takes the leadership by coming in slightly early at the end of a suspension or rest, and so on. The leadership of the breathing is continually changed until the group can do it seamlessly, without noticeably varying the breathing pattern, and the breathing rhythm changes organically.

Tips for Doing It Well

Think ahead Make your decision to take the leadership in advance and then choose your moment to do it. Don't decide in the moment and panic.

Be daring Don't wait to be offered the leadership; take it. Waiting results in a leaderless group. The best, most daring time to take over the leadership is the last possible moment before the group is about to take the next breath.

Use your ears to follow and your eyes to stay in sync Listen for the leading breath to know who the leader is. You don't need to see them to follow them, you just need to be able to hear them. You can make sure you are in sync by watching the hand movements of anyone in the group.

Breathe loudly to take the lead When you are the leader, make sure that everyone can hear you so that they can follow you. When someone wants to take over the leadership, they have to breathe as loudly as you – not louder – but come in sooner.

Things to Notice

'Sooner' does not mean 'faster' Be careful not to confuse getting in sooner with breathing more quickly. If your breathing is faster, the breathing of the group will speed up through the exercise, and you will lose your followers. In order to keep people with you, come in sooner to take the lead and then slow down to let people catch up. Breathe in such a way that by the end of your take over breath, everyone is in sync with you.

Followers want strong leaders Notice that when you are following you want to know who to follow and what to follow. In other words, the leader should be clear and strong with their takeover. Don't be shy; a shy leader is impossible to follow.

THE BREATH OF LAUGHING AND CRYING

In this exercise you manipulate your breathing to look as though you are laughing and crying. The movements and gestures associated with crying or laughing come from the need to support the breathing patterns that are created by these emotions. By copying the breathing pattern of these emotions, and then the movements that follow, it is possible to recreate the appearance of the emotions themselves. Ideally, the audience will interpret these movements as genuine crying or laughter when they see them.

You can use the same sequence of exploration, starting with the breath, to find the movements of any emotion. Once you are familiar with the breathing patterns of emotions and the ways in which they affect the movement of your body, you can apply them to your hands, and to how you move a puppet.

The Exercise

Make a circle around the room, facing each other. Have your feet parallel, shoulder width apart, and be aware of the 'string' holding you up.

STEP 1: Start with your hands together in front of you. Breathe in and bring your hands up to your mouth, as you did in the Tai Chi breathing exercise.
STEP 2: Now breathe out, push your hands in front of you, and make the sound 'Haaaaaa…'. Keep

STEP 2: Breathe out and say 'Haaaa!'.

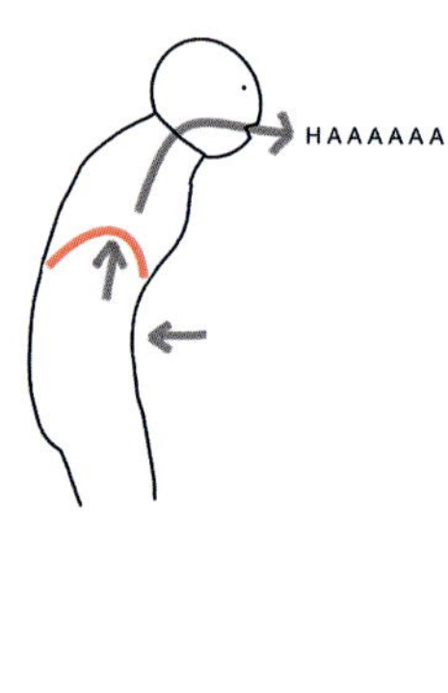

STEP 2: The tummy pulls in, and the diaphragm pushes up and pushes the air out.

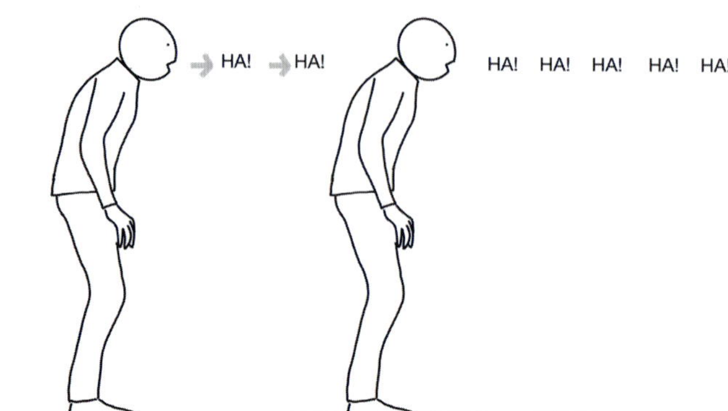

STEP 3: Use your diaphragm to breathe out in beats.

STEP 4: Use your diaphragm to breathe out in shorter beats.

going until you run out of air. Use your diaphragm to push out the last bit of air: pull your tummy in, push your diaphragm up and squeeze the air out.

Repeat this a few times, breathing in and out: 'Haaaaaaaaa....'

STEP 3: Now breathe in again and change your out-breath to two beats: 'Ha – Haaaaa...', using your diaphragm to push the beats of the air out. Repeat twice.

STEP 4: Change your out-breath to several beats: 'Ha ha ha ha ha haaaaa....' Repeat, breathing in and bringing your hands up, and out: 'Ha ha ha ha haaaaa....' In. And out: 'Ha ha ha ha....'

STEP 5: Now, make the 'Ha ha ha's grow bigger – louder, longer and faster. Let your mouth form into a smile and turn them into laughter. Keep driving the 'Ha ha ha...' sound with your diaphragm, but let it become more natural, building it louder and bigger.

STEP 6: Now, as the laughter gets bigger and bigger and you need more air to make it, start to involve your whole body in the effort. Make fists, clutch your sides and lean on your knees. Stamp your feet. 'Hahahahahaha.' Jump up and down. 'Hahahahaha.' Collapse on to your knees. Slap the floor. 'Hahahahaha.' Brace your arms on the ground. Point at someone across the room. Scream in pain. Shake silently with laughter. Do whatever you need to do to keep laughing. 'Hahahaha.'

STEP 7: Keep building your laughter into a crescendo, then, when you can't think of anywhere else to go with it, turn your smile over into a 'sad face', scrunch up your eyebrows into a frown, and keep going: 'Ha ha ha ha ha.' Keep the stamping, pointing, jumping up and down. Keep your unhappy face and keep the breathing going.

STEP 8: The laughter changes into crying. Keep crying. Wail at each other across the room. Shout at the sky. Plead with the ground. And then rest.

Things to Notice

Faked emotion is the same as real emotion While you are doing the exercise, look across the room at the other people doing the same thing as you. They look as if they really are laughing or crying. It looks real. Everyone is laughing and yet nothing funny has happened. Everyone is crying and yet no one is genuinely upset. The 'feelings' of laughter and crying come from the physical movements you need to support the breathing. The breathing pattern creates the emotion.

STEP 6: The breathing of laughter makes you double over and brace your arms.

STEP 8: Laughing.

STEP 8: Crying.

Real emotion. Fake emotion.

Laughing and crying are physically the same The breathing pattern and physical movements of crying and laughing are more or less the same. The only difference – the thing that indicates that you are crying – is the expression on your face.

The movement of the breathing leads to other movements As your breathing gets bigger and harder, you need to brace your chest by putting your hands on your knees or holding on to your sides. You may even collapse on the floor. The emotion becomes painful and you try to stop it by stamping or jumping up and down. You fall on your knees, roll on the floor, start groaning in pain. All this has begun with an exercise about breathing.

Emotions are physical feelings Emotions have physical effects on the body – they can make you cry, laugh, shake, vomit, need to pee. They turn you on, give you gut ache, headaches, make you feel cold. You feel butterflies in your stomach when you are nervous, you yawn when you are tired, and you cry in pain when you are unhappy. These physical feelings change your breathing, which affects how you move.

Emotions last a long time They may stay with you for a while – hours, days, sometimes even years – or your whole life.

MAKING YOUR HANDS BREATHE

Now that you have explored the movement of breathing in your own body, you need to learn to transmit that movement into your hands. In this exercise, instead of letting your hands move as an extension of your body, you use them to 'draw' the cycle of your breathing in the air in front of you.

Clutch your sides… … brace your arms… … roll on the floor.

You can do this on your own, or lead a group to do it together.

The Exercise

In this exercise, the aim is to draw a square in the air in front of you, following the patterns of your breath.

STEP 1: Breathe in and let your hand rise with the breath.
STEP 2: As your breath suspends, before you breathe out again, let your hand drift horizontally sideways.
STEP 3: As you breathe out, let your hand fall.
STEP 4: In the rest before the next in-breath, let your hand drift horizontally sideways back to the first position.
STEP 5: Breathe in again. Let your hand rise with the in-breath, fall with the out-breath, and move sideways on the suspensions.
Repeat a few squares to get used to doing it.
STEP 6: Try changing hand. Try making the upstrokes longer and shorter, slower and faster. Try different periods of suspension and rest.

Match the movement of your hand as accurately as possible to the breath. Get used to the idea that, in order to move your hand, you have to take some breath. To go up you have to breathe in, and to go down you breathe out. To move your hand faster you have to breathe faster. To stop your hand suddenly, you have to stop your breath suddenly.
STEP 7: Now, using combinations of long or short in-breaths, out-breaths and suspensions, make different patterns and journeys in the air.
STEP 8: Reverse the way your hands go: make your hand go down when you breathe in, and then up when you breathe out. How does this feel?
STEP 9: Use both hands. Move one hand at a time, in whatever combination you want to, but still following the basic rules that, to move your hand upwards you need to breathe in, to move it downwards you need to breathe out, and when you suspend, the hands move sideways. When you move one hand, keep the other hand still in the air where it last was.
STEP 10: Try moving your hand about in the air as if it is being blown by your breath. Let your hands go anywhere. Let each part of the breath give them more life and send them in a new direction. Let them hang in the suspensions and float on the

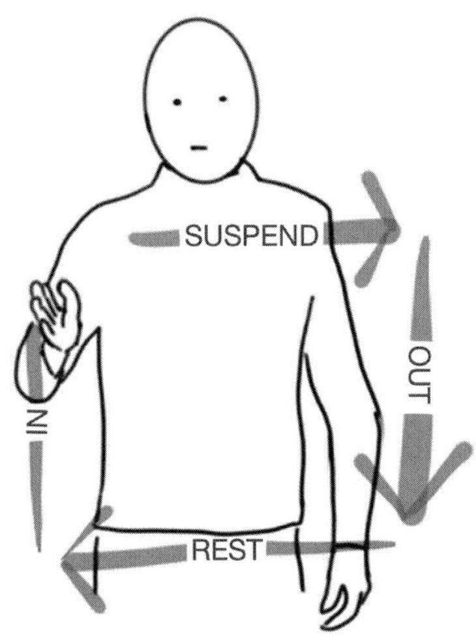

Draw a square in the air with your hand.

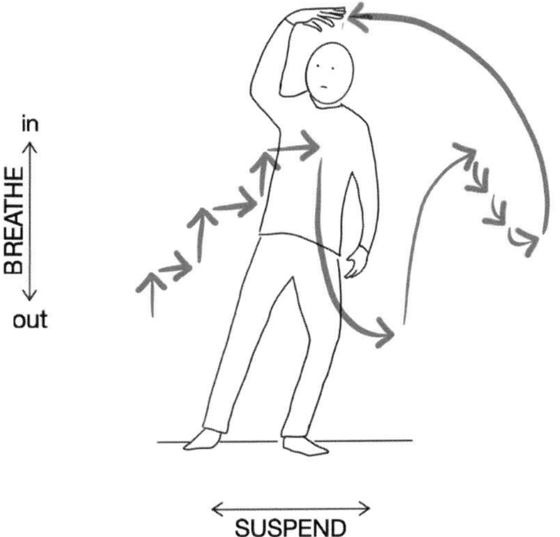

STEP 7: Improvise patterns, making your hand move with the breath.

STEP 10: Improvise free-form with both hands moving on the breath…

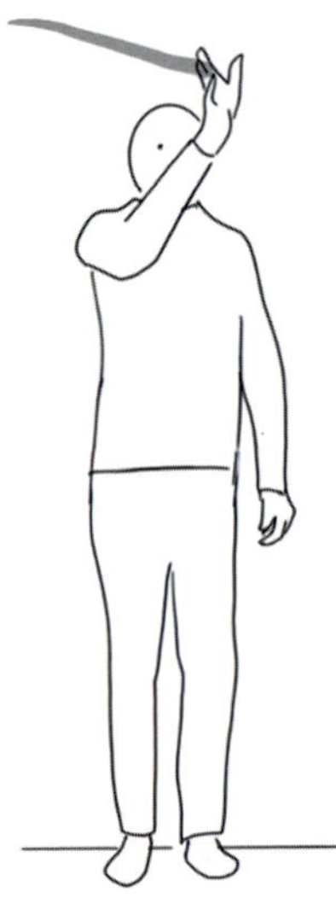

… wherever it wants to go…

… try changing hands.

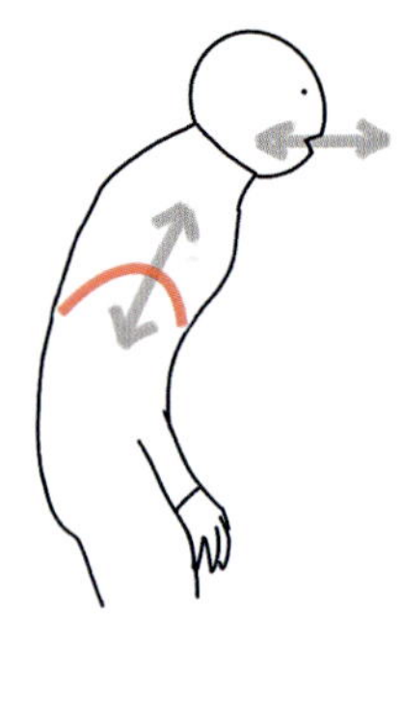

The diaphragm goes up when you breathe out and down when you breathe in.

breaths. Practise transferring the movement from one hand to the other, moving the hands together and separately. Try different kinds of breathing and different kinds of movement and let your hands play freely in the air.

STEP 11: When you stop moving, let your hands hang in the air, still, in front of you, and gently move up and down, almost invisibly, with your breath.

Things to Notice

Even with rules you have choices This is a creative exercise, not a sport, which means that you are allowed to break the rules. Or change them. The rules are there to be played with. You can do whatever you want. What makes having rules creative however is to notice what happens when you break them. Notice what it feels like, and see if it creates something new and interesting. The idea of rules is that something is more interesting if you follow them.

Going down while breathing in, and up when breathing out, feels wrong When you breathe in, you inflate and get a little taller: you 'go up'. When you breathe out, you deflate and get a little shorter: you 'go down'. That is the basic movement you have been trying to imitate: in–up, out–down. But in puppetry you can do whatever you want to do. You have a choice. You can go the other way if you want.

Why might you go the other way? It could be just because you want to, because you like to go against the flow. It could be to represent something that goes the other way when you breathe in and out. The diaphragm, for example, goes down when you breathe in, pushing out the abdomen and making room for the lungs. If you want to puppet the diaphragm, you will have to go in the opposite direction from the 'natural' in–up, out–down.

MOVING ROUND THE PUPPET CENTRE: FISH EXERCISE

'Centre' means 'centre of gravity' – a hypothetical point at which all of the weight of an object acts. You can find the centre of gravity of a flat object by balancing it on your finger. It will balance at only one point and that point is the centre of gravity.

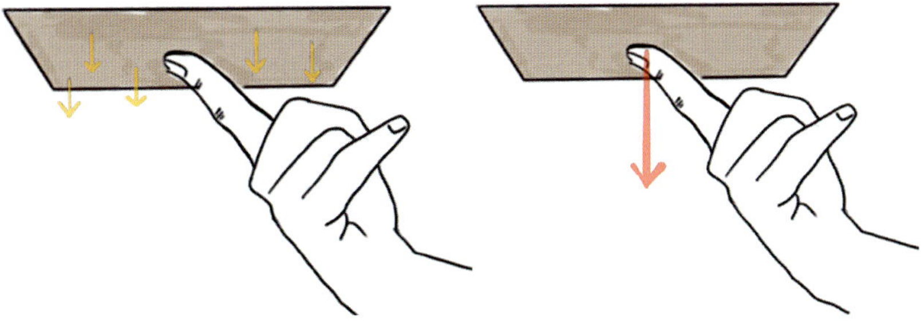

FAR LEFT: Every part of an object is pulled by gravity.

LEFT: The balancing point is the centre of gravity.

The centre of gravity of a person standing upright is, roughly speaking, about 10cm below the navel, about half way through to the back. It is the point about which that person moves.

This exercise explores the idea of creating an imaginary 'puppet centre' in your hand and moving around that. You make your hand become a fish. The centre of the fish is the point around which it turns in the water. This is approximately in the middle of the body of the fish, slightly towards the front. In your hand, it is just at the base of the fingers between the ring finger and the middle finger.

The Exercise

You can do this exercise alone or in a group.

STEP 1: Make your hand into a fish. Holding your hand flat, sideways on, your fingertips are the nose of the fish, your palm is its body and your wrist is its tail.

STEP 2: Start to make the 'fish' swim around. Turn it left and right, up and down, propelled by imaginary fins. Make it dart this way and that. Make it look here and there. It is alive. It is thinking. Explore how far it can swim without you having to move your feet.

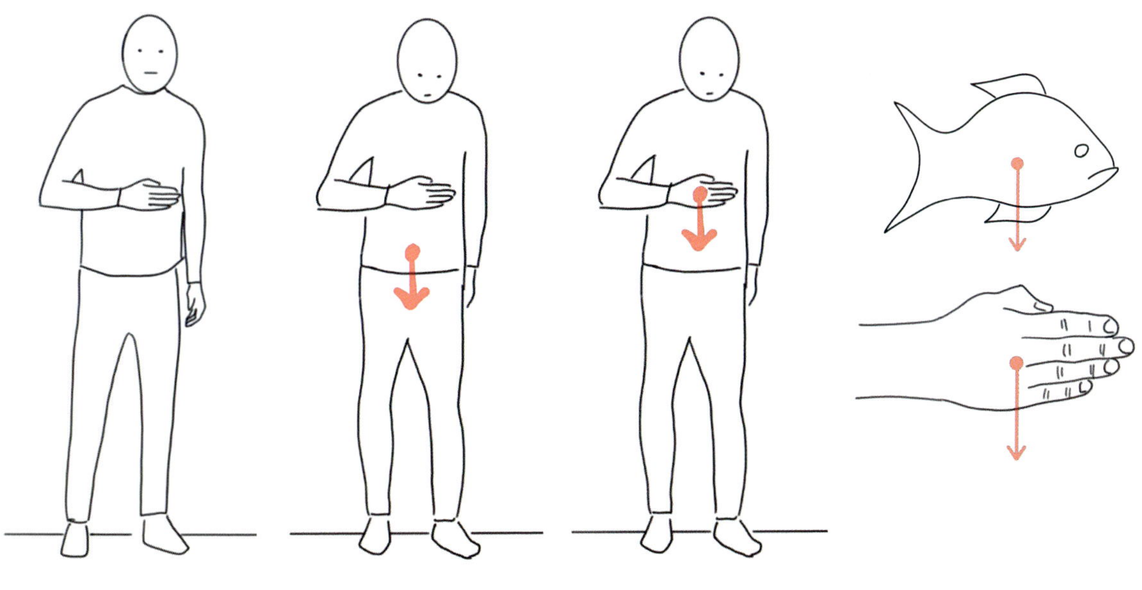

STEP 1: Your hand becomes a fish.

The puppeteer has a centre of gravity.

Imagine the centre of gravity of the fish in your hand.

The centre of gravity of a fish translated to your hand.

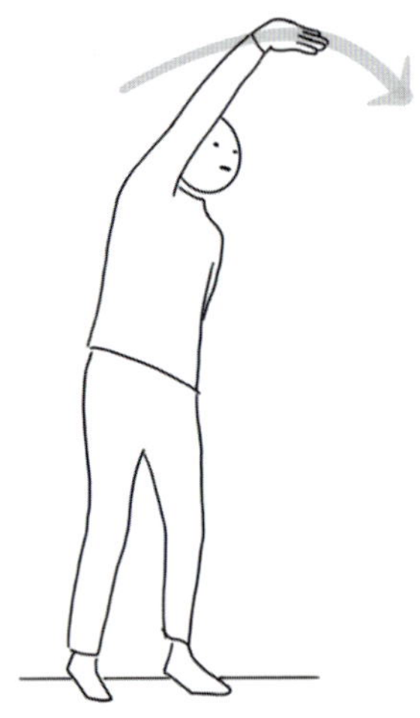

STEP 2: The fish swims high…

… and low.

STEP 3: The fish swims around you in a circle.

As the fish moves it pulls your arm after it. Then it looks somewhere else, changes direction, and swims away. It can stop still, swim backwards, look around, dart off in a new direction. It changes direction again. And again.

STEP 3: The fish swims around you and pulls you after it in a circle. Then it turns and circles the other way. All the time the fish moves first, pulls your arm and then pulls you after it. This is because you are following the fish, allowing the fish (your hand) to lead you, and you are moving around its 'centre'.

STEP 4: Now let the fish swim around the room, and follow after it. Make it swim high and low, close to you and far away, and explore all parts of the room.

Tips for Doing It Better

Don't flap! Flapping is what the fins and the tail do. Your hand is not being the fins of the fish, but the body, which stays fairly straight. Imagine the fins around your hand, causing the body to move. Have a look at fish in fish tanks for reference.

Use your arm As the fish starts to swim, extend your arm to let it swim some way before your feet and your centre start to follow. Then follow the fish on its journey with your arm extended. At the end of the journey, when the fish stops, bend your arm so you can stop after it. With your arm slightly flexed, your fish is ready to swim away again in any direction.

Follow the fish through its full journey When the fish turns right and left, it turns around an imaginary axis that runs vertically through its centre. When

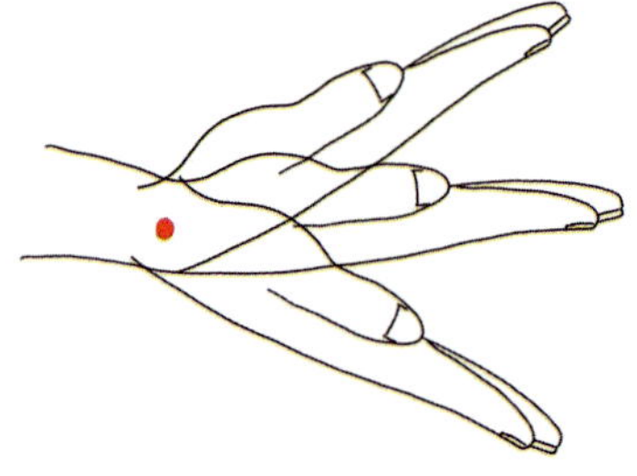

Moving around the centre in the wrist results in the effect of a hand flapping.

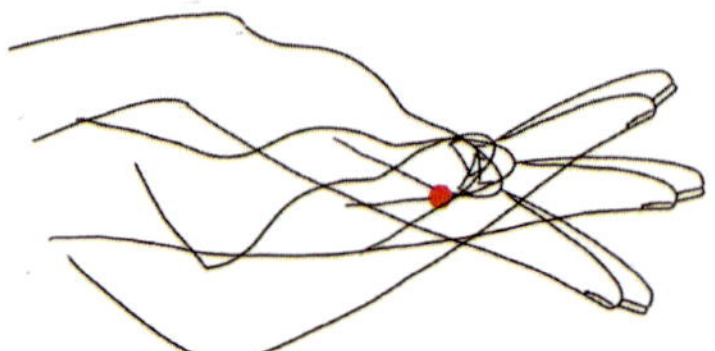

Moving around the centre in the fish results in the effect of a fish swimming.

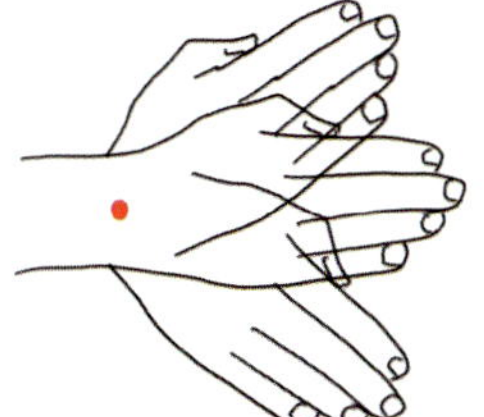

Moving at the wrist makes a hand waving.

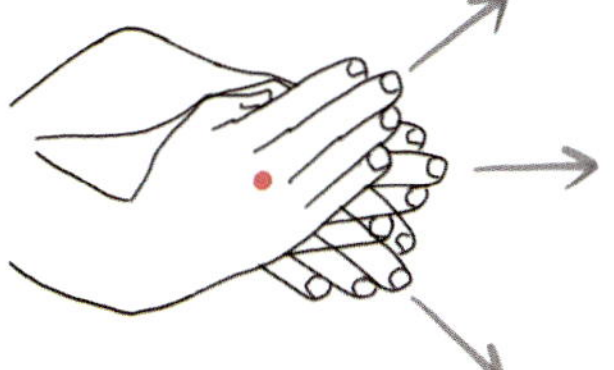

Moving round the centre makes your hand into a fish swimming.

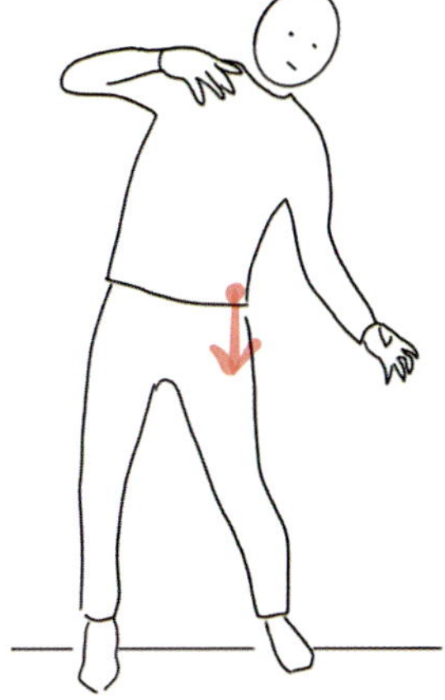

Your centre moves when you move.

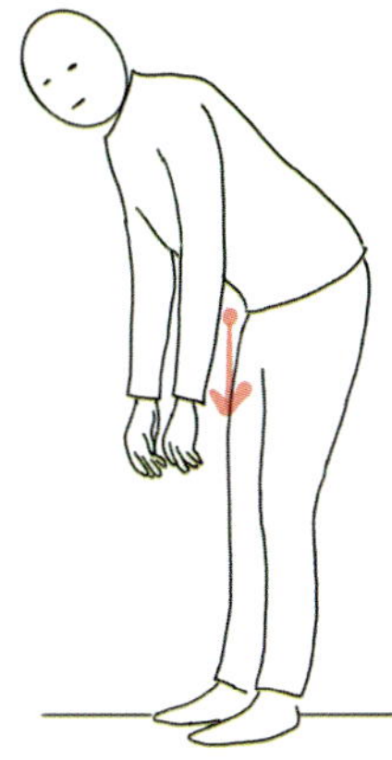

The centre even moves outside you when you bend forwards.

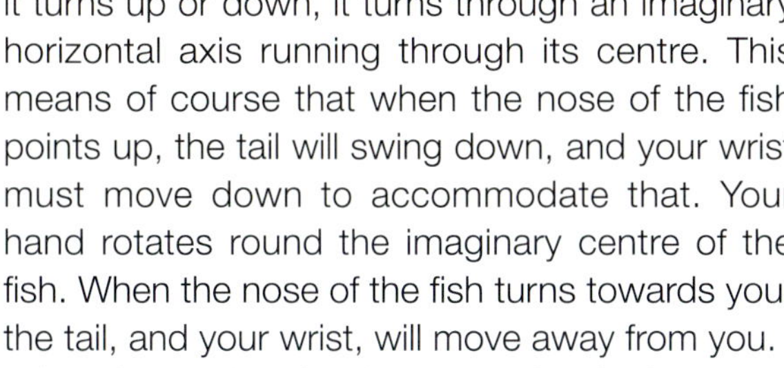

it turns up or down, it turns through an imaginary horizontal axis running through its centre. This means of course that when the nose of the fish points up, the tail will swing down, and your wrist must move down to accommodate that. Your hand rotates round the imaginary centre of the fish. When the nose of the fish turns towards you, the tail, and your wrist, will move away from you.

Imagine the line that the fish is 'drawing' in the air of its journey through the water. Try to follow this line. If the fish goes up, the tail will go down first and you will need to go down to make that happen.

Do not cut corners Follow the journey of the fish as fully as possible, to really make it look as though it is moving on its own. Cutting corners strengthens your centre and steals from the puppet. Take the line you would take if you did not want the fish to see you.

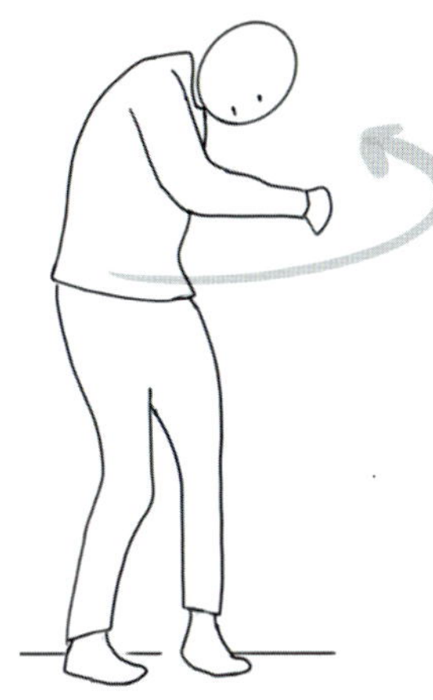

Forehand is easier…

… than backhand.

Things to Notice

The puppeteer's centre is 'real' The exact position of the centre of gravity varies from person to person, depending on their weight and shape, and from moment to moment as they move and change posture, as they do the puppetry. However, it always stays over the feet. If it really moved to the hand, the puppeteer would fall over.

The fish's centre is 'imaginary' The puppeteer creates the fish's centre by pretending that their hand is a fish. Although their hand – the fish – is held up and moved by their arm, they make it look as though it is held up by the water and propelled by its fins. The puppeteer pretends that they are following behind. It looks as if the fish's centre is real, and the puppeteer's centre is not real.

'Forehand' is easier than 'backhand' The wrist has more range when making the fish swim in the 'forehand' direction than in the 'backhand' direction. In the forehand direction your hand wraps around your body, while in the backhand direction you need to walk in a much bigger arc in order to follow the fish.

The audience looks at the thing that moves first If the fish moves first, and then you follow, you are moving from the fish's centre and the audience will look at the fish. If, on the other hand, you move first and the fish moves with you, then you are moving from your centre, and the audience will look at you. Look out for the mistake of moving a foot before your hand.

ARM AND FISH EXERCISE

In this exercise you practise changing between your hand being a hand, moving about on the end of your arm, and your hand being a 'fish', moving about underwater. The difference is that, in one instance, you are moving around your centre; in the other, you are moving around the fish's centre.

When you change from 'arm' to 'fish', you change between two states: an 'actor' state, where your arm moves around your centre, and a 'puppeteer' state, where you move around the fish's centre.

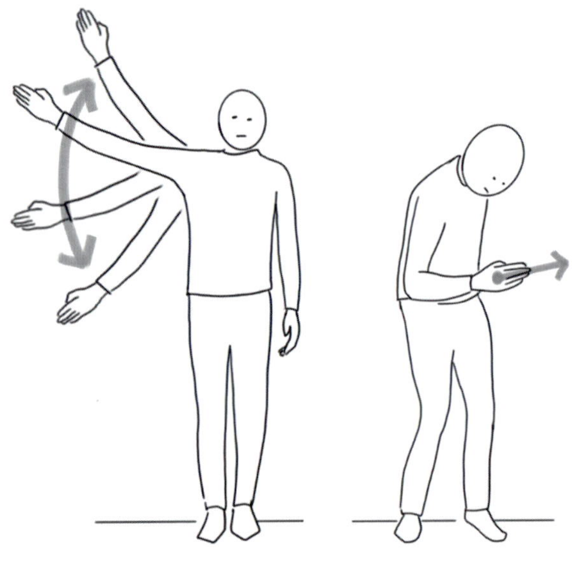

STEP 1: Move your arm like an arm.

STEP 2: The fish pulls the arm.

The Exercise

You can do this exercise alone or in a group.

STEP 1: Move your arm from your centre, like an arm! Wave it about from your shoulder. Make the most extreme example of moving your arm around your centre by keeping the arm straight. Walk around the room continuing to move your arm around from your centre. The arm remains in the same relation to your body as when you are standing still. You are moving from your centre. Your arm is an arm.

STEP 2: Now change to make your hand into a fish and move around the fish's centre – the imaginary centre in the middle of your hand. The fish moves around its centre and swims in the direction it is facing. The fish dictates where it goes and It pulls your arm after it. You follow after your arm. Bend your knees so that you can move quickly and silently after the fish. Your centre, the real centre, accommodates to the fish's lead.

STEP 3: Have someone call out 'Arm!' and 'Fish!', and respond instantly by moving your arm either as an arm or as a fish. The aim is to be as clear as possible, so that there is no ambiguity about when it is an arm and when it is a fish.

Things to Notice

There are two 'states' Notice that, in the 'actor' state, in which you are waving your arm about, the audience looks at you, the puppeteer. In the 'puppeteer' state, in which you are led by your hand, the audience looks at your hand, the fish. They look at the puppet.

Notice the changes in your footsteps The puppeteer's footsteps become quieter in the puppet-centred state. If the observers close their eyes, they should be able to tell, just by listening to the feet, which state the performers are in.

MOVING OBJECTS AROUND AN IMAGINARY CENTRE

A puppet is an object that has its own centre of gravity. In addition, if it has lots of parts, each part will have its own centre of gravity. As well as that, there is also a centre of gravity that belongs to the puppeteer, or puppeteers. In order to bring the puppet to life, it is necessary to create an illusion for the audience of a single, imaginary centre of gravity for the character, around which all the parts move.

In this exercise you practise moving an object around an imagined 'puppet centre'.

Cubist Fisherman puppet from *Le Rossignol* (Blind Summit).

Each part of the puppet has its own centre of gravity.

Each puppeteer has a centre of gravity (which moves about a bit when they move).

The puppet character has its own imaginary centre of gravity around which it moves.

The Exercise

This exercise is done with an object over a table or on the floor. You can do it on your own, but as always it is best with someone watching.

STEP 1: Take an object, for example, a cup. Hold it upside down so that the handle makes a nose. The cup is the head of an imaginary invisible character.

STEP 2: Hold the cup at a height above the table where you imagine the human body of the character to be. Visualize the body below the cup and where the centre of gravity must be: just below the navel, half way to the back, in the imaginary body.
STEP 3: Now move the cup around that imaginary centre. Make the cup look right and left, and up and down, make it bend over at the waist, forwards, sideways and backwards. All the time, think about moving the cup around the imaginary centre of gravity of the imaginary body.
STEP 4: Make the imaginary body walk around on the table, taking its 'cup head' with it. Focus on the puppet moving around the imaginary centre in the body that you have visualized.

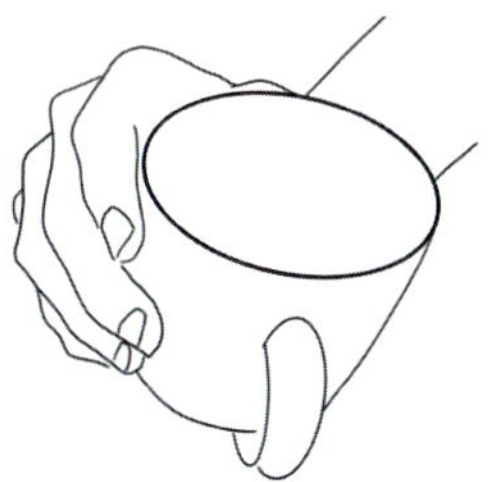

STEP 1: Take a cup.

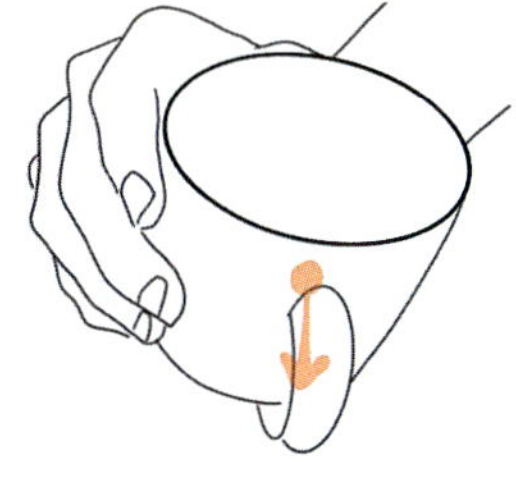

Note that the cup has a centre of gravity.

Tips for Doing It Well

Visualize the character To create the imaginary puppet character centre, you need to visualize the character and where its centre is in relation to the puppet object or objects that you are holding. If, for example, the puppet object is the head of the creature, then the centre of the creature will not be in the object but in the invisible body that you imagine below it.

Don't drop it! You need to be in control of the puppet's movement. If you let it move under the influence of gravity, it will move around the object's centre of gravity and not around the character's centre, and the character will die.

Something to Notice

The imaginary centre of gravity of the character is the important one By doing puppetry, you create a centre of gravity for the character that the puppet is playing. It may be in the object of the puppet itself, or it may be outside it. It may be in the space *between* the objects that make up the puppet. You create the centre of gravity of the puppet character by imagining it when you bring it to life.

STEP 2: Hold the cup above a table top as if it is the head of a character (right).

Visualize the puppet's body between the cup head and the table top (middle right).

The audience imagines the character's centre of gravity even though they see no body (far right).

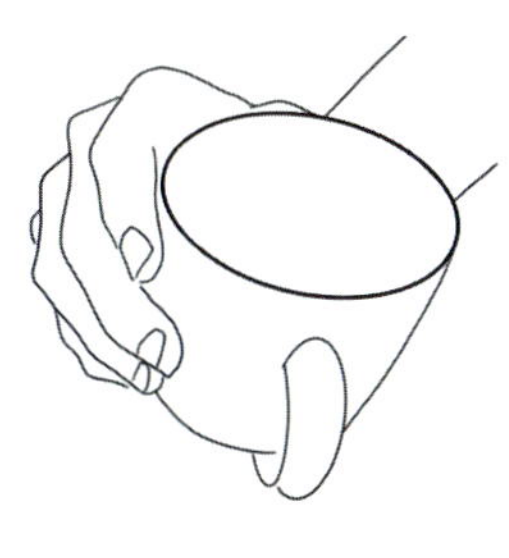

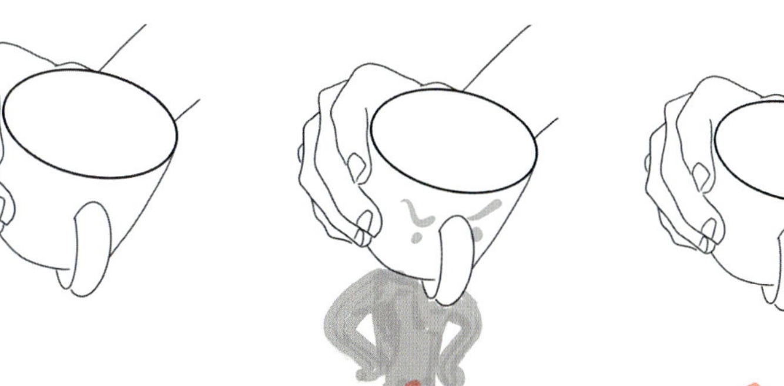

If you let go of your object it will move under its real centre of gravity and the character will die.

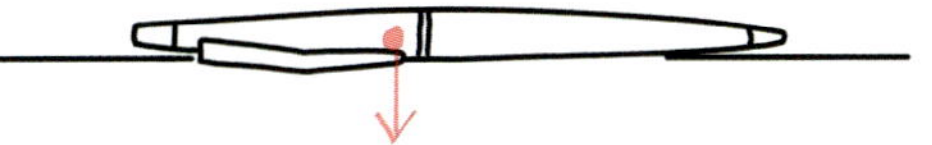

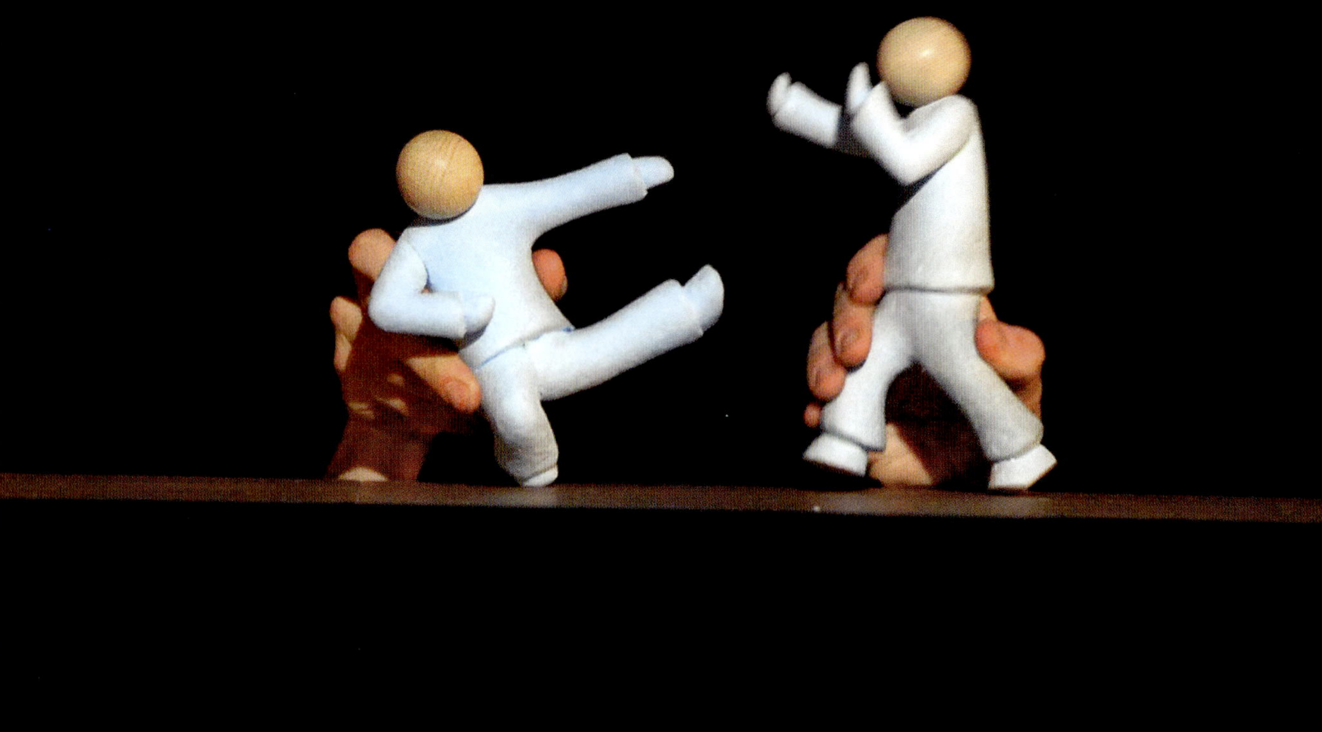

6
FIXED POINT AND FOCUS

Focus is the art of getting the audience to look where you want them to look, and fixed point is the art of creating still points on stage so that the audience can understand the movement.

This chapter provides a series of exercises to practise these elements and think about how they work in puppetry.

WHAT ARE FIXED POINTS?

A fixed point in puppetry is a pivot point around which parts of the puppet move. In real life, it is a point on which a person puts weight so that they can move another part of their body. For example, you will put your weight on to your back foot so that you can move the front foot forwards in preparation for walking. Another example is when you grip the edge of a swimming pool with your hands in order to pull yourself out. In these situations, the back foot or the hands cannot move because you are putting all of your weight on them, but in a puppet the puppeteer will need to hold these parts still in order to make them fixed points. If you are not held still, they will be dragged after the moving parts and the puppet will look weightless.

In this simple exercise, you explore how the feet act as fixed points in walking, with a simple finger puppet walking on a table top. Each stepping finger becomes a fixed point for the next step.

OPPOSITE: Blue Men from *Low Life* (Blind Summit).

The Exercise

You can do this on your own or with an audience to give you feedback. It is probably best done on a table top.

STEP 1: Make a finger puppet 'person' by standing two fingers on a table top. Put the weight on to one foot and then on to the other. When the weight is on one foot, that foot becomes a fixed point around which the other foot can move.

STEP 2: First, make the 'person' walk around on the table. Make it run. Make it go up to something on the table and kick it with one foot. Make it step over something. Make it jump in the air and land. Make it kneel and lie down. Can you make it sit on the edge of the table? Make it run in slow motion across the table, and take a giant leap like it is on the moon. Can you see a little person? Does it seem real to you?

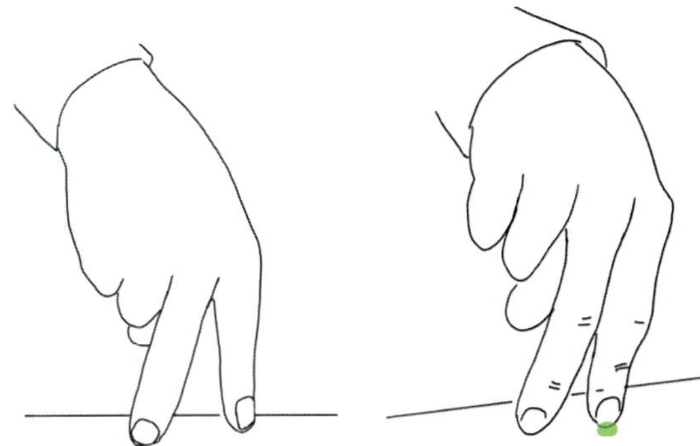

STEP 1: Make a puppet 'person' with two fingers.

STEP 1: The weight on the left foot makes it a fixed point.

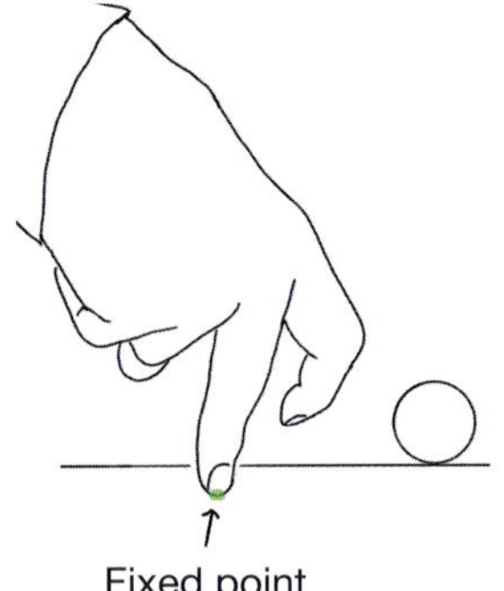

STEP 2: When the puppet kicks something…

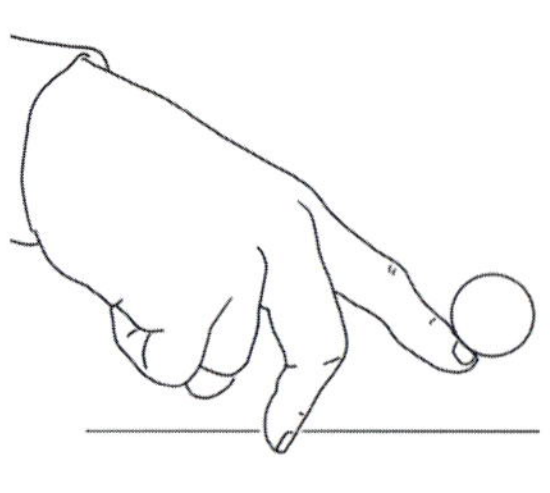

… the weight-bearing foot remains still as the fixed point.

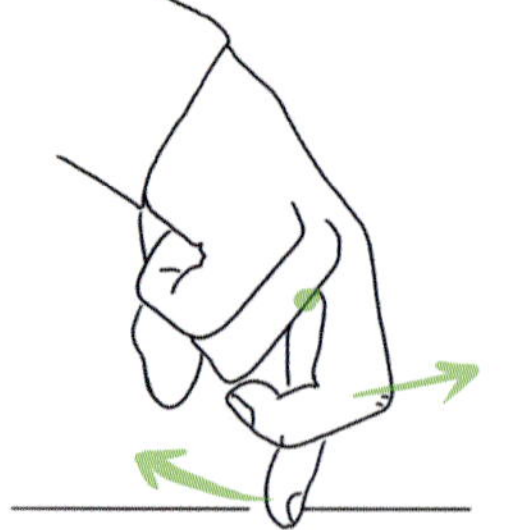

STEP 4: Running on the spot – the centre becomes the fixed point…

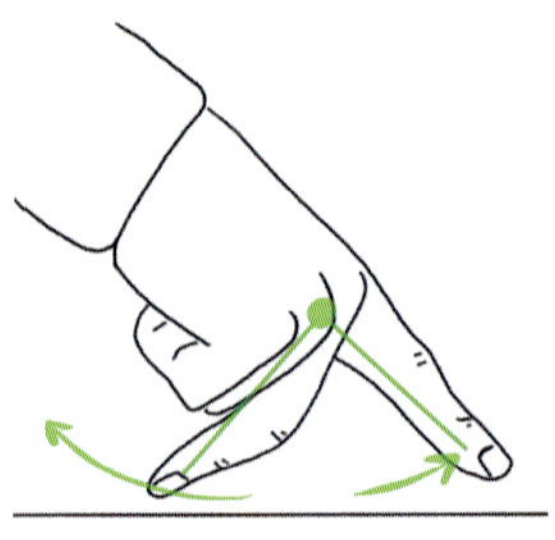

… around which the feet move.

STEP 3: Now make your two fingers slide around on the table top. Lift them up and down off the table. Now your fingers are just fingers sliding around on top of the table. It is no longer a little person. The little person has gone; they have changed back into fingers.

STEP 4: Now make your finger figure run on the spot on the table. To do this, instead of making the weight-bearing finger a fixed point and moving your hand forwards when it runs, you make your hand a fixed point and make your weight-bearing finger – the 'fixed point' – slide backwards during each step.

STEP 5: Make the puppet skip, jump, slide, skid, and come to a stop. Make it proceed stealthily forward, again moving on the spot. Make it stop suddenly and look around. Do all these actions 'on the spot'. Imagine a movie camera following the puppet. Make the puppet run in slow motion. Make it turn and run in profile, sideways on to the camera, still on the spot.

Things to Notice

Fixed points create the illusion of gravity working on the puppet In real life, a person stands on their feet. The feet hold up the legs, which hold up the body, which holds up the head. But the finger puppet is held up by the puppeteer: the hand is held by the arm and the fingers hang from the hand. The weight pressing down from above in the real person makes the feet into fixed points. To make the audience believe that the puppet is holding its own weight, the puppeteer has to hold the fingers down to make them into fixed points. Holding the puppet down makes it look as if the puppet is holding itself up.

The fixed points of the feet are connected through the legs Making your fingertip into a fixed point makes it look, to the audience, as if the weight of the puppet is on that 'foot'. And when the weight is on one foot, it looks as if it uses its 'legs' to lift the other foot and walk. Of course, this is an illusion. In reality, the weight is being held by your arm and you can just as easily slide your fingers around. When you do that, however, your hand is no longer moving around the imaginary fixed points of its feet and the puppet legs disappear.

The audience understands the 'camera' illusion Perhaps surprisingly, the audience has no difficulty understanding the idea of the moving camera when the puppet walks on the spot. They don't see the feet as slipping and sliding on the table – they don't see 'bad' fixed points. Instead, they see the table moving backwards under the feet of the puppet, and the world disappearing behind them. They don't see the puppet walking to the front of the table, but walking somewhere in the story. And when the puppet stops, they understand that the camera stops with them; when the puppet turns and walks sideways, they see the camera tracking beside them. The members of the audience watch the puppet as if it is 'on camera'. The audience/camera becomes the fixed point around which the whole world of the puppet is moving.

The puppet can perform an action on the spot better than any human performer For example, where a mime actor can only approximate walking on the spot, with a highly stylised convention, the puppet's feet can actually slide as if it were on a running machine. It is something that puppets can do better than people.

EXPLORING FIXED POINTS WITH TWO HANDS

There are many possible fixed points. When you are standing, your feet are fixed points. If you sit on a chair, then your bottom becomes a fixed point around which your upper body can move. If you cross one leg over the other leg, then where your knees cross is a fixed point for your free foot to move around. If you lean back in a chair, your back becomes a fixed point around which your arms and head can move. When you lie down, your whole body is a fixed point.

When you grab something to pull yourself up, or lean on your hand, or hang from something, then your hands are fixed points. If you lean on an elbow, that part of your body becomes a fixed point.

If you kneel on one knee, you have three fixed points: your foot on one side and your knee and foot on the other side.

When you walk with a stick, the tip of the stick becomes a fixed point every time it is placed on the ground. When you do something intricate with your hands, such as writing or typing or making something, then your hands are fixed points. You might hold one still while you reach with the other one for something, or you might hold them both still as you look around or stretch your back. When you bend over at the waist, your waist acts as a fixed point around which the top half of the body moves.

When you look at something, that thing becomes a fixed point while you are looking at it. As you move around, your eyes will remain fixed to the thing you are looking at as if attached by a string. This is a focal fixed point.

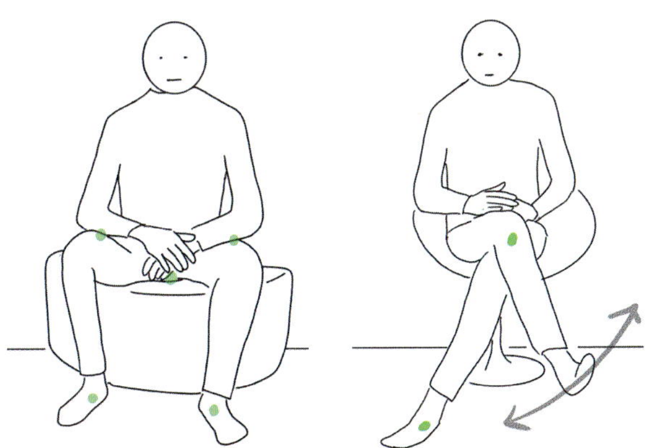

ABOVE: Weight creates fixed points: the feet on the ground, the bottom on the chair, the elbows resting on the legs.

ABOVE RIGHT: In this position, there are three fixed points: the left foot on the ground, the bottom on the chair, the right knee crossed over the left knee. The right foot is free to move around the pivot point of the knee.

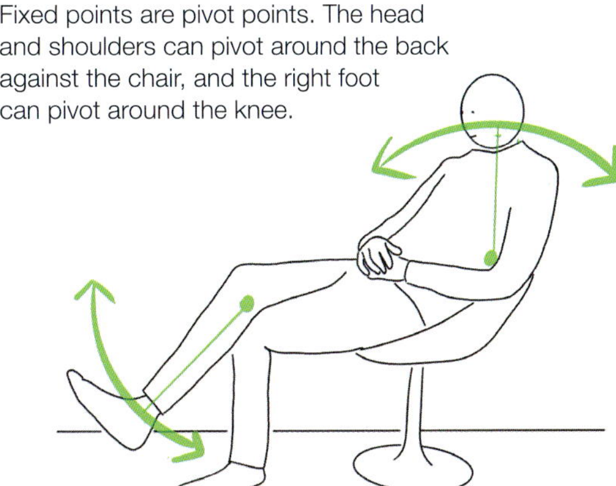

Fixed points are pivot points. The head and shoulders can pivot around the back against the chair, and the right foot can pivot around the knee.

If you hang by your hands, the hands are fixed points.

In puppetry you must create these fixed points in the puppets using your hands. In this exercise you practise making fixed points with your hands and moving around the space from point to point.

The Exercise

Stand behind a table. You can do this on your own or with an audience to watch you and give feedback.

When kneeling, the feet and the knee that is on the ground are fixed points.

STEP 1: Place a finger of your right hand on a table top. Then place a finger of your left hand somewhere else on the table top. Move the first finger (right hand) to a new spot, then move the second finger. Keep moving your hands, always keeping one finger as a fixed point on the table, when you move the other one. See how far you can reach without the other one moving. Let your fingers lead you around the table from fixed point to fixed point.

STEP 2: Now see a point in the air above the table and put one of your fingers on it, to make a fixed point in the air. Then find another one.

STEP 3: Move from point to point around the space, led by your fingers. Go to the floor, to the walls, to the back of a chair.

STEP 4: Move yourself around the fixed points without disturbing them. Walk up close to a point and then away from it without moving the point.

STEP 5: Swap around and watch someone else do the exercise. You should be able to see the fixed points in the air when they touch them and sometimes even after they let go.

Tips for Doing It Well

Control your own fixed points Make sure that your arms and body are free to range where they need to. It is easier if you are standing up than sitting down, because you can use your legs and back as well as your arms to move around. Bend your legs and have your feet well spaced. You, the puppeteer, need to be well balanced over your centre of gravity, so that you can move your arms to create fixed points.

Look out for false fixed points Leaning on your elbows is a common mistake when doing puppetry, as it creates two 'false' fixed points for your hands to move around. It is crucial that your arms are free to move, so that your hands can move around the puppet's fixed points.

Using your imagination is easier It is much easier to imagine seeing a point in the space and putting your finger on it, than trying to hold your finger still in mid-air. Your muscles still do the same work to keep it there, but your imagination controls them.

FIXED POINTS IN OBJECTS

An object multiplies the number of fixed points that you are able to control with each hand. An object with two ends, for example, such as a pen, gives you control over at least three fixed points with one hand. The more points and edges the object has, the more potential fixed points you can create. In this exercise you experiment with fixed points when puppeting a pen.

The Exercise

Take a pen in your hand and hold it upright on a table top. The top end of the pen is the 'head', and the bottom end is the 'feet'.

STEP 1: Keeping the head still, pivot the feet to a new spot on the table.
STEP 2: Then, keeping the feet still, move the head over it so that the pen is upright again.
STEP 3: Now move the pen around the centre – that is, the point where you are holding it. When the head moves forwards, the feet move back, and vice versa.
STEP 4: Now move the head first, keeping the feet still, and then pull the feet over in a second move.
STEP 5: Now move the feet first, then follow with the head, and then move the pen from the centre.
STEP 6: Continue to walk the pen around the table top, moving one point at a time. The two ends of the pen alternate as a fixed point around which the other end can move.

Something to Notice

The leading part defines the movement When the feet go first, the pen 'walks'; when the head goes first, the pen 'looks'. This is called 'leading with the feet' and 'leading with the head'. When the pen moves from its centre it can lean to pick something up, touch its toes, or do a handstand.

FOCUS GUIDES WHERE THE AUDIENCE LOOKS

The audience will be guided to look wherever you look. They look at what you look at. If you look at the puppet they will look at the puppet. If you look at something else, the audience will look at that. If you look at the audience, they will look at you. Making the audience look at something by looking at it yourself is called 'giving focus' in puppetry. In this exercise you practise making the audience look at different things by giving focus.

The Exercise

Stand in front of an audience, or another puppeteer, and make your hand into a 'frog': your fingers make the top jaw and your thumb makes the lower jaw. Imagine the frog's eyes are either side of your middle finger, or on the outer side of your index and ring finger.

Cat's head from *El Gato con Botas* (Blind Summit).

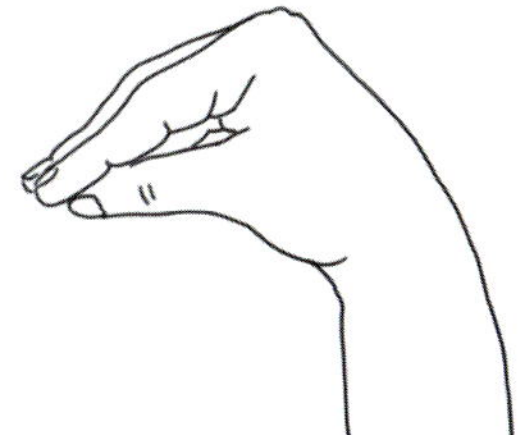

Make a 'frog' with your hand. This is the view from the side.

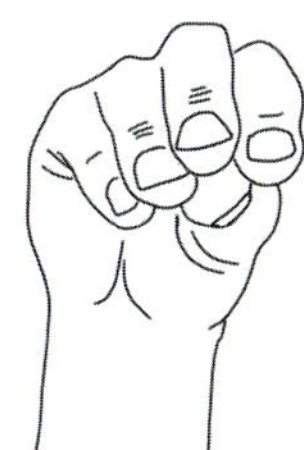

View of the frog from the front.

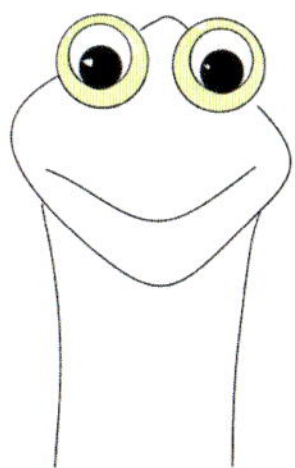

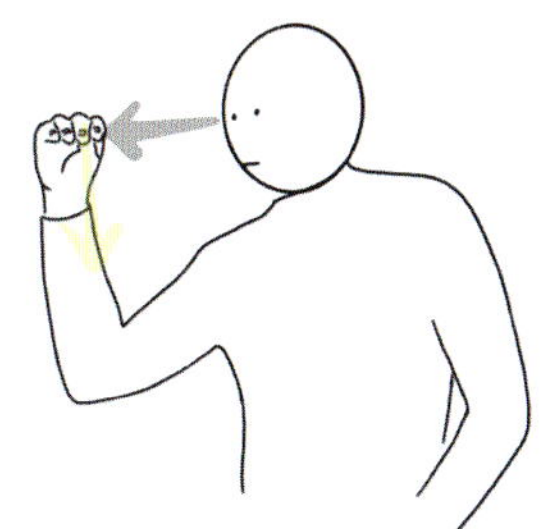

TOP LEFT: Frog.

ABOVE: The frog's eyes.

LEFT: Your hand as a frog.

STEP 1: Focus on the head of the frog (look at it), and make the frog look at things around the room (make the frog focus on things).
STEP 2: Make the frog look at the walls, the ceiling, the floor. Make it look out the window. Keep your focus on the frog, and let the frog look round the room. Make it look over your shoulder at the wall behind you. All the time, you keep looking at the frog.
STEP 3: Now try to be more specific: make the frog look at the light fitting on the ceiling, at a mark on the floor, at something on the table, at the handle on the door. Can the audience guess what the frog is looking at? How specific can you be?
STEP 4: Now you look up from the frog to the audience. What do they look at? Then look at the floor, look at the door, look at what the frog is looking at. Where does the audience look? Then look back at the frog. Can you feel when they are looking at the frog again?
STEP 5: Now turn the frog puppet to look at you. You are looking at each other.
STEP 6: Break your focus on the frog and turn to look out at the audience. Now the puppet is giving you focus. You, the puppeteer, are 'in focus'.
STEP 7: Now turn back to give focus to the puppet again. You are looking at each other again.
STEP 8: Turn the puppet to look out at the audience.
STEP 9: Finally, both you and the frog look out at the audience. Neither of you is in focus. Who does the audience look at?
STEP 10: Swap around and watch someone else do the exercise.

STEP 1: Look at the frog and make the frog look round the room.

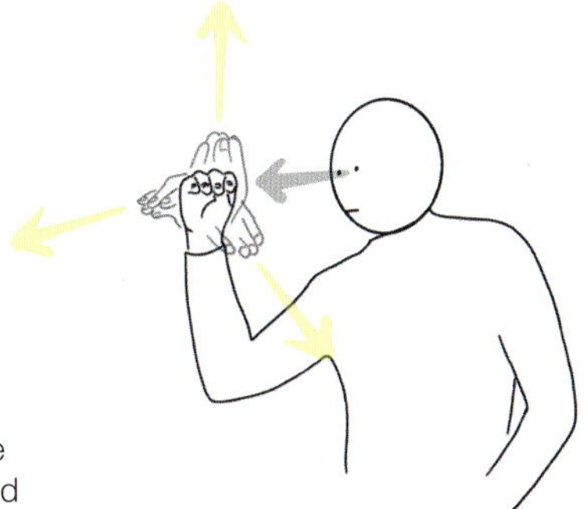

STEP 2: Make the frog look all around the room.

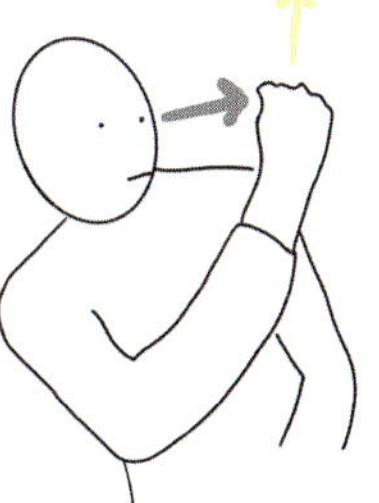

Things to Notice

You can direct the audience with your focus When you look at the puppet, they will look at the puppet. If you look at something else, they will look at that. If you look at them, they will look at you. You are their guide as to where they should look, and what they should see.

There are many ways to do it wrong The purpose of focus is to make the audience look at the frog. If you look at the audience, they will look at you and not at the frog. If you look where the frog is looking, the audience will look at you, wondering what you are looking at. If you look through the frog, lining it up with what it is looking at, like a gun, they will look at you, trying to work out what you are doing.

There are four states governing you and the puppet The puppet can be in focus; you can be in focus; you can both be in focus; or neither of you can be in focus. When you are both in focus, you are brought into the puppet's reality. When neither of you is in focus, the puppet is brought into your reality and the audience sees a puppeteer holding up their hand. When you look back at your hand, the frog reappears.

You need to be in focus to be 'in the scene' When the puppet looks at you it brings you into the scene. You, the puppeteer, become visible all of a sudden. You can turn to look out to the audience, talk to them, or do whatever you want to do. In a sort of role reversal, the puppet is giving you focus. The puppet is puppeting you.

When you turn and look back to the frog, you give focus to the puppet and it can turn to the audience and say or do whatever it wants to. You are in a scene together with the frog. You are puppeteering the frog, and the frog is puppeteering you.

The puppet is always looking at something The only time the puppet looks at nothing is when it closes its eyes. Even when it looks away from something, it will look at something else. You should always know what your puppet is looking at. What the frog looks at tells the audience what it is thinking about. What the puppet is thinking about tells the story.

FAR LEFT: Wrong! If you look at the audience they will look at you, not at the frog.

MIDDLE LEFT: Wrong! If you look through the frog it becomes a gun.

LEFT: Wrong! If you look past the frog, the audience will look at you.

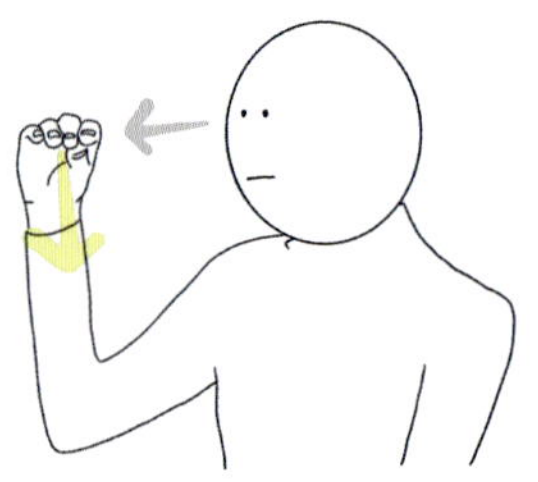

The puppet is in focus and is looking at the audience.

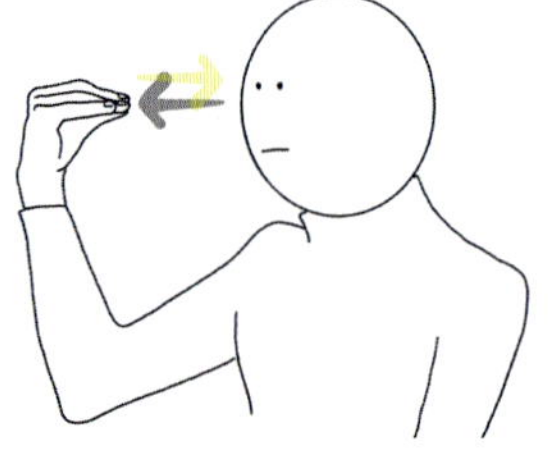

The puppet is in focus and is looking at the puppeteer.

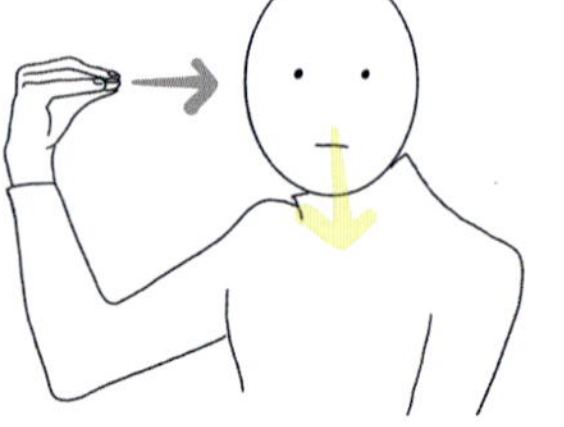

The puppeteer is in focus and is looking at the audience.

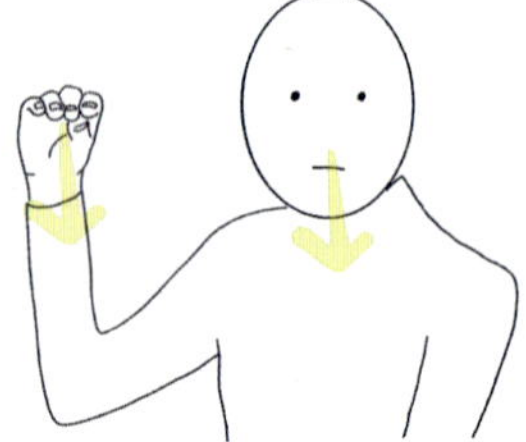

The puppeteer and puppet are both looking at the audience, and neither of them is in focus.

LOOKING AT THE AUDIENCE: 'CLOWNING'

When a puppet looks to the audience it shares its thoughts. If it looks to the audience between each thing it does, it appears to tell a story. This is called 'clowning'. It is very useful in puppetry because, as well as drawing the audience into the puppet's story, looking to the audience keeps the puppet alive. In this exercise you explore using the puppet's focus to make a story.

The Exercise

Set up the room to have an audience and stage area. Go on stage one person at a time and make a frog with your hand (*see* previous exercise).

STEP 1: Look at your frog and make the frog look at the audience.
STEP 2: Turn the frog to look at something on stage; it can be something as simple as a mark on the floor.
STEP 3: Then make the frog look back at the audience.
STEP 4: Make it turn to look at the mark on the floor again, and then back to the audience. Repeat: look at the mark, look at the audience, mark, audience.
STEP 5: Then make the frog look at different people in the audience. Pause on one of them for a moment, and then look back at the mark on the floor.
STEP 6: Make the frog look off to stage left, then back at the mark on the floor.
STEP 7: Make it look stage left, then at the mark, then at the audience, then back at the mark.
STEP 8: Make the puppet look at you, then look at the audience yourself. Look back at the puppet and then make it turn and look back at the mark.
STEP 9: The puppeteer looks past the puppet at the mark so that both of them are looking at the mark, then the puppet and the puppeteer look at each other, before turning slowly to look at the audience. Then the puppeteer looks at the puppet, and the puppet looks back at the mark on the floor.
STEP 10: And so on. Keep playing with sequences of looks, always checking in with the audience between each look. Try different sequences and different timing.
STEP 11: Swap with someone who is watching and watch them doing it. Pay attention to where you look when you are watching, and to what you think the frog is thinking.

Tip for Doing It Well

Don't lose your nerve You may feel that it is too slow, that the puppet is looking at the audience too much, and that you want to get on with the scene. However, the opposite is usually true. More often than not, the audience will want you to go more slowly. They like to see the puppeteer break down the puppet's thoughts and each time the puppet looks out at the audience, they engage more with its story.

Things to Notice

Clowning tells a story When the puppet looks at the audience, the audience sees it thinking about what it has just seen. The frog seems to be asking them, 'Do you see that mark on the floor?' When it looks at them again, it seems to be asking, 'Do you know what it is?' When it looks at one specific person, it seems to ask again, 'Do *you* know what it is?' When it looks off stage it seems to be thinking, 'Should I tell someone about this?' The looks start to tell a story.
Looking at the audience reinforces the puppet The frog exists only because the audience members are imagining that your hand is a frog. This is the premise – 'that person's hand is a frog'. What the audience are really looking at is your hand, but every time it turns to look at them, they see it as a frog. The face-off reinforces its 'frogness' in their imagination.

The looks at the mark on the floor progress as the story progresses, and the looks out to the audience reinforce the puppet.

WORKING WITH TWO PUPPETS AND ONE PUPPETEER

With a puppet in each hand there are three of you in the exercise: you and two puppets. In reality, you are playing all three characters, so you need to direct the focus of the audience at all times. The audience can only look in one place at a time so there is always only one of you 'in focus'. This exercise helps you practise putting the characters in and out of focus.

In this exercise you are visible, but the principles apply when the puppeteer is out of sight.

The Exercise

Make a frog with each hand: think of them as Left Frog (LF) and Right Frog (RF).

STEP 1: Make Left Frog look out at the audience, while you and Right Frog focus on it.
STEP 2: Turn LF to focus on RF.
STEP 3: Turn your focus to RF.
STEP 4: At this point, RF can turn out to look to the audience.
STEP 5: Reverse the process: turn RF to focus on LF, turn your focus to LF, and then turn LF out to the audience. The audience follows your focus and looks from frog to frog with you. Your focus acts as a guide to where the audience should be looking and when.
STEP 6: Practise passing the focus back and forth, keeping all the movements separate, until it feels easy and natural. It will take a few goes.
STEP 7: Now turn LF and RF so that they are looking at each other. You will need to split your focus between the two!
STEP 8: Turn them both to look to the audience.
STEP 9: Last, turn both frogs slowly to look at you, while you look out at the audience.

Things to Notice

You need to give the audience time to look from one frog to the other Changing your focus from puppet to puppet tracks where the audience is looking and how long it takes them to change their focus. You need to wait for them.

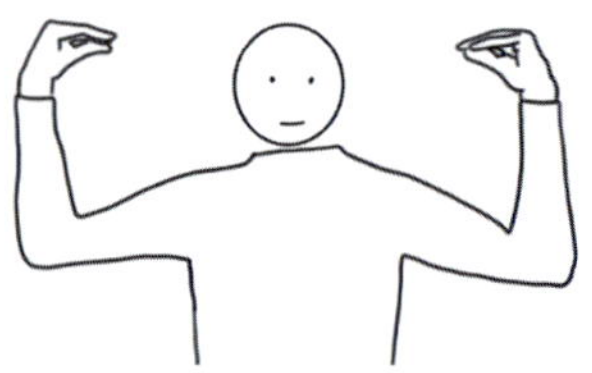

Make two frogs.

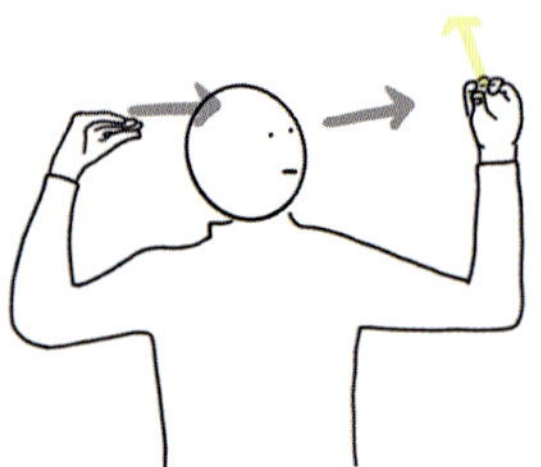

STEP 1: Right Frog and puppeteer focusing on Left Frog; Left Frog looking at the audience.

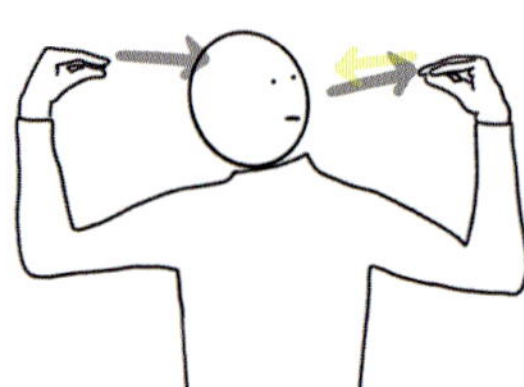

STEP 2: Right Frog and puppeteer focusing on Left Frog, Left Frog looking at Right Frog.

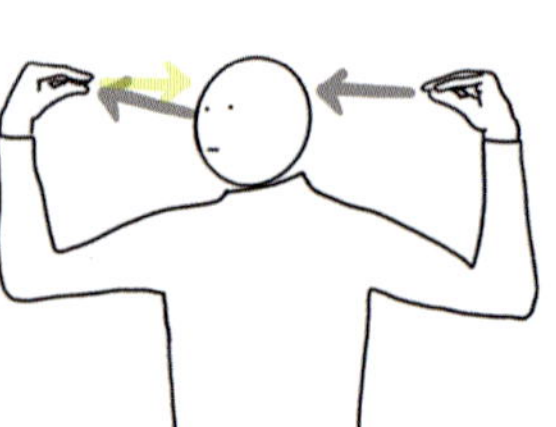

STEP 3: Puppeteer switching focus to Right Frog.

STEP 4: Left Frog and puppeteer focusing on Right Frog, Right Frog looking at the audience.

Puppets look out Counterintuitively, puppets look 'out' to the audience when they are in focus to act or speak; when they look 'in' at one of the other characters on stage, they put that character into focus. When the puppet looks at another puppet on stage, it looks like it is listening. Puppets talk to each other through the audience.

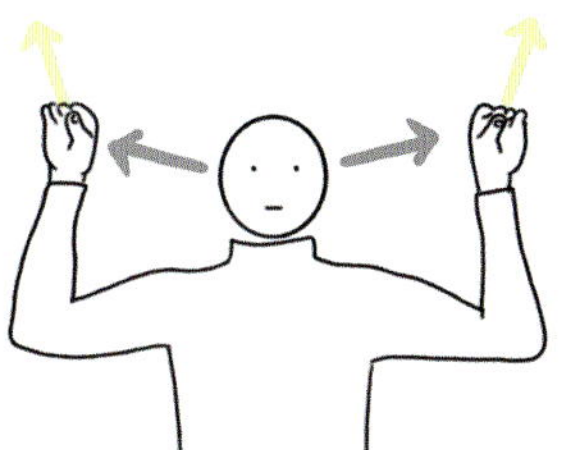

STEP 8: Both Frogs looking out, puppeteer's focus split.

BELOW: The puppet is always looking at something (Blind Summit).

The parabola.

IMITATING GRAVITY – THE PARABOLA

Anything flying through the air – a ball, a bullet or a person jumping – will describe the same shape in the air, called a parabola.

The parabola is the result of gravity acting on an object that is moving upwards into the air, pulling it back towards the ground. As it gets higher, it slows down. It gets slower and slower until it reaches the apex of its flight, where it hangs in the air for a moment and then begins to fall, getting faster and faster until it lands on the ground.

Gravity is part of every movement the puppet makes – to a greater or lesser extent. When it is off the ground, gravity will play a big part. When it is on the ground, gravity will play a less significant part, but it will still play a part. You can think of life as the resistance of gravity. Since, as a puppeteer. you are controlling the centre of gravity of your puppet, you need to practise imitating the way gravity works.

The Exercise

Stand with plenty of space around you.

STEP 1: Draw a parabola in the air with your hand. Make your hand start fast and then slow it down as it ascends towards the apex of the parabola, where it stops and hangs for a moment. It then accelerates as it falls back to its original position. Try to feel gravity working on your hand to help you.
STEP 2: Now draw the parabola again in slow motion. Try slowing it down further, as if the slow motion were doubled, then double the slow motion again, so that it feels as if the object will never arrive at its destination. Add more detail to the movement as it slows down more.
STEP 3: Make the parabola wider. Make your hand take off from your left side, pass up in front of your face, and land on your right side.
STEP 4: Make the parabola even wider so that your hand travels across the room. Make your hand take off on one side of the room and land on

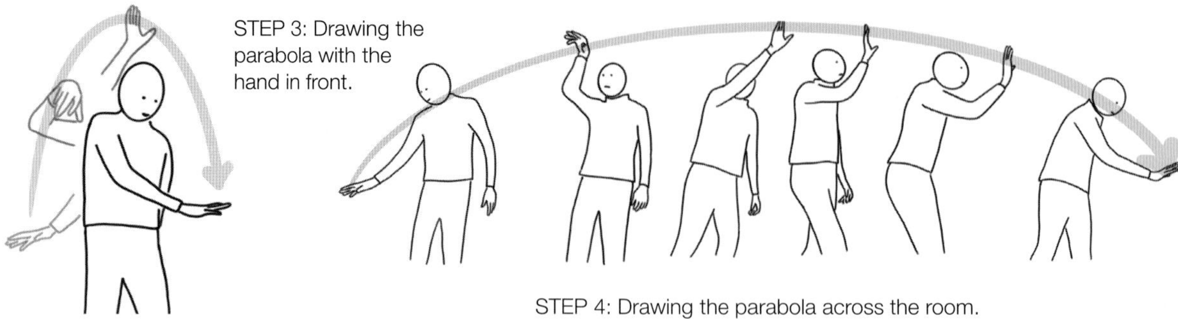

STEP 3: Drawing the parabola with the hand in front.

STEP 4: Drawing the parabola across the room.

the other side of the room, fitting your steps into the flight of your hand so that it draws the perfectly smooth line of a parabola across the room.
STEP 5: Make your hand go straight up and down, describing a vertical parabola. Your hand bursts into the air, slows down as it gets higher, reaches a completely still moment at the apex of the flight, and then accelerates back towards the ground, until it goes 'Smack!' at the end.
STEP 6: Keep practising until you can feel the parabola in your hand and can do it at all speeds, lengths, heights and variations.

Things to Notice

The parabola is symmetrical You can stretch out the parabola into long and short versions, expanding time or the distance over which your hand travels, but the overall shape always remains symmetrical and the same.
Air resistance interrupts the parabola Because of air resistance, a falling object reaches a top speed – terminal velocity – and does not get any faster. This will depend on the shape and weight of the object. A feather, a leaf, a parachute or a glider, for example, will float on the air currents.
Muscles work against gravity Whether it is breathing, standing, sitting, rolling over, walking or speaking, the puppet's muscles are working to resist the gravity that would otherwise pull it to the ground and flatten it out.
Machines also work against gravity When the puppet is in a car, or a plane, or buffeted by the wind, or swept along by a current, then mechanical forces overcome gravity and carry the puppet away. However, when those forces end, the puppet will fall to the ground in a parabola.

TAKE-OFF AND LANDING

Every movement has a take-off moment that starts it and a landing movement where it ends. For example, the knees bend and straighten to propel a person into a jump, and compress and extend to absorb the impact on landing. Before taking a step forwards, the weight moves back on to the back foot to push off. Before you speak, you take a short in-breath.

The take-off and landing vary depending on the nature of the movement. If you are having difficulty making a movement in gravity seem real, take a moment to think about the preparation and landing. Are you doing them? Are they right?

The Exercise

Begin by making a five-legged puppet with your hand standing on fingertips on the table top.

STEP 1: Drop the heel of the hand on to the table top, and 'bounce' the hand into the air.
STEP 2: Describe a parabola in the air.
STEP 3: Land the palm on the table top and bounce on to the feet.

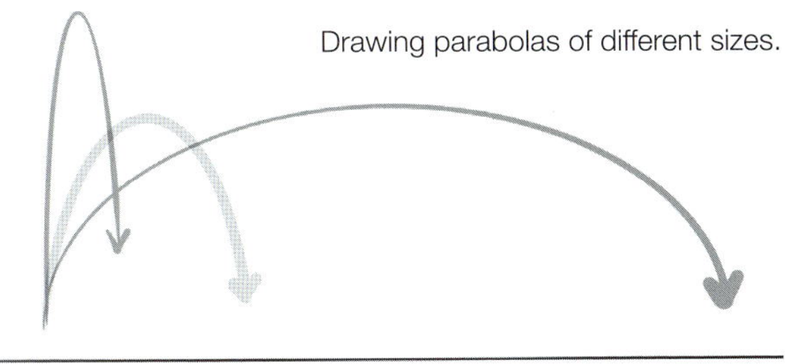

Drawing parabolas of different sizes.

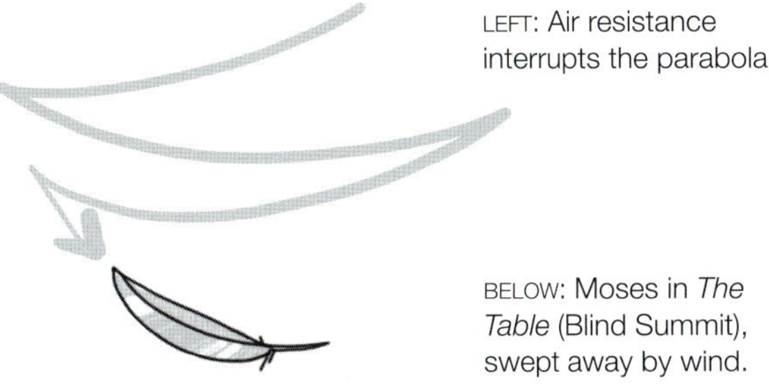

LEFT: Air resistance interrupts the parabola.

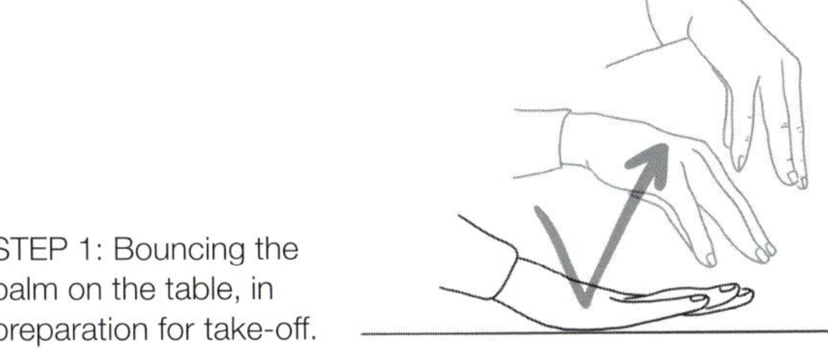

STEP 1: Bouncing the palm on the table, in preparation for take-off.

STEP 3: Landing on the palm and bouncing on to the feet.

BELOW: Moses in *The Table* (Blind Summit), swept away by wind.

Something to Notice

The audience anticipates the parabola from the take-off They can see when you start the movement where it is going to end; they can see the parabola. When someone walks on to the stage, the audience can tell pretty much straight away where they are going. They can see if they are going to walk across and off the other side, or if they are going to stop in the middle. They might even be able to predict whether they will stop three-quarters of the way across, or at the back or the front. They can see the parabola of the journey.

If you do what the audience expects, they will be satisfied. If you interrupt the anticipated journey, they will be surprised. And if you suddenly extend the journey, they will see that.

For example, think of someone walking on to the stage as if they are going to come to the downstage centre and make an announcement. Imagine that, when they get there, they don't stop but keep going, step off the front of the stage, walk through the audience, and leave the building. The audience will laugh. Why? Because they thought they knew where the performer was going, and then they went somewhere else. There was a beginning, a middle and a different end.

This can happen in everyday life. For example, you think you recognize someone and go to say hello but, as you get closer, you realize you don't know them at all. Now you have to change the 'end' of your movement. At the beginning of your journey you had set your centre of gravity on a parabolic path to one place, but you had to interrupt that path. This throws you off balance as you try to change direction. The beginning and the middle have a different end.

7
LEADING AND FOLLOWING

In puppetry you tell stories through a series of moving pictures that lead the audience's eye around the stage, from puppet to puppet, from one part of the puppet to another part of the puppet, through movements that change who is leading and who is following. These changes, between leading and following, are a visual representation of changes in power: the drama of the scene. The stage becomes a single giant puppet.

In these exercises you practise leading and following, first with your hands and then in a big group.

THE TWO-HAND PUPPET: LEADING WITH THE FEET

In the two-handed puppet, your upper hand represents the head and the lower hand represents the feet. In this exercise you practise leading with the feet and following with the head, to make the puppet move – walking, running or stepping – from place to place around the stage. The feet move first and the head follows. The feet make the puppet 'travel' around the space.

OPPOSITE: Howie and Lewie from *Citizen Puppet* (Blind Summit).

The Exercise

Each puppeteer uses their two hands over a table. You can do this in a group or on your own.

STEP 1: Make your hands into fists and hold one above the other, about 30 centimetres apart, on a table. You now have a two-handed puppet. Use your dominant hand (generally the one you write with) as the head and your other (subordinate) hand as the feet.
STEP 2: Make the puppet move around on the top of the table by jumping the bottom hand first and then following with the top hand second. Repeat this pattern to make the puppet move around the table.

Imagine that the two parts are connected by a piece of elastic. When the hand representing the feet moves, it stretches the elastic and then pulls the

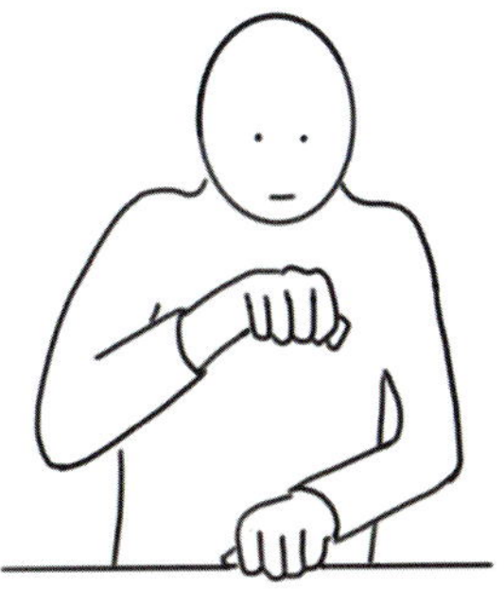
STEP 1: Making a two-handed puppet from your fists.

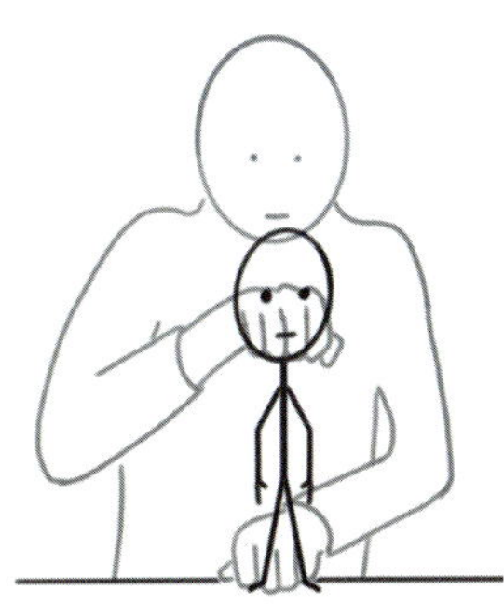
STEP 1: The top hand is the head and the bottom hand is the feet.

STEP 2: Lead with the lower hand and…

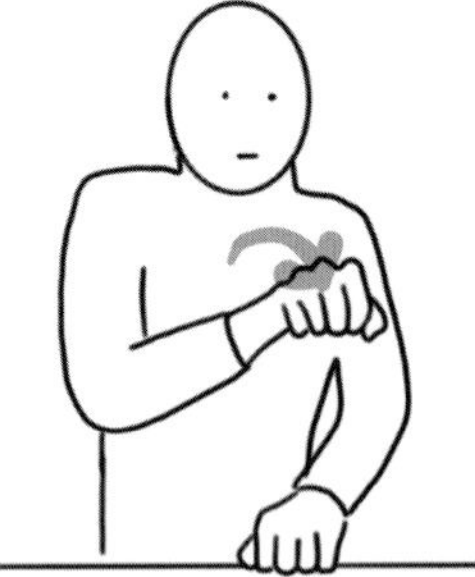

… follow with the top hand.

STEP 2: Leading with the lower hand…

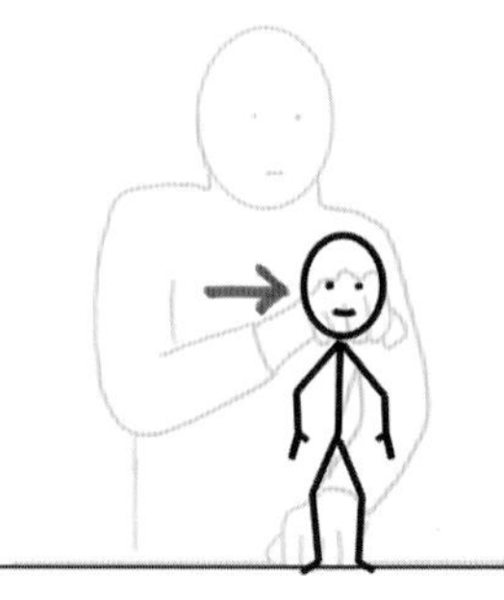

… represents stepping or walking.

head hand after it in the second movement. As a result, the movements are separate but connected. The puppet is leading with the feet and following with the head: feet, head… feet, head… feet, head.
STEP 3: Vary the speed and character of the movements. Make them calmer and softer, or quicker and more agitated. Try sliding the feet on the table top and sliding the head after it. Try making the puppet 'waddle' by rocking your bottom hand on the knuckles to 'walk' on the table, with the head hand following a beat behind. Try hopping and jumping. Try big moves and little moves.
STEP 4: When the head catches up with the feet, make sure it is looking at something. You can make it look in the direction in which it is heading, or back where it came from. You can make it look at the floor, or fix on one point as it moves. Always move the feet first and the head after. Move the feet on the first beat of the movement and the head on the second beat.

Tip for Doing It Well

Beware of 'neutral' moves with the head When you move the head after the feet, make sure that it does not 'go blank'. As the head moves over to the feet, pulled by the feet, make sure it is always looking at something. It may change what it is looking at as it is pulled after the feet, or remain fixed on the same thing, but it should not be neutral just because it is following.

Things to Notice

The feet and the head play equal parts The timing of the movements of the feet, followed by the head, are two equal beats. Each movement forms half of the movement: the movement of the feet starts the movement, and the head finishes it.

Make sure you give the feet and the head the same amount of time for their movements, to create an even rhythm between them. If one beat is long, both should be long; equally, if one beat is short, both should be short. Let the feet play an equal part in the storytelling. Beware of favouring the head movement over the feet movement.

The two actions – the movement of the feet and the movement of the head – are locked in an endless cycle of cause and effect. The feet move somewhere and the head follows that movement. If the feet move quickly the head responds quickly; if the feet move slowly, the head follows slowly.

Travelling movement can represent many things When you move the two-handed puppet on a table top, you are making a stylised version of movement around the stage. That movement does not simply represent walking. It could represent running, or taking a single large step, or jumping, or hopping, or skipping. It might not even represent real-time travelling. It could represent an edit, as in a movie or a graphic novel, or it could represent a piece of 'blocking', put in by a director to tell the story of the scene: 'The character was here and did this, and then it was there and did that.'

What the audience sees in the movement depends on the rhythm and timing of the movement of the two hands, and the intention behind them. Try to be as specific as possible about what you want the audience to see the hand puppet doing when you move it. For example, when the feet hand jumps or slides across the table top, it can represent the stepping of one leg. The movement of the head in response to it will represent the movement of the second leg catching up with it.

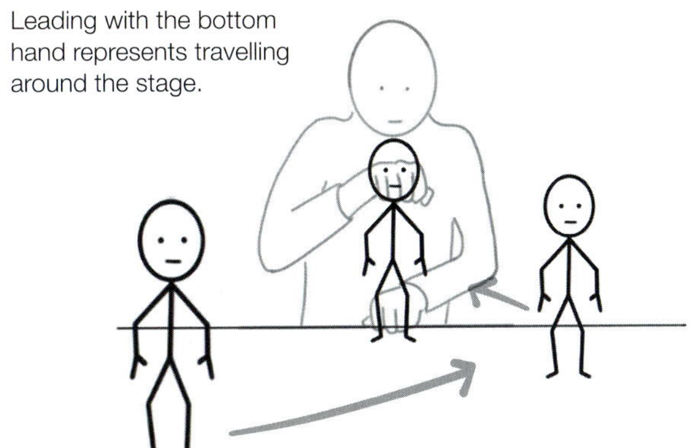

Leading with the bottom hand represents travelling around the stage.

THE TWO-HAND PUPPET: LEADING WITH THE HEAD

Moving the top hand – the head – makes the puppet look at something. It can also change the posture of the puppet, and create body language. If the puppet feels too close to something it might pull its head away from it, making it lean backwards. If the puppet cannot see what it wants to see, it might crane its neck and lean its head forwards to see further. This exercise explores leading with the head.

The Exercise

Make a two-fist puppet again (*see* above), standing on a table.

STEP 1: Turn your head hand around on the 'neck' to make it look at something in the room – maybe a mark on the table top, the ceiling, a wall, the door.
STEP 2: Make a small movement with the feet in response to the head's movement.
STEP 3: Turn the top hand to look at something else and make the bottom hand respond again. Every time the head hand moves to look at something, the feet hand responds: head, feet…head, feet, and so on.

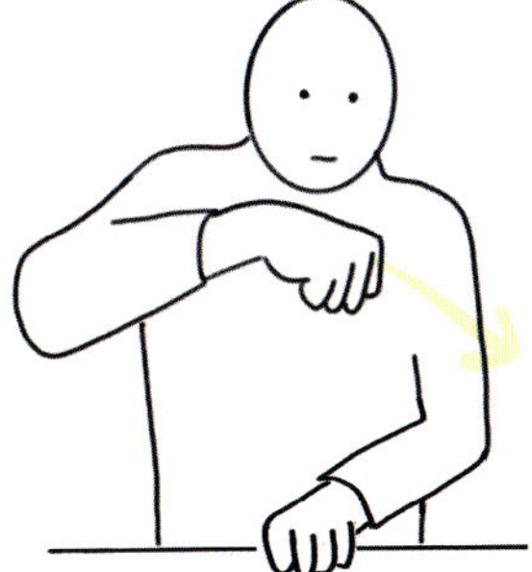

STEP 1: Turn the head hand to look at something…

STEP 2: … and react with the feet hand.

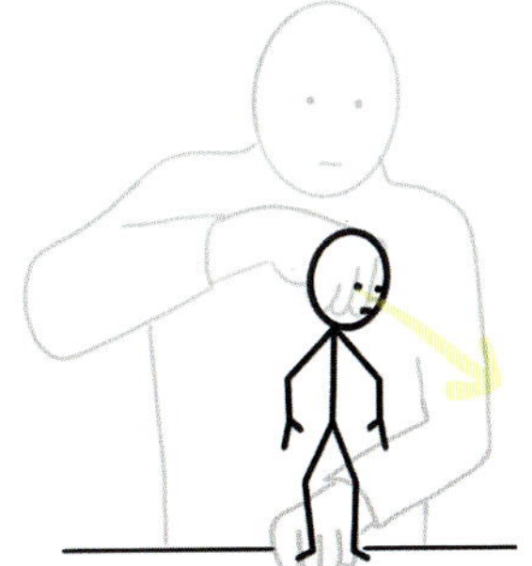

STEP 1: Leading with the top hand makes the puppet look at things…

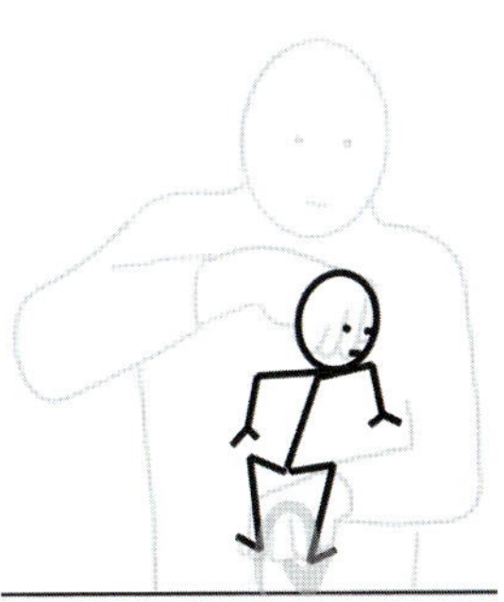

STEP 2: … and see them.

STEP 4: Try varying the response of the feet to the head turning. Make it big or small. Make the feet jump in fright, or make just a small adjustment in the weight. See how small you can make the response: it may be just a twitch or a slight shift. It should not be so big that the head has to follow it, and it becomes the leader.

STEP 5: See how accurately you can make the puppet look at things. Make it look at the ground and then make it look at its own feet. Make it look behind itself and then make it look at you. Make it look back and forth between two things. Every time the head moves, make sure there is some kind of reaction from the feet.

Tips for Doing It Well

Give both beats the same amount of time Just as when leading with the feet, make sure that the head and the feet movements share two halves of a single beat, whether they are big or small.

Be specific with the head movements Make sure when the head turns it ends up looking at a specific thing. Don't just move it; know what it is looking at when it moves. The head moves to look at things. The head is always looking at something.

Things to Notice

The head does not walk and the feet do not look at things When the head is leading, the feet move in response to what the puppet sees, not in response to where it moves. The head does not move the puppet around the table. The head cannot make the puppet travel, but what it sees might make it want to move its feet.

The head does not always look where it is going The head can be facing one way and the feet the other way. People often look around them while they are walking somewhere. They don't always look where they are going but they are always looking at something – the sky, the ground, a poster on a wall, other people walking past, trees, the clouds, a view.

Leading movement with the head makes the puppet into a fish If you make the head pull the feet into a movement, your puppet starts to swim. It becomes a swimmer or a fish. Changing how the parts of the puppet lead movement makes it read as something different.

There are times when a walker will lead the feet with their head, ducking under an obstacle, for example, or craning the neck when they are desperate to see something, or to discover the source of a smell or a sound. They will also lead the feet with the head when backing away from something they don't like. As a general rule, however, fish and other swimmers go head first, and walking creatures go feet first.

Travelling head first…

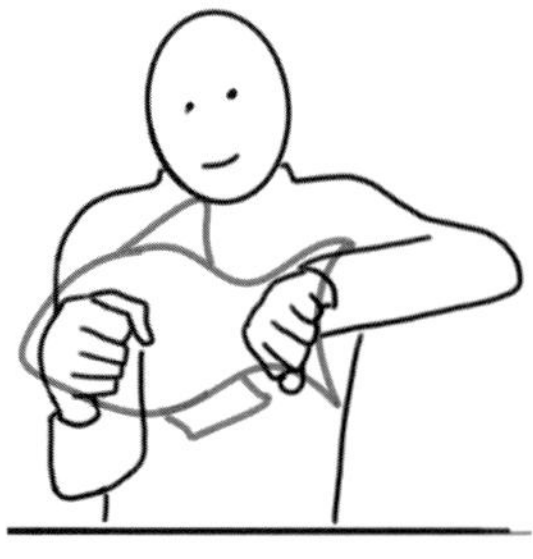

… makes the puppet into a fish.

Travelling feet first…

… makes the puppet into a person.

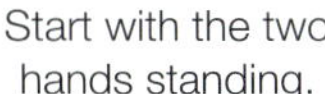

Start with the two hands standing.

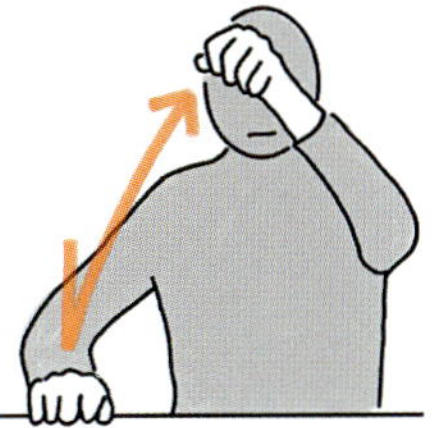

STEP 1: The head takes off…

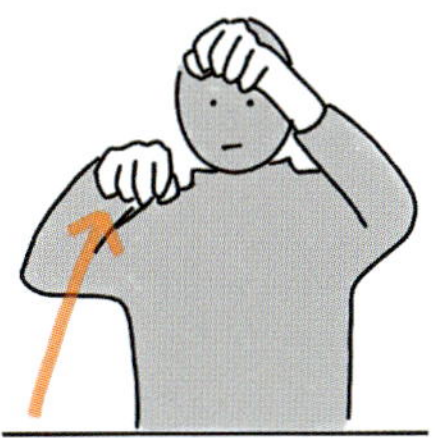

STEP 2: … the feet follow…

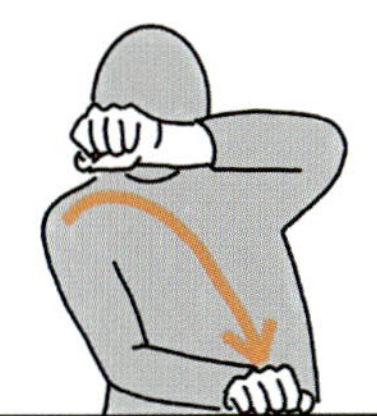

STEP 3: … the feet land…

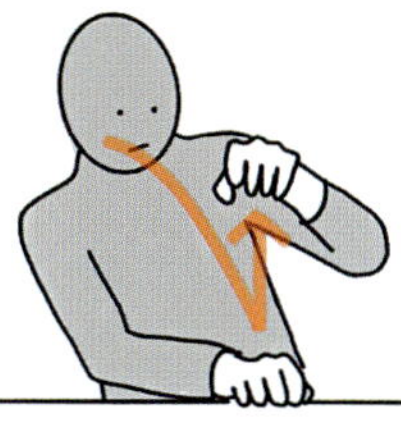

STEP 4: … then the head lands.

MAKING A TWO-HANDED PUPPET JUMP

To make a two-handed puppet jump, the head hand starts by compressing and extending the knees to make the puppet take off. It suspends in the air while the feet catch up, then the feet overtake the head and lead the puppet into the landing. The head and the feet swap the lead between taking off and landing.

In this exercise, you break down the movement and practise it. The important thing to get right is the rhythm of the movements.

The Exercise

Position your hands, one above the other, on the table (*see* above).

STEP 1: A jump is made of four half-beats, which are all separate but connected. In the first half-beat, the head compresses down towards the feet, then springs up to the top of the arc of the jump, where it stops, suspended in the air.
STEP 2: In the second half-beat, the feet are pulled up after the head. They compress up under the head, and the puppet hangs for a moment at the apex of the jump.
STEP 3: In the third half-beat, the feet take over the lead from the head, accelerating back towards the ground, where they land.
STEP 4: In the fourth half-beat, the head is pulled out of suspension by the feet, compresses over the feet, and then springs up to full height.

Something to Notice

Every movement of the two-handed puppet is a variation on a jump The puppet can make big jumps and small jumps. It can jump the whole way across the table in one move or it can make very small jumps on the spot. If the head looks somewhere, the feet respond with a small jump on the spot, and the audience can see that the puppet saw something.

PUPPETING THE STAGE: THE SCHOOL OF FISH

A school of fish is a group of fish, all of the same species, swimming together in the same direction. There can be thousands, even millions, of fish in a school. A school is different from a shoal, which is made up of different species of fish swimming in different directions.

In this exercise you begin with individual fish and build up to make a school. You can do part of the

Shadow line-up from *The LIttle Match Girl* (Blind Summit and Improbable).

exercise with as few as two people and there is no maximum number.

The Exercise

Clear the room and have everyone on their feet to start the exercise.

STEP 1: Everyone makes a 'fish' with their right hand (*see* Chapter 5) and starts them 'swimming' around the room. Each person focuses on their fish and lets it lead them, moving from the fish's centre. There should be no 'flapping'!
STEP 2: When one fish meets another, they stop for a moment and say 'Hello', and then move on. When they meet another fish, they greet it, and then swim on. The exercise continues until the fish have all met each other.
STEP 3: Once all the fish have met each other, the instruction is changed. so that when a fish meets another fish they pair up and start swimming together, side by side. After a while, they break off, pair up with another fish and swim with them. If a third fish joins a pair, one of the fish leaves, so that they are a pair again.

Everyone keeps focusing on their fish and letting their fish lead them, resisting the temptation to look round at the other fish. Let the fish do the looking. The front fish of the pair leads the other.
STEP 4: Next, the pairs join other pairs to become schools of four. Now there is a front fish, a back fish and two side fish in each school. The front fish is the leader.
STEP 5: The schools of four join up to become schools of eight, then the eights become sixteens, and so on, until the group is split into two schools of roughly equal numbers.

STEP 1: Making the hand into a fish.

STEP 2: Two fish greeting each other.

STEP 3: The fish swimming in pairs, the front fish leading.

STEP 4: Pairs joining up to form schools of four fish.

STEP 6: Ask one school to come out and watch the other school. What do they see? Do they see a school of fish? Or do they see a group of people doing strange movements together? Do they look at the fish or at the puppeteers? Do they watch individual fish or one big school of fish? Do they feel that they are watching puppetry, or contemporary dance, or some sort of strange ritual?
STEP 7: Ask the observers for feedback on what makes it work and how they think they can improve on what they are seeing. See if you can develop rules together.
STEP 8: Swap the groups around and get them to show each other what they saw.

Things to Notice

Notice how you feel It is extraordinary how much social tension can be experienced in a meeting between two hands pretending to be fish. Some meetings feel too long and awkward, while others feel cut off short; sometimes it feels just right. Be aware of how your fish meetings feel.

It gets crowded As the number of fishes in the schools increases, it gets harder to get the spacing right. If everyone tries to get to the front, they end up in a row and not in a school. If more fish join, the row may become a circle, with all the fish pointing towards the middle like a cocktail party, and your fish can't go anywhere. The groups become entangled, people become uncertain who to follow, and the swimming slows down. To make a school of fish, some fish need to hang back to be the middle fish and the back fish. In fact, it is the back fish that defines the size of the school.

Fish need space When the fish get too close, the puppeteers get tangled up in each other and the audience cannot see what is going on. The fish do not need to be close together for the audience

If the fish end up forming a circle, they cannot go anywhere.

to see that they are part of the same school. The fish will look as if they are 'together' when they are swimming in the same direction, and turning at the same time. See how far apart the fish can be and still clearly be 'together'.

Puppetry is not contemporary dance Sometimes, people watching puppeteers doing a school of fish may feel they are seeing a group of contemporary dancers doing synchronised arm movements. Both versions – the contemporary dance version and the school of fish version – are equally valid artistically, but the school of fish is puppetry and the contemporary dance version is contemporary dance. This exercise is about making puppetry.

SCHOOL RULES

This exercise introduces a few rules on how to be a school of fish: how the fish relate to one another and how the puppeteers should interact.

Every time the school changes direction a new fish becomes the front fish (the leader fish). No one single fish is the leader and the leadership keeps changing, depending on the direction in which the school turns. This process is called 'emergent leadership'. Every fish is a leader and every fish is a follower. This is how a real school of fish organizes itself. To an audience the school of fish will appear to be moving with a mind of its own.

As long as they act according to a few simple rules, every participant will always be aware of whether their fish is leading or following:

- RULE 1: Everyone focuses on their fish and allows their fish to look where it is going, without looking up to check what else is going on. They need to let the fish lead them, and trust it to see where it is going.
- RULE 2: The fish should be spread out so that they have room to turn without bumping into another fish or one of the other puppeteers.
- RULE 3: Each person makes their fish copy what the fish immediately in front of it does: it swims when the front fish swims, turns when it turns. For example, if the fish in front turns right, the following fish turns right. If the fish in front swims up, the follower swims up. If it turns left, the follower turns left.
- RULE 4: Finally, when the leader fish changes direction, it must make another fish the leader. For example, if there is a fish on its right flank, when it turns right, that fish will become the front fish. If it turns left, the fish on the left flank becomes leader. If it turns through 180 degrees, the back fish becomes the new leader.

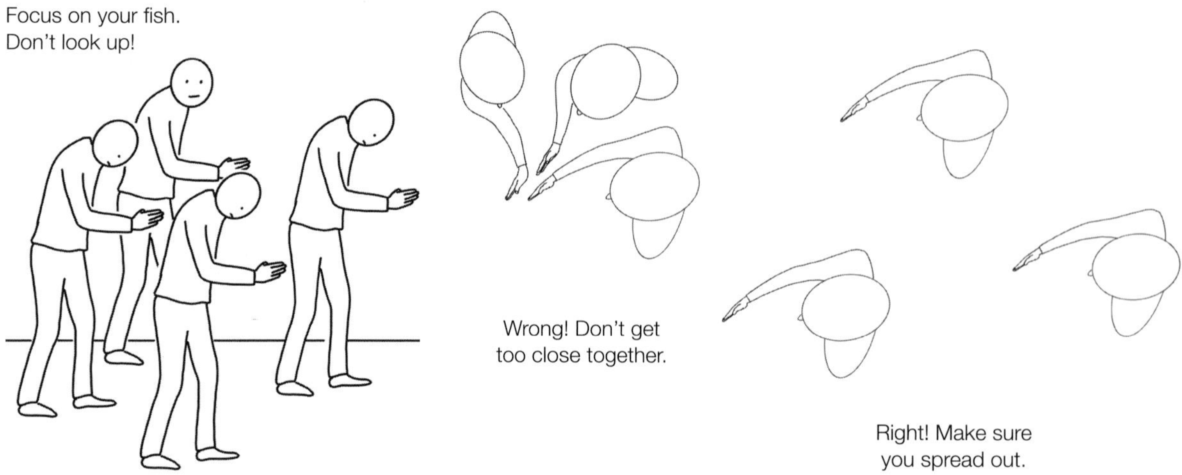

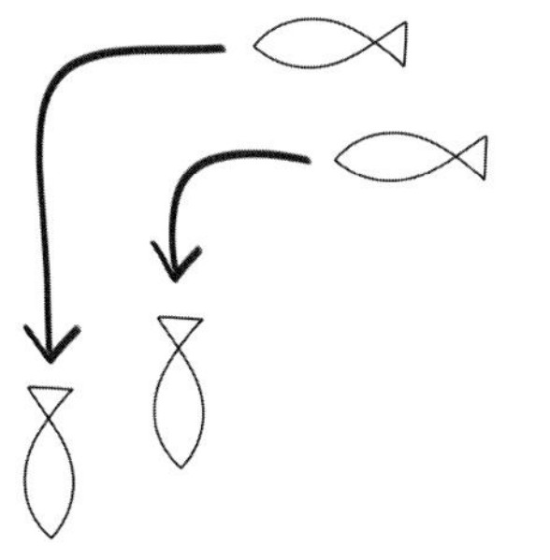

Wrong! The fish follow each other round the corner and the lead fish remains the leader.

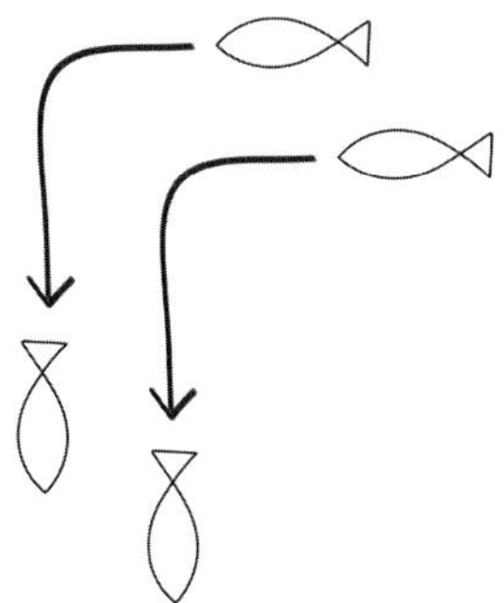

Right! The fish all change direction at the same moment and the leadership changes.

The Exercise

STEP 1: Make two schools of fish again and this time follow the above rules.
STEP 2: Get the two schools to swim around the space, using the rules, changing leader every time they turn.
STEP 3: Ask one school to come out and watch the other school practising. Get them to give feedback on what they can see and then swap around and have a go at improving on it.

Tips for Doing It Well

Turning your fish around its centre makes it easy to follow As a leader you want to make choices that are easy for the other puppeteers to see and to follow. Make your fish turn sharply and clearly around its centre (the centre of your hand, as described in Chapter 5). Don't turn your body to follow your fish until the other fish have started turning.

The fish turning is easy for the other fish to see and to follow and the audience will see the fish following one another. Turning your body will distract the audience from the fish, and catch the other puppeteers out. Instead of seeing a school of fish swimming, they will see soldiers marching.

Think about how to make a new leader fish as soon as you become leader As leader, when you turn, you must turn in a direction that makes someone else the leader. If the school is mainly to your left, by turning left you can be fairly sure that you will make a new leader. If you are unsure which side most of the fish are, a 180-degree turn will always make a new leader.

The audience only knows what you tell them People are scared of getting it wrong. They worry that their fish will go off on its own and look silly. But that doesn't matter at all to the audience, who will enjoy 'the funny fish that went off on its own'. As long as your fish keeps following the rule of turning when

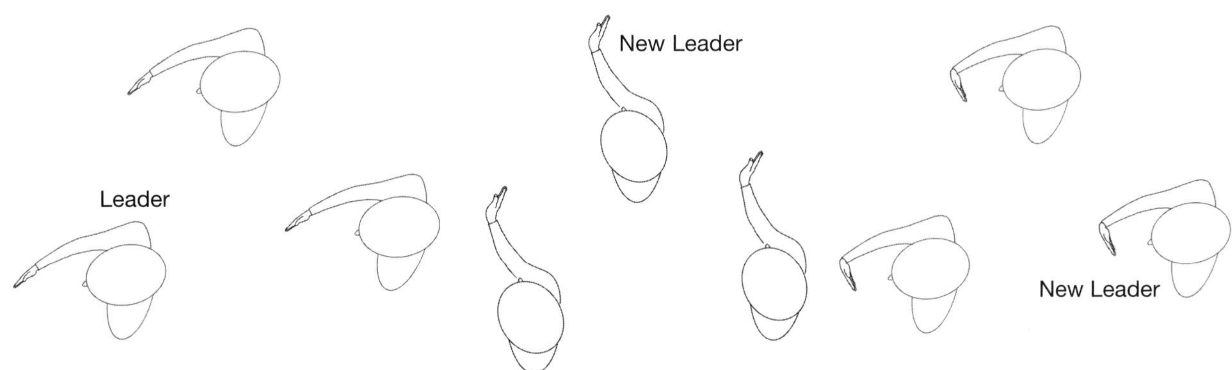

The leadership changes every time the school changes direction.

If the school turns right, the fish on the right becomes leader.

If the school turns left, the fish on the left becomes leader.

the nearest fish to it turns, it will find its way back to the school, and no one will be any the wiser. If, on the other hand, you correct yourself by looking up to see what is going on, then you show the audience that something is wrong.

Prepare to become the leader When you are following, think about what will make you the leader. If you are on the right flank of the school, you know that the lead fish turning right will make you leader. If you are on the left, you are looking out for the leader to turn left. If you are at the back, you know that you will become the leader if the current leader turns through 180 degrees. Knowing this in advance means you can relax and accept the leadership confidently when it comes.

Hang back after giving away the leadership It takes time for the new leader to realize they are the new leader. There is a brief moment when there is no leader. When you change from being the leader to being a follower, you need to hang back while all the other fish in the school change direction, until the new leader fish starts to lead. The better the group is working together, the shorter this time becomes.

The back fish is important It is a common mistake to think of the back fish of the school as insignificant. In fact, the back fish defines the size of the school, showing the audience how far the school extends. In addition, if the leader turns 180 degrees, the back fish will become the leader fish.

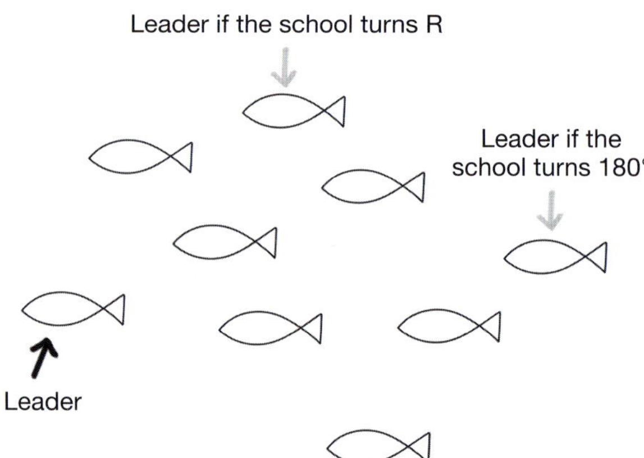

Think ahead to what will make you the new leader.

Things to Notice

It is difficult to change status fast When you pass the leadership on to another fish, you change from leader to follower, and the status of your fish falls. Conversely, when your fish becomes leader, its status rises. This means that the status of your fish is constantly changing. It is hard to change status from leader to follower and follower to leader quickly. Naturally, you will want to check: 'Do you really want me to lead?' Equally naturally, you will want to resist being demoted. Part of getting better at this exercise is learning to accept and let go of leadership quickly and easily.

The power of the leader fish is to appoint the next leader People often think of leading as pulling people where you want them to go but that is not how it works in the school of fish. In the school of fish, the power of the leader is to give away the leadership, to make another fish the leader. What is interesting for the audience is not only that the school of fish changes direction, but also that the leadership changes. The power changes.

WHEN TO CHANGE LEADER

A change in leadership of the school of fish is a visual representation of a power shift on stage. A leader is demoted to follower and a follower is promoted to leader. And the school keeps swimming. The power shift is the moment that the audience is most interested in, so you need to know when to make it happen.

If the school of fish holds on to the same leader for too long it becomes prosaic, but if they try to change too soon and the school will break up and the scene will descend into chaos. Both are boring for an audience.

In this exercise you explore when the audience wants you to change the leader, how to judge it and how to practise doing it in your schools of fish.

The Exercise

Divide the group into two schools of fish. Have one school on stage and make the other school an audience.

STEP 1: The onstage school of fish starts to swim about the space, changing leader every time they change direction, as before.
STEP 2: The audience shouts out 'Change!' when they want the leadership to change.

Anyone in the audience group can shout out 'Change!' They should shout out whenever they are bored, or are about to be bored. 'Change!' 'Change!' 'Change!'
STEP 3: As soon as they hear the audience shout 'Change!', the leading fish must turn and make another fish the leader.
STEP 4: The audience then shouts 'Change!' again. They should have fun with it. How quickly can they make the school change the leader? How long can they extend the time between changes? What happens if they do it too soon? Or leave it too long?
STEP 5: Then, instead of the audience shouting out, anyone in the school of fish can shout 'Change!' when they want the leadership to change. Any puppeteer, except the current leader fish, can shout out.

The audience watches to see if they agree whether the moment is being judged correctly.
STEP 6: Swap the groups around and do it again.

Things to Think About

When is too early to change? Each time the leadership changes, there is a short period when there is no leader. For example, if the lead fish turns 180 degrees to make the school of fish swim in the opposite direction, at that moment there is no front fish, no leader. If someone shouts 'Change!' now, there will be no fish to make it happen.

The next thing is that the fish immediately behind the leader turn 180 degrees, then the fish behind them, and so on, until the back fish turns and becomes the new front fish, leading the school in the opposite direction. Now that the school has a new leader, it is possible for it to change direction again.

In other words, the earliest possible moment a school of fish can change leader is as soon as a new leader is established. The quicker the school has a new leader, the sooner it will be able to change again.

When is too late to change? If the observers of the exercise have to shout 'Change!', then you have probably missed the moment. Real audiences will

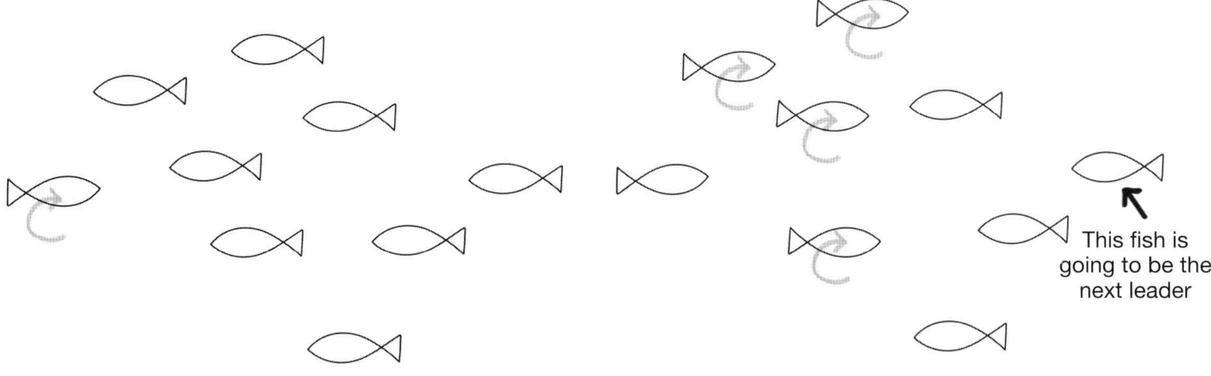

If the lead fish turns 180 degrees, there is no leader to lead a change of direction.

Half the school has turned 180 degrees. There is still no leader to change direction.

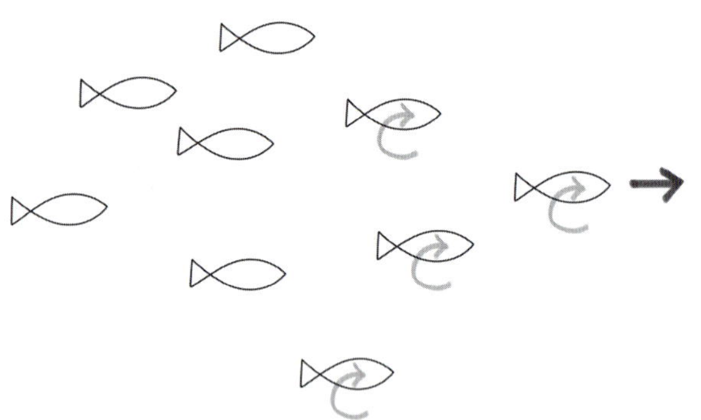

All the fish have turned. There is now a new leader that can lead a change of direction.

probably be too polite actually to shout out, but they will feel the moment. As the puppeteers in the school of fish your goal is to internalize the audience's shout of 'Change!', so that you hear it without the audience saying it, and recognize that it is time to change the leadership.

The leader does not decide when is right to change In this exercise, the only person who never shouts 'Change!' is the leader fish. They don't need to, since they can simply make the change. The instruction 'Change!' only determines the timing of the turn. The shout of 'Change!' controls when to change, not which way. The direction of the change is directed by the leader fish.

USING BREATH TO TIME THE CHANGES

In this exercise you use breathing together to time when the changes should occur. Breathing together 'drives' the story of the school of fish. The puppeteers feel instinctively when the fish should change direction, and the suspensions of breath hold the audience's attention and allow you to extend the time between changes.

Of course, fish do not breathe in this way, but this is not a biological breath, it is a 'story-telling breath'. You are breathing the way you want the audience to breathe. You are controlling the drama with your breath and using breath to direct the audience's eye around the stage.

The Exercise

Set up the exercise as before, with half the group making a school of fish in the space and the other half watching.

STEP 1: When the school of fish makes the first change of direction, and the leadership changes, the puppeteers take a breath in together. They then suspend their breath until the next change of direction, when they breathe out.
STEP 2: On the next change of direction, the puppeteers breathe in again, then suspend, and so on. Can you make the audience wait for you by holding your breath? Can you make them give you more time between changes?
STEP 3: Swap round and repeat the exercise. Give feedback to each other on what was worked and what did not work.

MAKING TWO SCHOOLS SWIM THROUGH EACH OTHER

A great way to finish working with schools of fish is to try to make two schools swim through each other. The aim of the exercise is that the two schools should still be visible all the time as they swim through each other, and do not become entangled or slow down. Instead, there should be an explosion of excitement, as there is when fish do this in real life.

The Exercise

STEP 1: Form into two schools of fish, in opposite corners of the room.
STEP 2: Make the two schools swim towards each other, pass through each other, and arrive in the opposite corner of the room, without losing their 'togetherness' as two separate schools of fish.

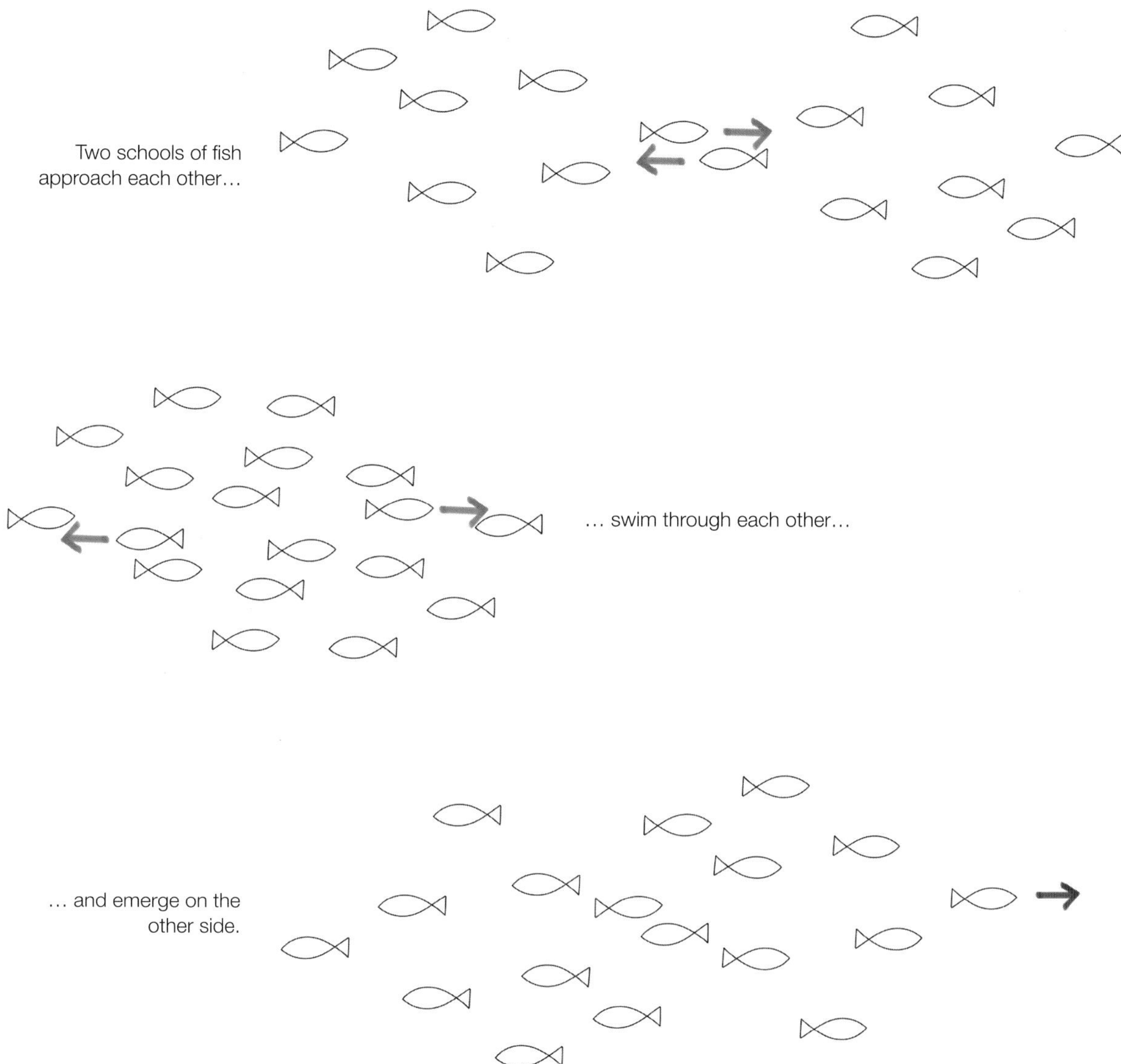

STEP 3: Discuss how to make it better and repeat the exercise a few times. Think about how to use breath, focus, moving from the centre, leading and following, to make the two schools swimming through each other as fast, dramatic and real as possible. Your aim is to capture the explosion of excitement that would occur if two real schools of fish were to swim through each other.

Tip for Doing It Well

Use the breath to tell the story Take a deep breath in together before the schools of fish set off and hold your breath until you meet in the middle of the room. Breathe out as the fish pass through one another in a flurry of excitement, and then hold your breath until the schools arrive at the other side of the room.

8
GROUP PUPPETRY AND IMPROVISATION

With three puppeteers you can bring to life six one-handed puppets, three two-handed puppets, one four-handed puppet and one two-handed puppet, one six-handed puppet, or any other combination that you can think of with six hands.

All these puppet arrangements work on the same general principles: each puppeteer has an object in each hand, which they operate separately to create dramatic movements on the stage. The difference is the degree to which the objects they are working with are joined together. In this chapter, you will explore the various ways to use different combinations of puppeteers working separately or together on a puppet (*see* box, p.130).

WORKING WITH ONE PUPPETEER ON A WORKSHOP PUPPET

With one puppeteer on each puppet the workshop puppet is a two-handed puppet. With only two hands you hold the head with one hand and the feet with the other hand and make the puppet stand and move about on the stage (like the two-handed puppet in Chapter 7). In this exercise, three puppeteers have a puppet each and improvise simple scenes together.

OPPOSITE: Moses in *The Table* (Blind Summit).

The Exercise

Everyone has a puppet each. You can do this exercise on a table or on the floor.

STEP 1: Hold your workshop puppet by the head and the feet. Hold the head with your dominant hand (the hand you write with) and the feet with your subordinate hand.

Hold the head between finger and thumb, just behind the ears, and the feet with the other hand, using the index finger to hold one ankle, and the middle finger to hold the other. Keep this grip throughout the exercise. Focus on the head of the puppet.

STEP 2: Make the puppets move around the space with the feet, and look at things with the head. Lead with the feet to travel, and lead with the head to look at things. Move one part of the puppet after the other.

STEP 3: Explore what the puppet can do. Make it kneel, sit and lie down. Make it walk and run and jump. Make it float and fly and stand on its head. Make it lean and slide.

THE WORKSHOP PUPPET

The workshop puppet is a training tool for practising general principles. You can use it on your own, as a two-handed puppet, with two people as a four-handed puppet, or with three people as a six-handed puppet.

There are two versions of a workshop puppet: a specially made cloth one and a home-made newspaper version.

The cloth workshop puppet is made from calico and filled with pillow stuffing. It may be as simple as two cut-outs of cloth sewn together, with joints made simply by sewing across. More complicated versions may have webbing joints and special patterns, and limbs stiffened with wooden dowels inside the stuffing. They come in a variety of sizes and shapes, but are usually about 50–60cm high. However they are made, they take on a lot of character when you start to puppet them.

It is also possible to create a simple workshop puppet with newspaper. These are easy to make, in about 10 minutes. The best way is in a group of three. Take three sheets of newspaper and roll them up lengthways to make a tube. Fold the tubes in half, hook one inside the other to make the body and the legs, and then wrap the third one around the neck, like a scarf, to make arms. Twist the top to make a head, and secure the legs and arms in place with tape. As an extra detail, you can tape an object to the neck to make a more sophisticated head.

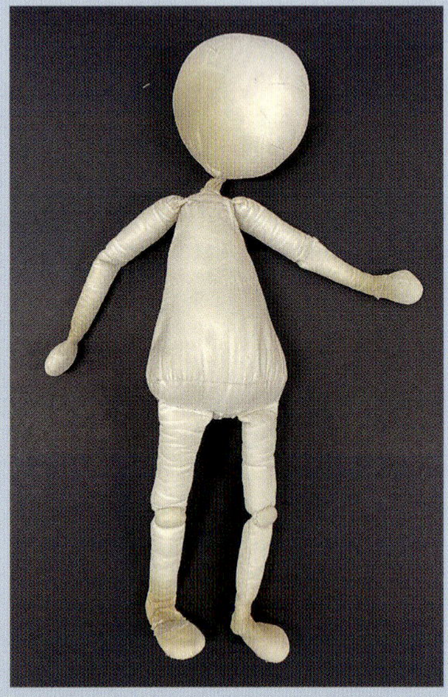

LEFT: Workshop puppet.

BELOW: Workshop puppets can be all sorts of shapes and sizes.

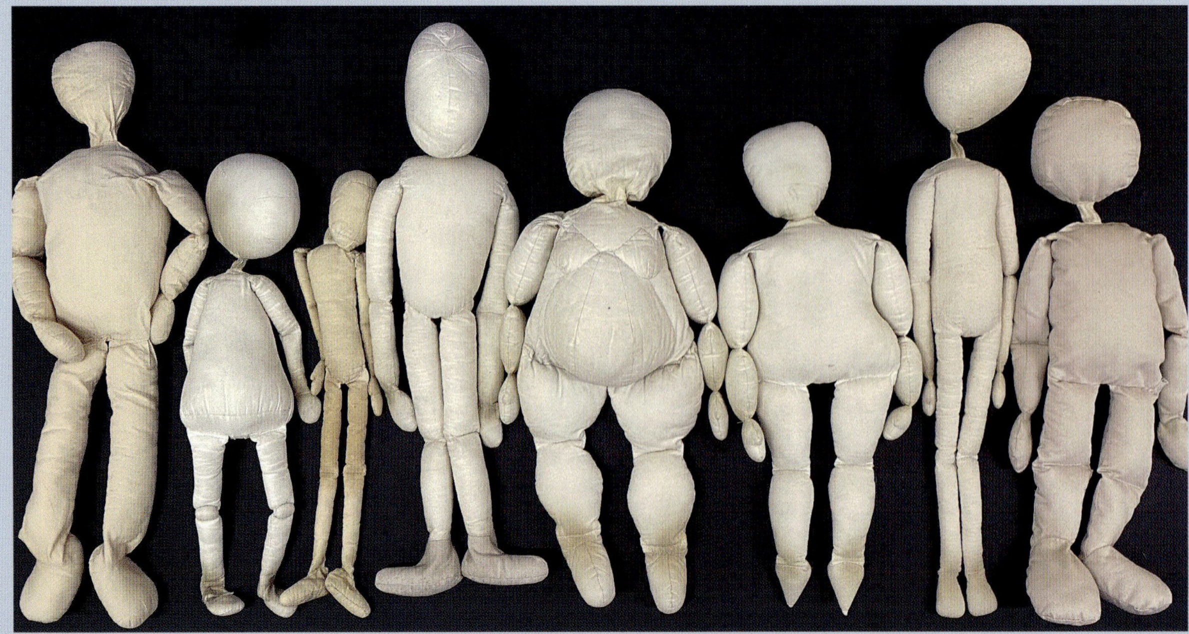

Creating a simple workshop puppet

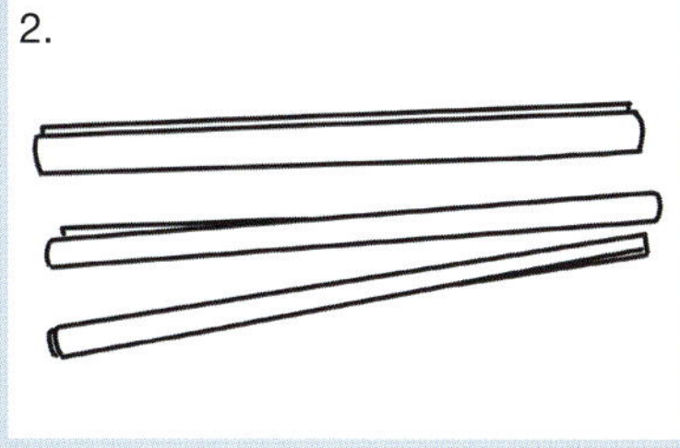

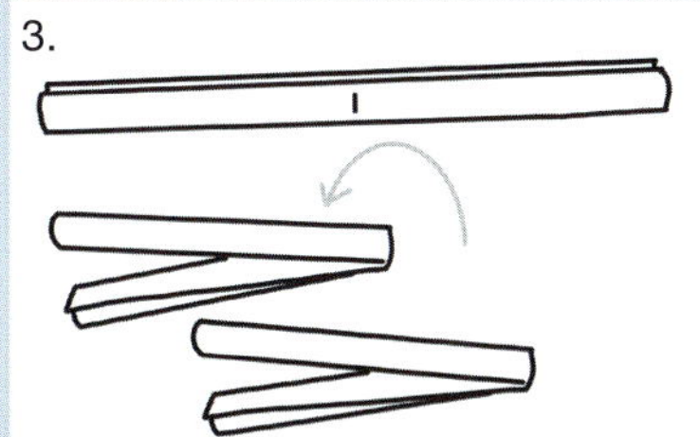

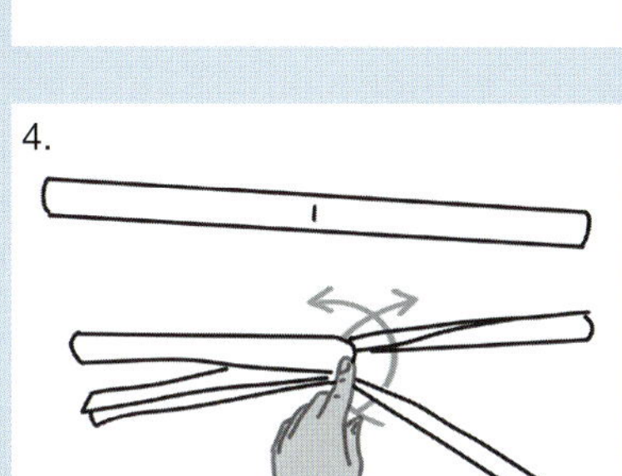

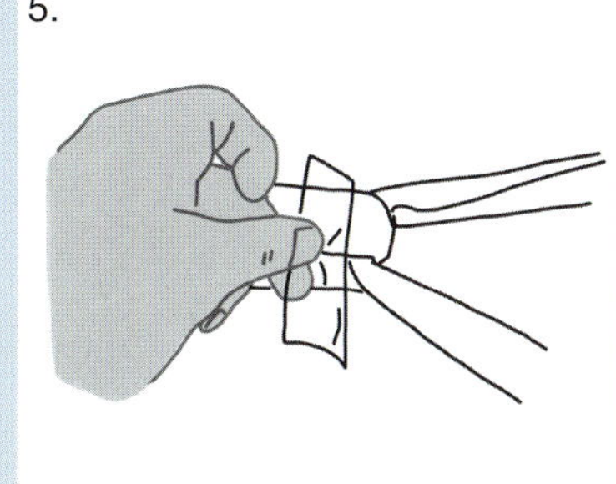

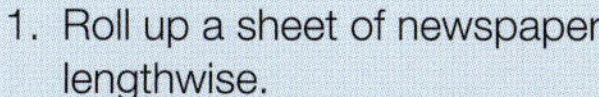
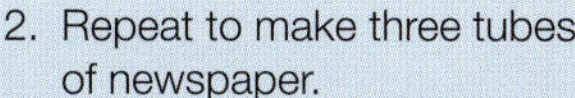

1. Roll up a sheet of newspaper lengthwise.
2. Repeat to make three tubes of newspaper.
3. Fold two of the tubes in half.
4. Hook the two tubes together to make the body and legs.
5. Fix the waist with tape.

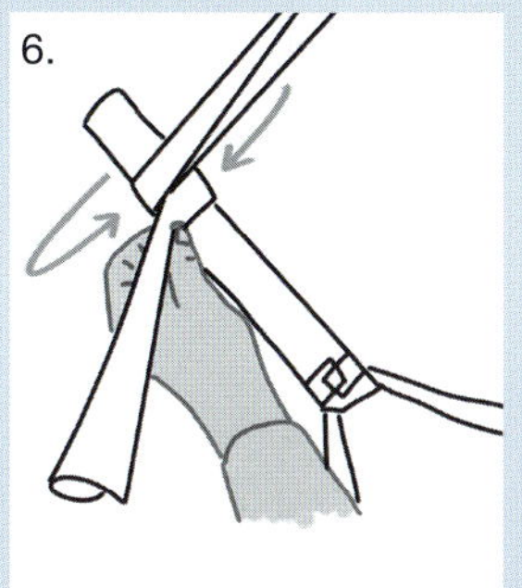

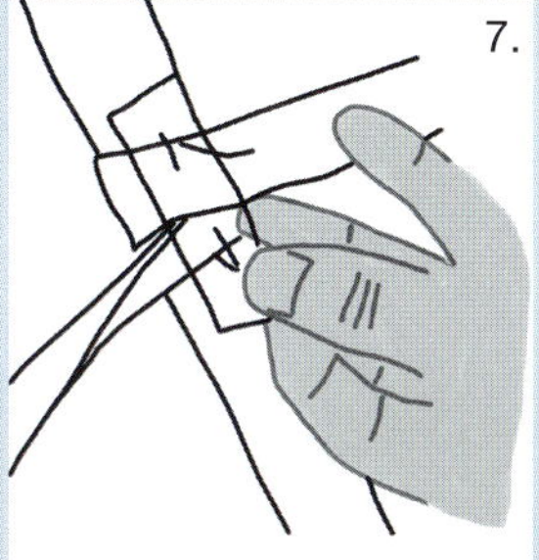

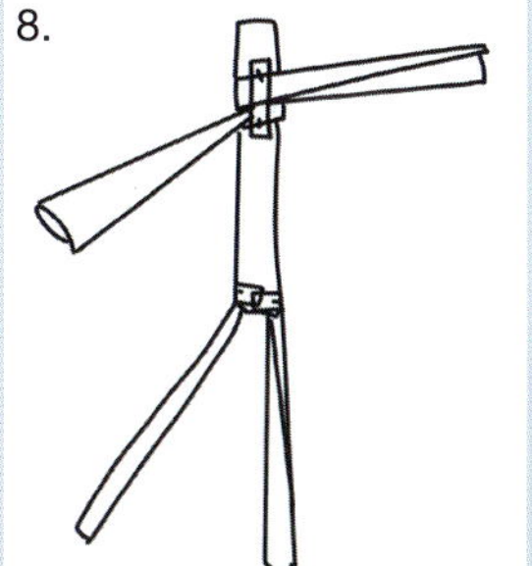

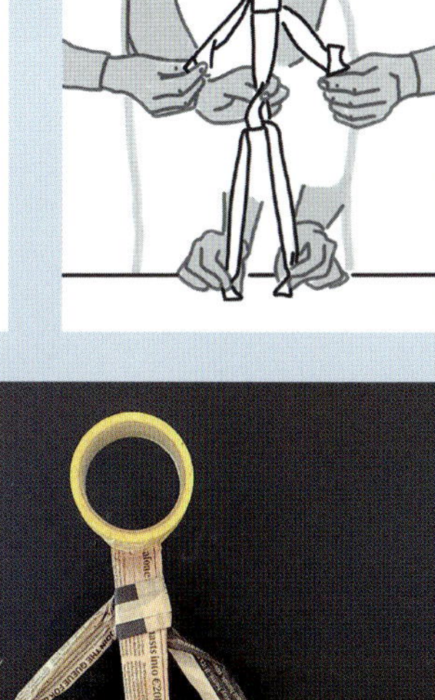

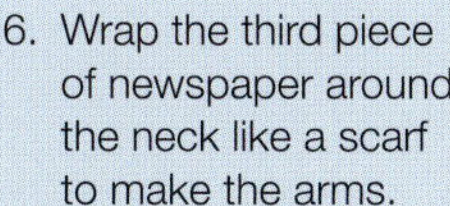

6. Wrap the third piece of newspaper around the neck like a scarf to make the arms.
7. Secure with tape.
8. The final puppet.
9. Add an object to be the head, and three puppeteers to operate it.

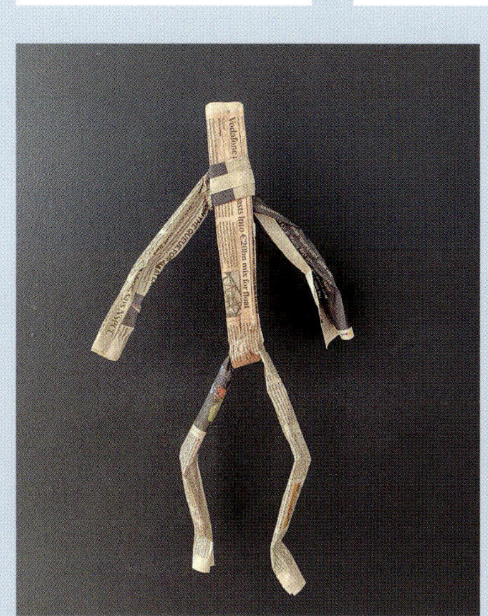

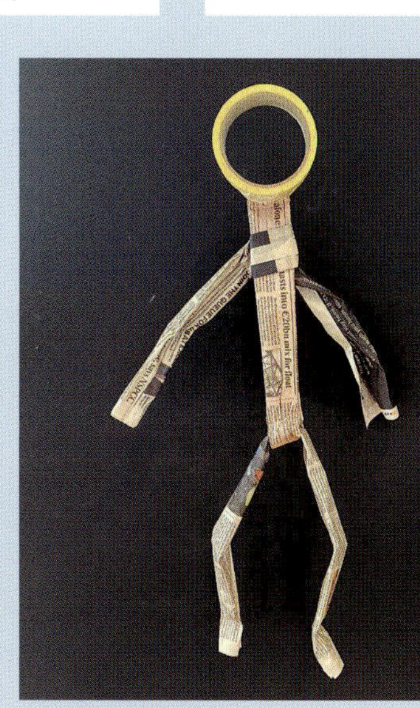

RIGHT: The newspaper puppet.

FAR RIGHT: The newspaper puppet with a roll of tape for a head.

With only two hands to operate the puppets, the movements you can do are simple but recognizably reference real stage movement, or 'blocking'. STEP 4: Now make the puppets breathe. Show the expansion and contraction of the lungs, with a tiny increase and decrease in the height of the puppet.

Connect the movement of the puppet around the stage to the breathing, by making it take a breath in before it moves, and then breathing out when it arrives: breathe in, turn the head, react with the feet, and breathe out. Breathe in, move the feet, follow with the head, and breathe out.

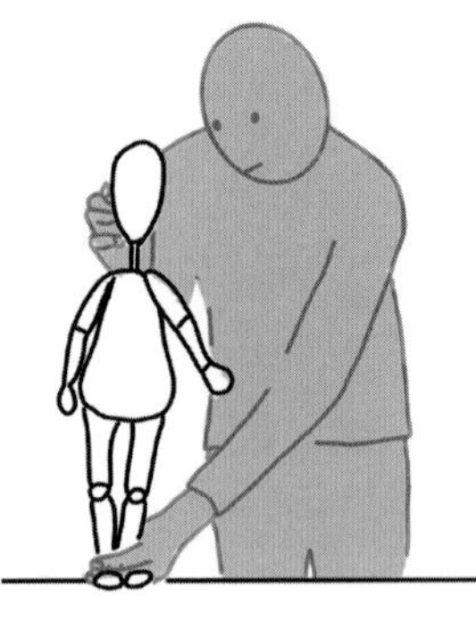

STEP 1: Holding the workshop puppet by the head and the feet.

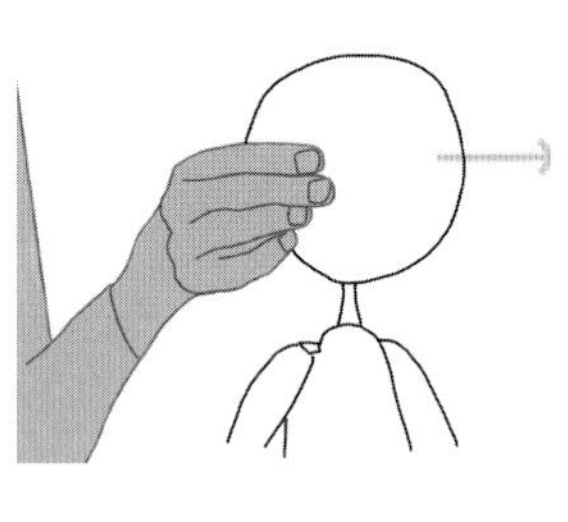

STEP 1: Holding the head

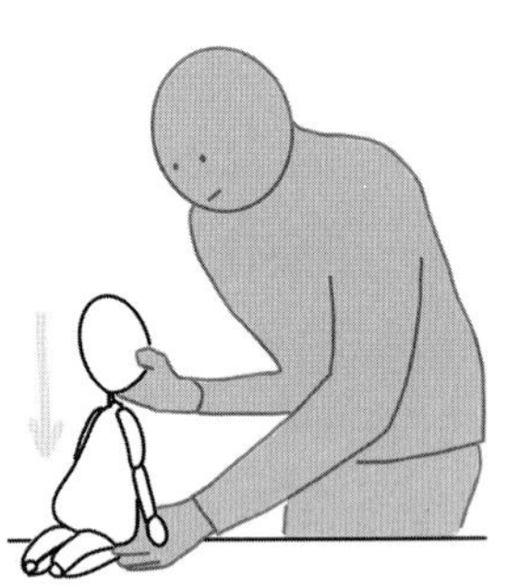

Make the puppet kneel…

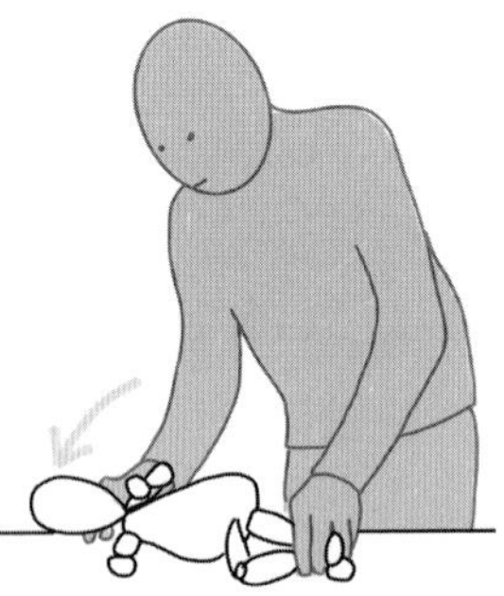

… lie down.

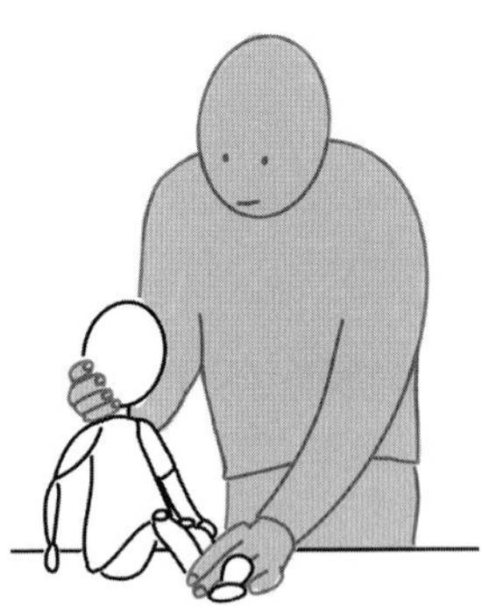

… sit.

… float.

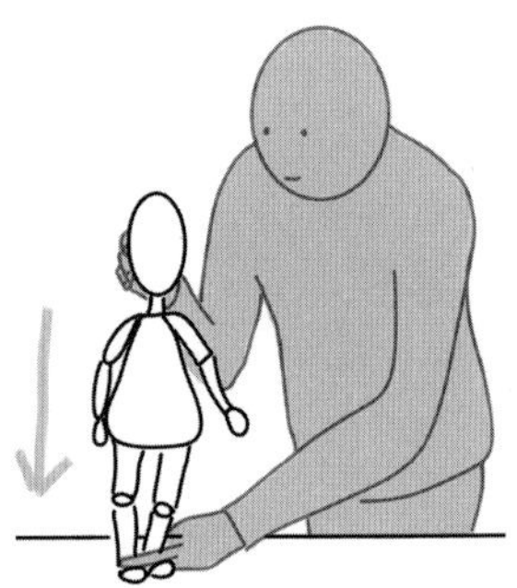

Make the puppet breathe out…

… stand on its head.

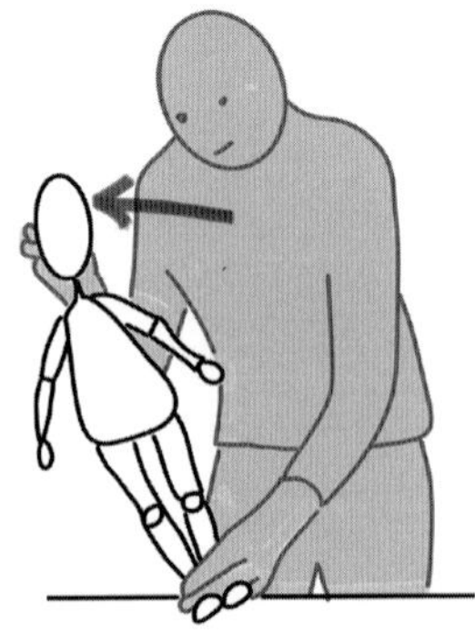

Make the puppet puppet lean.

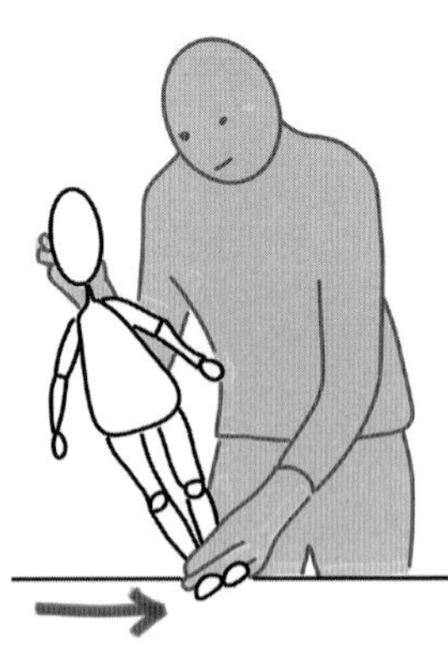

Make the feet slide.

STEP 5: Now bring three puppets together to perform in the same scene. Move them one at a time. Each time one puppet moves, the other two puppets react. Move, react. Move, react. Explore the shifts in power dynamics as they move around the stage.

Things to Notice

The midline of the puppet controls its head and centre By holding the head and feet of the puppet you can make it look at things, breathe and travel. These are the fundamental elements of making the puppet perform. The arms flap about and the legs are not able to move separately, but by controlling the midline of the puppet you control the puppet's centre and head.
Movements read as the thoughts of the puppet By letting only one puppet in the group move at a time, they appear to think about what they are doing, and respond to the others. The audience's focus passes from puppet to puppet as they become active – leading – and then passive – following. Each movement reads as thought and leads to a change in the power dynamic on the stage.

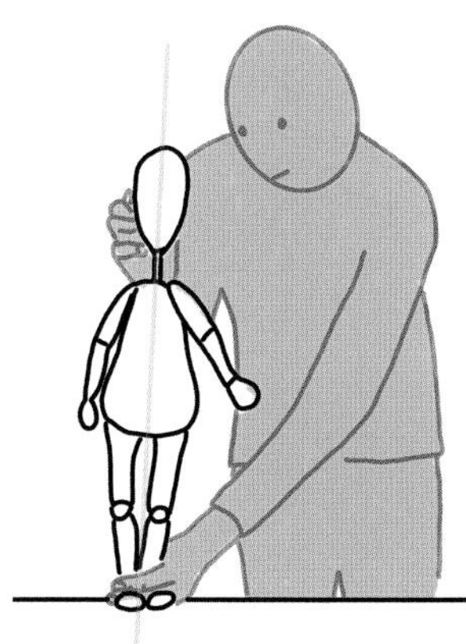

With two hands you control the centre of the puppet.

TWO PUPPETEERS ON A PUPPET

With two puppeteers there are a variety of ways to hold the puppet. Each different arrangement makes a slightly different puppet, with different conventions for how it works. If feet are not crucial in a scene, it makes sense to hold them and operate them with one hand. If, however, they are essential to tell the story, then you need to use an arrangement that gives you two hands to move them separately.

This exercise looks at the different ways two puppeteers can work on a workshop puppet and what each arrangement gives you.

The Exercise

In this exercise, you work in pairs to make four-handed puppets.

STEP 1: Test each of the two-person arrangements (*see* box, p.134) for holding the puppet. Move the puppet around the space leading with the feet, and make it look around the space leading with the head. Make it reach for things, point at things, and gesture leading with the hands. Make it sit, kneel, stand, walk, jump, and so on. Try making it talk.
STEP 2: Share what you have discovered with the rest of the group and then swap around to watch them.

Tip to Do It Better

Remember to lead and follow With four hands it is easy to make the puppet move too much, so that the audience cannot follow what it is doing. You can think of the puppet as being made of three parts: the head, the body (including the hands) and the

TWO-PERSON ARRANGEMENTS

ARRANGEMENT 1: Sharing the midline
Puppeteer One takes the head and a hand, and Puppeteer Two takes the feet and the other hand. They take the head and the feet with their 'inner' hand, and use their 'outer' hand to take the hands. Puppeteer One takes the head with their dominant hand. The puppeteer's hand should match the puppet's hand – hold the puppet's right hand with your right hand, and the puppet's left hand with your left hand.

This is the best arrangement for most two-person puppet improvisations.

ARRANGEMENT 2: Two-feet mode
Puppeteer One holds the head and a hand, and Puppeteer Two takes a foot in each hand. In this arrangement the puppet has working legs to walk around, but it has one arm hanging loose. (This is sometimes referred to as the 'dead arm problem'.) It is a useful arrangement if you want working legs but only have two puppeteers.

ARRANGEMENT 3: Midline only (head–bottom–feet mode)
Puppeteer One takes the head and the bottom, while Puppeteer Two takes the two feet. This means that you have control of the centre. It is very good for practising puppeting the body or the feet. It is not ideal for performance, since it leaves two hands hanging.

ARRANGEMENT 4: Crossing the midline (speaking mode)
Puppeteer One holds the head and the feet, while Puppeteer Two holds both hands. This means that the midline is controlled by one puppeteer and the two hands by another. This is particularly good if you want to improvise with speaking and hand gestures.

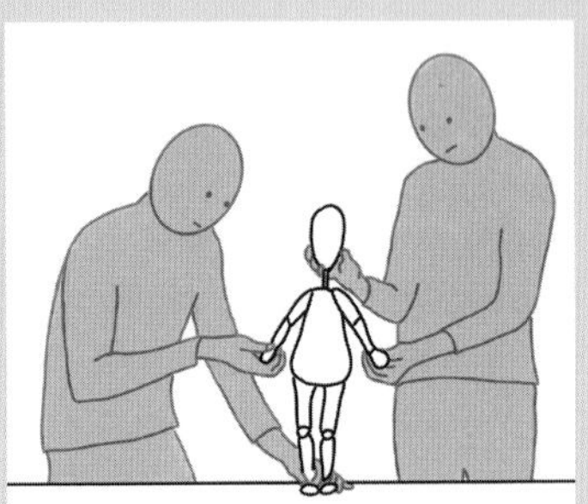

ARRANGEMENT 1: Sharing the midline.

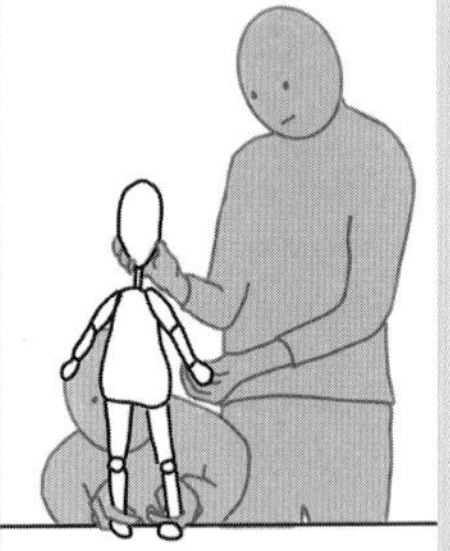

ARRANGEMENT 2: Two-feet mode.

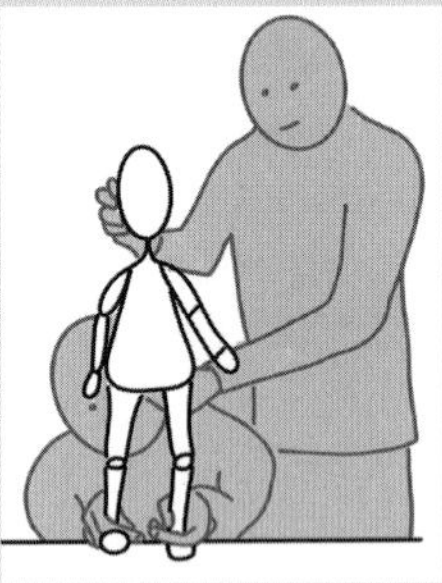

ARRANGEMENT 3: Midline only.

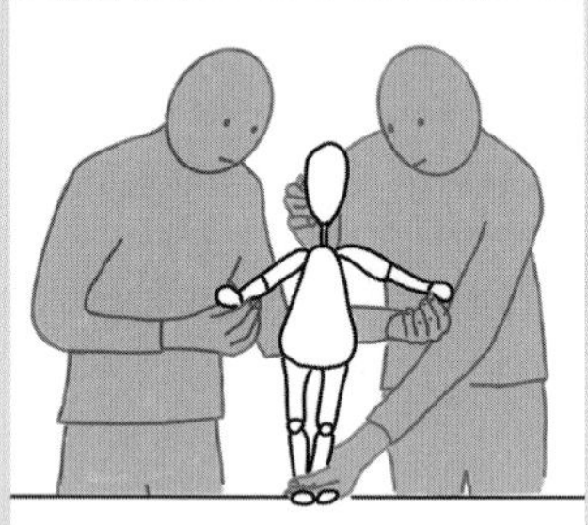

ARRANGEMENT 4: Crossing the midline.

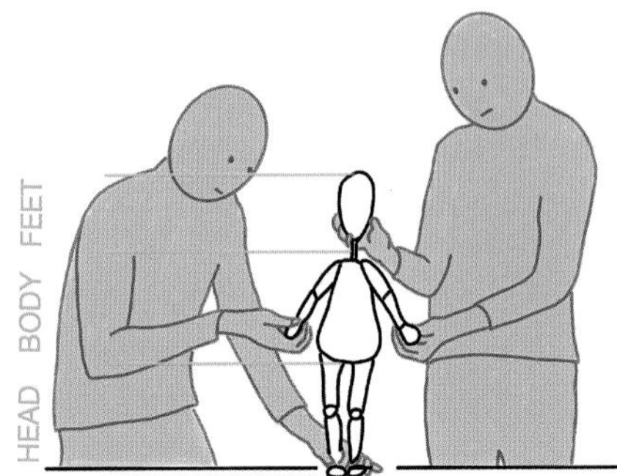

Think of the puppet as head, body and feet.

feet. Try to think of your hands as part of these three parts. When one part moves, or 'leads', the other two parts stay still and then they react, or 'follow'.

THREE PUPPETEERS ON A PUPPET

With three puppeteers on the workshop puppet, all its limbs can be moved. This offers huge possibilities for movement, but it can also cause confusion about which part should be moving and which part should be still. As a result, it becomes more important than ever to understand which parts of the puppet lead which actions.

This exercise explores who does which parts when you have three puppeteers on one puppet.

The Exercise

Three puppeteers take one puppet and stand it on a table.

STEP 1: Puppeteer One holds the head and a hand and stands on one side of the puppet. Puppeteer Two holds the rear end and the other hand and stands on the other side of the puppet. Puppeteer Three goes in the middle and takes the feet.

The three puppeteers arrange themselves behind the puppet so that the head puppeteer can hold the head with their dominant hand.

STEP 2: Focus on the midline of the puppet. The head puppeteer focuses on the head, the puppeteer holding the puppet's bottom focuses on the spine, and the feet puppeteer focuses on the feet, or the space between the feet.

STEP 3: Make the puppet breathe. To do this, all the puppeteers breathe together and the body puppeteer makes the chest move up and down with the breath. Connect the puppet's movement to the breath by making the puppet take an in-breath before performing an action, and breathe out after it has completed it.

STEP 4: Start bringing the puppet alive by leading with different parts. Begin with the feet. Make the feet go up and down and lead the puppet around on the table.

Move each part of the puppet – the head, the body and the feet – separately, so that there is always only one part leading at any time, with the rest of the puppet following.

STEP 5: Try leading with different parts of the body. Try making the puppet point at something and let the puppet follow the hand towards that thing. Make the puppet kneel. Make it sit down. Lead with the head. Turn the head to look at something and make the rest of the body react.

STEP 6: Give the puppet thoughts by saying 'Thought' every time you make it move, and develop the emotion using the breath of the puppet.

Something to Notice

The three-person puppet has working legs Legs are a luxury for a puppet, not a necessity. Most puppets work perfectly well without legs. They are unique to a few puppets, including the three-person table-top puppet and string puppets. Expressive moving legs are really what define the three-person puppet.

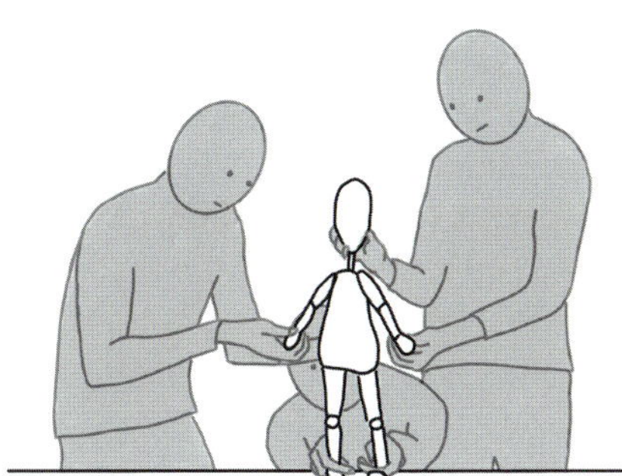

STEP 1: Three people on the puppet.

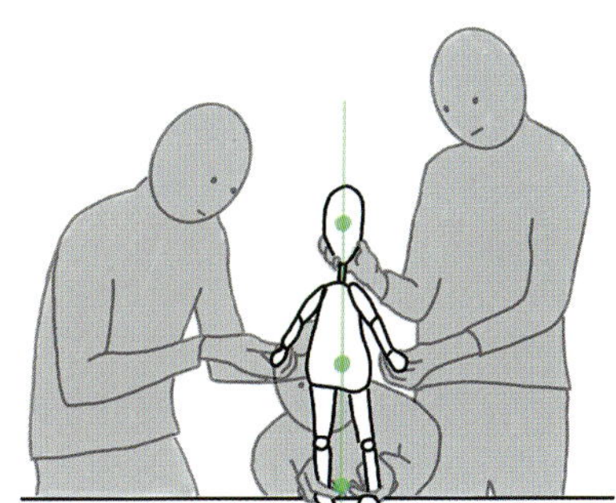

STEP 2: Focusing on the midline.

Kevin in *Low Life* (Blind Summit): 'alcoholic puppetry'.

IMPROVISING IN GENRE

A puppeteer does not play the characters in the show. They are played by the puppets and the puppeteer plays the show. Instead of thinking about the characters *in* the show, the puppeteer has to think about the character *of* the show – that is to say, the 'genre'.

Genre is to puppetry what character is to acting: it gives the puppeteers motivation and backstory. Genre ties together what the puppets look like, how they work, and how the puppeteers move them. When you are making a show, working out a puppetry genre tells the puppeteers how and why they are performing with puppets.

In this exercise you learn how to puppet in genre and how to find the right genre for what you are doing.

The Exercise

In this exercise you work in groups of three with a workshop puppet on a table.

STEP 1: Take a sheet of paper and make a list of genres to try. You might choose a theatrical genre such as Shakespearean Theatre, *Commedia dell'Arte*, Children's Theatre, or a musical genre such as Broadway Musical, Lloyd Webber Musical or Grand Opera. You might think about a movement genre such as Contemporary Dance, or Performance Art; a film genre such as Disney, French New Wave or Manga; or a puppetry genre such as French Object Theatre. Alternatively, you can make something up: what about Eastern European Fairytale Puppetry or American Improvisation Dinner Theatre?

STEP 2: Take the first genre from the list, say, Shakespearean Theatre. Divide into your groups of three with a puppet and spend two minutes improvising a short scene in the genre. Think about how the performers move in that genre, typical characters of that genre, the type of gestures they make, how they relate to the audience, how they speak, and what sort of things they do and say.

For example, if you are working in the genre of Shakespearean Theatre, you might say that typically the performers move in a grand, slightly over-acted way, making big gestures to the gallery. They speak in verse, and talk about battles and inheritances and uncles and love. A prince would be one typical character.

STEP 3: Having spent a couple of minutes improvising with your ideas, present your genre improvisations to each other. Don't worry about being 'good'; just do them and see what happens.

STEP 4: After each presentation, give feedback to each other on what you have seen. Did the puppet capture the genre? How could you make it more specific and more clear? If an observer did not know what genre it was, would they be able to guess?

STEP 5: Once everyone has presented their improvisation, move on to the next genre and work through the list.

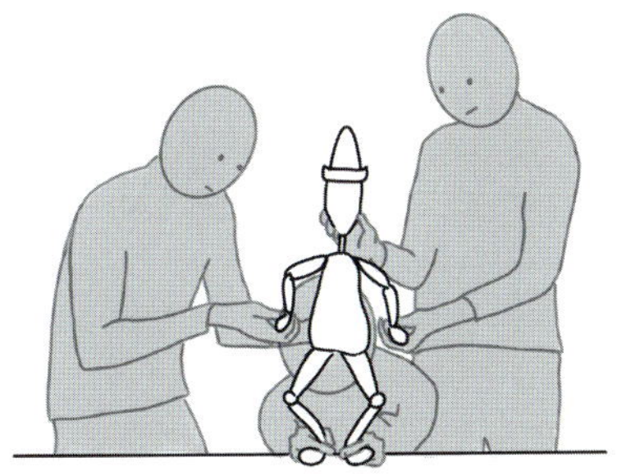

Commedia dell'Arte puppetry.

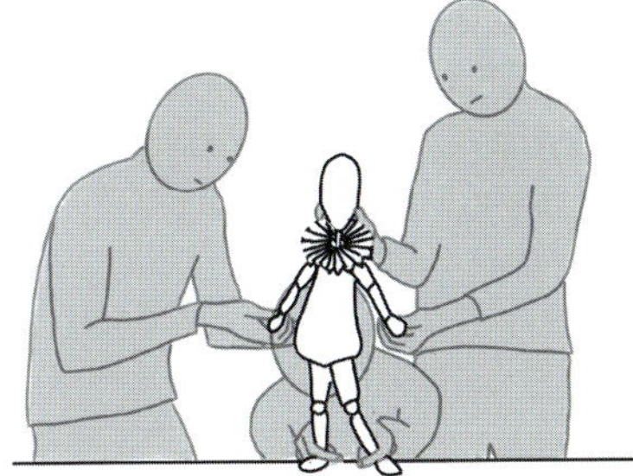

Shakespearean puppetry.

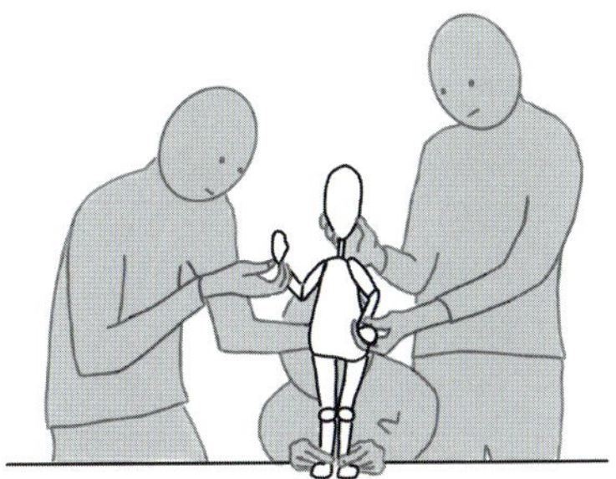

Children's entertainer puppetry.

Things to Notice

Puppets imitate performers Puppets exist only on stage, so their references for performing are other performances given on stage. They copy other performance genres: for example, Punch and Judy is a puppet version of pantomime, string puppet shows are imitations of grand theatre, and the Muppets copy TV presenters. Genre gives a reference for how the puppets should behave on the stage – they should do what a performer in that genre would do. In order to know how to make the puppets move and speak, you need to know what sort of show you are copying. For example, although a puppet is not real, a puppet can copy realism as a genre.

Performing in genre means everyone knows what to do The puppeteer may be puppeting many puppets or they may only be puppeting one part of a puppet, so they cannot know – just from thinking about the character – what they should do with their part. However, if they think in terms of genre, they will know what to do. A feet puppeteer knows how, when and why a Shakespearean actor walks. A hand puppeteer knows how, when and why an opera singer gestures with their hands. A head puppeteer knows the sorts of things a Commedia actor says. A Punch and Judy puppeteer knows how actors behave in a pantomime scene. If you are not sure how performers move and speak in a particular genre, you can always research it.

Improvising in genre generates content The primary goal of using genre is to make the puppetry come alive, but as you explore genre you will also develop content. Genre tells you how the characters approach a particular scene, how they introduce a subject, what they say about it, who they speak to, and so on. The puppets generate material from the situations that arise, as a result of having to use the conventions of a genre to explore them.

THE PUPPETRY GENRE

When you do puppetry you go into character as the puppeteer. At the end of the show, you stop being the puppeteer and become yourself again. It is you, the puppeteer, who has to get into character for a show, not the puppets. The puppets are always in character. They are already in character before you begin and after you stop. They are not living, but they are in character.

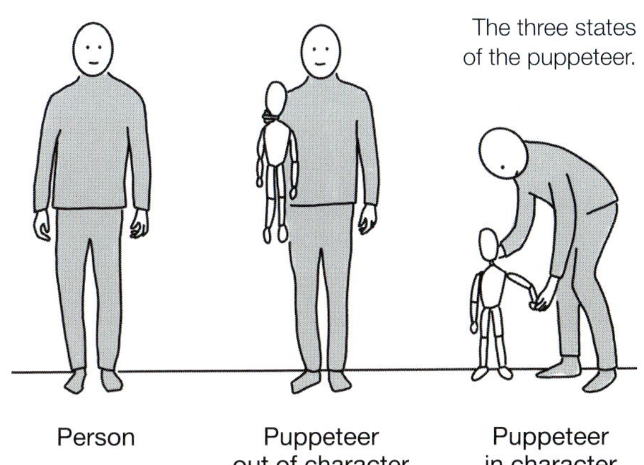

The three states of the puppeteer.

The puppeteer's character is determined by the genre of puppetry they are doing. The last exercise explored the genre in which the puppets are performing. The next step is to change it into a 'puppetry genre' that includes the motivation of the puppeteers.

In this exercise you practise becoming different kinds of puppeteer to see what difference it makes to your puppetry. You can then choose a suitable puppetry genre for whatever show you want to make.

The Exercise

Divide the room into a stage area and audience and let people come on stage as individuals or in groups, depending on the needs of your show.

STEP 1: Take the list of genres that you have been using to make different kinds of puppetry. Start at the top of the list and add the word 'puppeteers' to the genre. For example, if the genre was 'Shakespearean', then the puppeteer genre is 'Shakespearean Puppeteers'.
STEP 2: Now go off stage and come on again in character as a Shakespearean puppeteer. Walk around as a Shakespearean puppeteer; stand in front of the audience and greet them.
STEP 3: Think about how a Shakespearean puppeteer would walk, what they would wear, how they would talk, and what they would say.
STEP 4: Now see how the Shakespearean puppeteer would do puppetry. Go and get a puppet in character, bring it on stage, and bring it to life. How do you do that? Do you do it in front of the audience or do you need to hide behind a screen to do it? Can you be in the same space as the puppet or do you need to disappear before the puppets appear? Is your Shakespearean puppeteer the type of puppeteer who is never seen by the audience at all?
STEP 5: Now see if you can bring the puppet to life as the Shakespearean puppeteer. Think about how they would do puppetry. Are you rough and ready, or painstaking and precise? Are you good or bad at it? Is your puppetry quiet and intimate or loud and demonstrative? Do you like to be impressively serious, or make people laugh? When you are in character as the genre puppeteer, can you make the puppet perform in genre?
STEP 6: Now try coming out of character and come to the front of the stage to bow. Do you bring the puppets out with you to show the audience? What is your attitude when you take a bow?
STEP 7: Work through the list, trying different kinds of puppeteer genre. Notice which ones make doing the puppetry easier, and which ones make doing the puppetry harder. Which genres work for the puppets and which for the puppeteers?

Things to Notice

The genre must always be some kind of puppetry or puppeteer Only puppeteers do puppetry; it is not done by anyone else. Unlike acting or singing or dancing, which people do in lots of other settings, puppetry is done only in front of an audience, and the person doing puppetry is always some kind of puppeteer.

There are of course lots of things that are *like* puppetry – actions that are done with the hands – but the motivations are different. Only a puppeteer brings an object alive in order to tell a story.

The genres that work are 'showing' genres Puppetry is visual and as a puppeteer you show your puppetry to the audience. Your motivation is a desire for the audience to watch the puppets. For this reason, you need a genre that implies that you want to show them the puppets. This can be any descriptive genre that informs how and why you would hold up your puppets and make them perform.

The puppeteer's genre is the puppet's backstory A puppet does not have a father and mother; a puppet has been made in a workshop. The audience assumes that the puppeteer has made the puppet in much the same way as they think an actor has made up their words. Although they may not have made the puppet, the puppeteer is standing in for the maker. To the audience, the puppeteer represents the origin story of the puppet, and by inference gives a clue to the origin story of the show.

The 'puppetry genre' tells you how to costume the puppeteers The puppeteers are the people behind the puppets. By working out what genre of puppeteer they are – the genre they are using to show puppet – they are given an identity that not only guides how they move and do puppetry, but also how they should dress and look.

The design of the show and of the puppets, the costumes of the puppeteers and puppets, and how the puppets tell the story, all come from the puppetry genre.

RIGHT: Cubist puppeteers.

BELOW: French New Wave puppeteers.

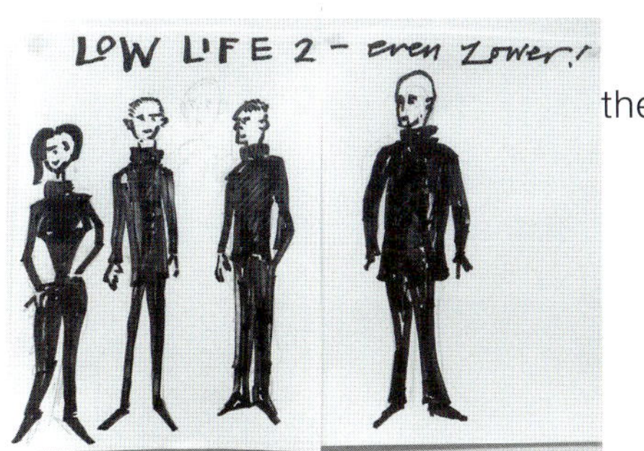

the

Paper Story (Blind Summit).

9
DESIGNING PUPPETS

Using puppetry to tell a story is not a neutral decision. It is an art that will attract some people to come and see it and will put other people off. Additionally, it means something. The use of puppetry is in itself an interpretation. What, where and how you use puppets in the story tells the audience what sort of metaphorical meanings they should look for in your production.

The process of developing puppetry involves changing an idea into a performance by three-dimensional, physical, moving objects that you can bring to life and make perform. Your puppets need to be able to perform the functions you set them in the script and your stage has to be capable of accommodating the kind of puppet you decide to use. The two go hand in hand. The stage makes the puppetry work and controls how the audience sees it. The challenge for a designer is to work within the necessary restrictions of the chosen form to create a fresh, new stage for the puppet to appear on.

There is no such thing as a standard puppet show, so you need to create a core concept around which you can build something. The core concept is based on who the puppets are, how you are going to make the show, and who is going to watch it.

This chapter suggests various ways to think about making puppets that will do what you want them to do.

OPPOSITE: Designing Japanese Envoy puppet for *Le Rossignol* (Blind Summit).

STARTING POINTS: THE PUPPETRY CONCEPT

Puppet shows have people and puppets in them and you need to decide what roles they are going to play. Are all the characters going to be played by puppets? Are all the people going to be puppeteers? Are some characters going to be played by puppets and some by people?

When you decide the casting of the people and puppets, you establish the conventions of your show. You set up who the audience can see – the characters – and who they should think of as invisible – the puppeteers. In doing this, you determine how the puppetry is going to work in your production, and what it will mean.

In this exercise, you consider the options and what they mean.

The Exercise

This is a thinking exercise, which can be done on your own or in a creative group. The task is to decide what form the casting of your production is going to take. It boils down to four options:

1. 'The Puppet Show': a 'normal' puppet show, with all the characters in the story being played by puppets, and the people in the show being invisible puppeteers moving in the background. One of the puppets will take the role of the protagonist. This kind of show is a re-creation of an imagined theatrical production, by puppets. The puppeteers are storytellers, and the

puppets are their tools, to represent the characters in the story. The underlying message for the audience is 'we are all puppets'.

2. 'Alice in Puppet-land': in this type of show, one character is played by an actor and all the rest are played by puppets. The other people in the show are invisible puppeteers manipulating the story. The audience understands that the puppets and the actor cannot see them. The audience identifies with the actor and sees them as a guide to puppet-land. The show becomes the story of a person entering a strange world of puppets: it may be a dream for them, madness, or an hallucinatory state.
3. 'All the world's a stage': in this type of show, some characters are played by people and some are played by puppets manipulated by people. Everyone can be visible and invisible. Everything is declared. The audience understands that the cast are storytellers and all the characters are being created on the spot by actors and puppets. The underlying message is that all of life is theatre and everyone is acting all the time. The story of your life is whatever you say it is. All the world's a stage.
4. 'ET': here, one character is played by a puppet, the rest by people. Among a cast of actors, a puppet is used to play one specific role, for example, a baby, an animal or a ghost. The characters in the show behave as if the puppet is the real thing. They don't see the puppeteers. The audience understands that the puppeteers are invisible servants of the storytelling. In this type of show, the puppet becomes a central metaphor encapsulating your interpretation of what the story is about. The puppet is probably not the protagonist of the story.

Things to Notice

Certain 'numbers' feel right When you look at how many puppets, puppeteers and actors you are going to have, you need to ask yourself if it looks right. Can you imagine them on stage together? Are there enough? Are there too many? Do you have odd numbers or even numbers? Odd numbers give you a 'middle' person, and even numbers give you two equal halves. An even number can also be an odd number plus a 'spare'.

One puppet surrounded by people.

Puppetry comments on performing Puppet shows imitate theatre, dance, comedy and pantomime, and draw the audience's attention to the construction and nature of the performance. Acting, singing and dancing hide the author's intention by making the story appear to be driven by the decisions of the characters, puppetry reveals the author's intention by showing that the decisions of the characters are driven by the story. Puppetry shows the performances and reveals the underlying mechanisms of the play. When you watch a puppet do something, you see the storyteller at work.

DESIGNING A REHEARSAL PROCESS

Since no two puppet shows are the same, no two rehearsal processes will be the same. When designing a rehearsal process, think about what you specifically need to do in the sessions to deal with the challenges ahead of you, and formulate your process round these. Some processes will need a lot of research and development; some will need lots of design time and some will need lots of puppet training.

The Exercise

Write down the specific challenges of the performance and design a rehearsal plan that allows for time to tackle them. There are a number of issues to consider:

Allow time for the design and construction of the puppets Some projects need to be more heavily weighted towards making puppets that work properly rather than spending time creating a story. For example, if you are building a giant puppet to walk through the streets, you may only be able to rehearse at the last minute, but you will need to spend a significant amount of time testing the puppet during its construction. You will need to set up days with puppeteers that allow plenty of time in case you need to redirect the way the puppet is being made. During these workshop days, the puppeteers will also be developing their skills on the puppets.

Use 'Research and Development' (R&D) days to solve script problems Much of puppetry rehearsal is about problem solving, especially if the puppets are going to be technically complicated. This is best done without the pressure of an opening night looming. Getting as much of this done well in advance, with pre-rehearsal R&D days, frees up the actual rehearsal period to refine the performances and storytelling.

Identify challenges in the script and put aside some individual days ahead of rehearsals to solve them. A day with some puppeteers and some materials in advance of rehearsals lets you work free from pressure and gives you time afterwards to process what you have learned. Plan to do whatever days you need to, spread over the pre-rehearsal period, so that you go into the rehearsal period feeling properly prepared.

Allow time for puppetry training If the puppetry is particularly demanding, you might want to set aside some special time to work with them, either in advance of rehearsals, or in special sessions during rehearsals. Even starting a day early can make a big difference. A little time well spent goes a long way.

Decide on the rehearsal period required to make the show Actually making the show can be quite quick if you are well prepared, and have answered as many questions as possible *before* you get to the rehearsal room. Allow between two to six weeks.

Consider trying out material with an audience If you can arrange for people to see part or all of what you are making, it can be extremely valuable. If you do decide to try out material in front of an audience, make sure that you go into it with a clear purpose. It can be very easy to be put off course by audience reactions. Ask for feedback with clear questions that an audience can answer, such as, 'Do you understand what's going on?' or 'Is this funny?'

Pre-rehearsal training on *Madam Butterfly* (Blind Summit).

IMAGINE THE VENUE AND THE AUDIENCE

Puppetry is a technical art form, which depends entirely on being seen by the audience. Thinking about the venue, or kind of venue, where it is going to be performed should inform every decision. This means that you need to know how big the puppets are, what the puppeteers look like, and how you will manage the audience's journey through the show.

The Exercise

STEP 1: Think about where you are going to perform the show. What sort of building is it? How many seats are there? What sort of stage? What sort of auditorium? Is the stage a flat floor? Is the seating raked? What are the sight-lines like?
STEP 2: Imagine the puppets in the space. Are they going to be on the floor or raised up? Are they going to be on the stage, or on a stage within the stage?
STEP 3: If you already have a venue, go and visit it with a puppet to see it in the space. Test the sight-lines. Look at it on stage from all four corners of the auditorium and make sure you can see it. If you are not able to visit, can you get plans or photographs of it? Can you visit a venue like it?
STEP 4: Think about your audience. Who do you want to come and see it? Are they puppetry aficionados, puppet-curious, or sceptics?
STEP 5: Think about the experience of the audience coming into the theatre. What do they see when they come in? What time of day or night are they going to watch it? How will they be feeling? What will they expect to see and why are they coming? Imagine the atmosphere: are they excited, or apprehensive, or judgemental?
STEP 6: Think about the audience at the end of the show, or in the interval if there is one. What do they say to each other about it? What do they tell their friends about it afterwards? What will they say about the puppets? What will they say about the images? About the story?

Questions to Ask Yourself

Have you seen something like it before? What other shows is it like? How is it different? Do you need to be original or similar to something that already exists? Is there a version without puppets that you can refer to? Can you learn from what other people have done before and from how it has gone?
Does your idea feel 'complete'? Can you say what is missing? No idea is ever fully formed and much of the show will have to be found in rehearsal, but the core idea needs to be there. That is the element around which you will assemble everything.

MAKE A VISUAL TIMELINE OF THE SCRIPT

When you decide to use puppets in a show, you are adding new people – puppeteers – to the cast. A script tells you what the characters in the story do, but not how to represent them with puppets, how the puppets work, how many puppeteers you will need, or what the puppeteers do.

In this exercise you make a visual timeline of the script, to see when the characters come on and off stage, when the stage is busiest, and when it is most empty, and start to think about what it is going to look like when you stage the scenes using puppets.

The Exercise

You can do this exercise on paper and pencil or on a computer spreadsheet. If you do it on a computer, make sure that you print it out afterwards so that you have a hard copy to hand, on which you can make notes.

STEP 1: Make two axes: put 'time' along the top and list the characters down the side.
STEP 2: Divide the timeline along the top to make each column worth a minute. Mark in the breaks between acts and scenes.
STEP 3: Down the side, allocate a row to each character, and give each character a different colour.

Research and Development workshop (Pinto and Pollack Dance, and Blind Summit).

Mark in their exits and their entrances, and fill in with colour when they are on stage.
STEP 4: Mark in key moments that stand out to you in the story: these may be moments of action or lines that you think are important.
STEP 5: Give a row to locations so that you can see where they change and how long the show will spend in each place.
STEP 6: Print out your timeline on three or four pages of A4 paper in landscape format, tape it together and put it on the wall.

Things to Notice

Which scene has the most characters on stage? Find the scene with the most characters on stage. How many characters are there? This scene is going to be the most demanding in terms of puppets and puppeteers. Do you have enough puppets to stage the scene with a puppet for each character? Have you got enough puppeteers to hold them? Have you got enough space on the stage?
Which are the biggest scene changes? Scene changes where the stage goes from one character to many, or many characters down to a few, are dramatic moments that you will want to recreate somehow. How many puppets do you need to make them happen? What is the best way of making them happen with puppetry?
Which scene has the fewest characters? If there is a scene where one character has to hold the stage alone, then that needs to be a puppet that can do the job. It needs to connect to the other scenes and create a strong contrast.

MAKE A GALLERY

This exercise is about collecting images inspired by the script. Try not to edit yourself; simply put everything up on the wall, around your timeline, and stand back and look at it. The purpose is to change the words into tangible objects that you can see, hold and maybe even puppeteer.

Print out pictures and pin them on the wall.

The Exercise

STEP 1: Search for pictures in magazines and books and on the internet. Print or cut them out, and do your own drawings and paintings. Look for images that inspire you in art, paintings, photographs and fashion. Find pictures of different types of puppets and costume ideas for the puppeteers. Pin your pictures up on a board around the timeline so that you can see them accumulate. Make them physical. Make them begin to take up space.
STEP 2: Read through the script and write down or draw images that come into your head for puppets, regardless of how strange they might seem. Make

ABOVE: Cardboard binoculars made while preparing *Peter and the Wolf*.

RIGHT: Workshop for *Peter and the Wolf*.

a note of props, costumes and set ideas that occur to you. Look at videos or pictures of old productions, and, if there are any pieces of music that are in any way relevant, listen to them. Make a note of anything that inspires you from these sources and anything that you like from them. Collect a brainstormed list of ideas for puppets and puppetry.

STEP 3: Use cardboard to make some rough objects inspired by what you have seen and liked. You might make an actual puppet, or a small bit of furniture, or you could make a puppet head, or some hands or bodies. You might just cut out some shapes inspired by a theme or a genre.

Things to Notice

Images take up space When you print images out, or paint them or draw them, you create something that takes up space in the world. You create an item that a puppeteer could hold and move around in space – even a simple piece of paper can be puppeted. You have begun to change the script into a three-dimensional form. You have taken the first steps to making your show.

Don't leave the images online or on the computer or your phone. Digital images are no use to a puppeteer.

Making things helps you think You can think while you are making, drawing or painting. The process is meditative but it also makes you face the realities of your ideas. If they stay in your mind, it is easy to ignore any inconsistencies and contradictions in them. If, for example, you want to end a scene by cutting the puppet's strings because you like the metaphor, that puppet cannot be a glove puppet.

Do your images balance with the script? Do you have more images for one part of the script than for others? Do the busy parts of the script generate lots of images? Are there holes in the script? Do you have several ideas for one scene and nothing for another?

Do you like it? Stand back and look at your gallery. Can you see a colour palate emerging in your images? Is there a vibe? Does it do what you want it to do? Is it clear? Will the puppets speak for themselves or are you going to be constantly having to explain it? Do you like looking at it?

SCENES TO 'SOLVE'

In this exercise you turn the script from a story that works by the interaction of psychological characters into a list of items that you can actually try out with objects in a space.

The Exercise

Referring to the timeline and your collection of images and objects, scribble down a list of all the things the puppets need to do in the show, and any ideas you have for how to do them. Write down elements that you can try out with puppeteers in a rehearsal room.

You might consider writing down some of the following ideas for the show:

- A puppeteer pulls a puppet out of a box at beginning of the show
- A puppet introduces the puppeteers to the audience
- Do the puppets sing?
- How do we do 7 *characters* at end of Scene 1? Can they be 1-person puppets?
- Puppet and person dancing at beginning of Act 3?
- Underwater fight scene at the top of Scene 2?
- Try getting the puppeteers to whisper the story to the puppet and the puppet relating it to the audience
- Try getting the puppets to 'read' the script
- Final act: just two puppets on stage together for 10 minutes
- What can the puppet do that an actor can't?

Things to Notice

A lot of the items on the list are questions You can't be sure if something is going to work until you have a chance to try it out with puppets in a rehearsal room. This list acts as a prompt of things to work through in R&D workshops.

Prototype for dinosaur bird in Verona Arena.

The list contains contradictions As well as trying each thing out on its own merits, you will need to see if elements that do not seem to go together can actually go together. Can you have two different kinds of puppet in your show? Is the colour palette too broad? For now, keep the contradictions in the air; it is much better to tackle them when you are actually in the rehearsal space.

PUPPET DESIGN (R&D) WORKSHOP

Before you can start rehearsing a puppet show you need to have puppets. Designing and making the puppets involves thinking about what they need to do, what they need to look like, what sort of stage they will need and what puppeteers will be required to work with them. It is difficult to think all this through on paper. A research and development (R&D) workshop is a space where everyone can think in three dimensions, test out ideas, and design the puppets in the hands of puppeteers.

At the end of the R&D workshop you should know how the puppets will work, what they are going to look like, and how many puppeteers they will require, so you or a puppet-maker will be able to set about making them. You may need to revisit the rehearsal room to test the puppets during the making process, but the basic parameters are worked out in the R&D workshop here.

Arranging the Workshop

An R&D workshop is the first step to developing your idea. First, you need to book a rehearsal room. This will provide you with an empty space in which to gather some people together, along with some puppets and materials, and work with them to make rough versions of all the ideas you have. The workshop is a place to try things and see what works, and what doesn't, what to keep, and what to let go.

You are going to design the scene first and then make the puppets.

You need to be able to think freely, invent, ask difficult questions, try silly things, and maybe go off at a tangent. For example, a jumper tied to two sticks might become a cat puppet, or a few cardboard boxes may end up being a lion. In order to feel the necessary freedom, you need to arrange a workshop far enough in advance, so that you don't feel the pressure of having to find a solution straight away. Try to make it at least a year before rehearsals. Allow roughly three months to manufacture puppets, and another three months to make mistakes and rethink. Make sure that your schedule fits in with the production schedule for the set design and costumes.

Three or four days is a good length of time to aim for. It takes at least a day to get things on their feet, and going on longer than a week rarely yields better results. If you run out of time, you can always organize another session.

If you are going to have a workshop over more than one day, you will need to arrange for the puppets and materials to be kept safely overnight. You need exclusive use of the rehearsal room, or secure storage elsewhere. Puppets and materials are valuable, and you might want to leave things set up in the room overnight, to come back to in the morning.

Participants

You may be making a show on your own, or with a large team of people. There are a number of people you might want to invite to the workshop, including yourself!

Make sure that you are clear about your role going into the workshop. Are you performing, directing or designing, or all of these? Maybe one of the goals of the workshop is to establish roles.

Invite the most skilled and inventive puppeteers you know. If you are going to perform the puppetry yourself, hire a puppeteer to stand in for you in the workshop, so that you can be on the outside and see what you need to see. The workshop is also a good opportunity for casting.

Ideally, you should have the puppet-maker in the workshop, making and adapting puppets with you, as you experiment. This time together, with the puppeteers, will be an invaluable reference for you both later, when you are making the puppets on your own.

You might also want to invite other creatives, such as the director (if this is not going to be you), designer, writer, lighting designer and sound designer. This is your chance to start working together, and you want them to be involved with the puppetry from the beginning.

If there are singers, actors or dancers who will work with the puppets and puppeteers in the show, the workshop is a great chance for them to meet the puppets, and have a go.

Consider inviting the producer, marketing department, and other venue staff along to the workshop, so that they can see the logistical challenges of putting on the show. It is much easier to show people what puppetry involves than to try to tell them. Make sure they know they are welcome. Puppetry involves lots of stuff and lots of people, so a good stage manager is invaluable, too, to help you manage the room, and anticipate things that get overlooked such as transport, storage of the puppets, safety and maintenance.

Materials and Tools

Collect together a 'kit' of materials and tools, so you can quickly make rough puppets in the workshop. When anyone has an idea, you want to be able to fashion something quickly out of cardboard or cloth, so that it can be held up in the space, and you can get an idea of what it would look like, and how it would work. If you have any specific

A 'MAKING KIT' FOR AN R&D WORKSHOP

Cardboard This universal material is useful for quickly making things in the workshop. It can be ordered online in one-layer and two-layer sheets in packs of 20, or you can pick up old boxes from shops for free. White goods stores and furniture stores are good for big boxes.

Cloth A cotton sheet or some swatches of silk are very useful for quickly making into puppet bodies.

Big roll of paper Lining paper can be used for making into puppet arms, legs, and so on. You may be able to get roll-ends for free from a printer.

Glue gun and glue sticks For making 3D structures from cardboard. You can buy glue guns online or in a hardware store for £10–20. Make sure you have plenty of glue sticks.

Gaffer tape For attaching cardboard structures to walls, stands, chairs, ropes, sticks, or puppeteers. Available online or in hardware stores.

String Ordinary white string is useful for hanging things.

Bamboos Useful for strengthening big cardboard structures, for rods on puppets, or for making stands. The best place to get bamboo is a garden centre or a hardware store.

Green cutting mat To protect that expensive dance floor in your workshop space, or someone else's table top, while you are cutting cardboard.

Scalpel and lots of blades For cutting cardboard. Cardboard blunts scalpel blades quickly so you will need change your blade frequently.

Sharps box For used scalpel blades. You can make one out of an old coffee pot with a slot cut in the lid.

Steel rule A 1-metre rule is most useful.

Scissors For cutting and shaping paper and cloth.

Markers, poster paints and brush For drawing or writing on cardboard to make signs or to decorate what you have made.

A4 paper For taking notes, drawing and writing things down. A4 sheets can be stuck together with tape and displayed on a wall.

Blu-tack To put things up on the wall so that the whole room can share and be reminded what you are all thinking about.

Old puppets and puppet parts Old bits and pieces can be adapted with card and cloth to mock up new puppets.

Camera and/or video recorder To capture improvisations and puppet creations. The camera on a phone or tablet will do.

Glue guns.

materials that you think will be relevant to your show, bring those along.

Exercises

The point of the workshop is to try things out with puppets and see if they work. If you have an idea for a puppet, you need to see it. If you have an idea for a scene, you need to see the puppets do it.

In these exercises you are looking for potential, not the finished product. Someone holding up a cloth puppet, facing someone dressed in cardboard armour and holding a bamboo spear, might be very rough, but if you can see how it will work, you can take it away to design and make and it will flourish once you get to the rehearsal stage.

STEP 1: Share your list of 'tasks'
State clear simple aims for the workshop, such as, 'I need to find a puppet that can carry a one-hour show', or 'We need to make six animal-puppet sequences, each about five minutes long.'

Share the list with everyone in the workshop at the beginning, then put it on the wall so everyone can see it and it can be worked through. Don't get drawn into side discussions about story, character and other aspects until the second or third day of the workshop, when everyone has got used to the main task.

This gets everyone to look at the show through the other end of the telescope and see it from the point of view of what the puppeteers need to do, rather than what the characters in the story do. Everything a puppet does in the story will have to be facilitated by a puppeteer.

STEP 2: Stage the problems
Tell the puppeteers what a scene needs to achieve, for example, 'The puppet has to do ballet for five minutes.' Don't get into why, or how, or what it means right now, just say what you want to see. Keep the focus of the exercise on seeing the problem.

Ask the puppeteers to take hold of some objects, bring them on stage, and do the scene. Set a stopwatch and run the scene. This will allow you to experience the parameters of the scene with objects in the space and see what the puppetry needs to achieve. And sometimes you stumble across an idea of how to do it.

STEP 3: Get everyone to do 'puppet-making'
Give the group half an hour to make a puppet character in the show. Encourage them to work in small groups and use the materials you have brought. It does not need to be complicated; it can be as simple as a collection of cardboard boxes with a face drawn on them.

Make an audience and 'meet' the puppets. Each puppet has a simple task: come on stage, introduce itself, say something about itself, pose for a photo, and then leave. Have a line-up of the puppets and take a group photo.

Cubist Geisha in a design workshop for *Le Rossignol* (Blind Summit).

People usually come up with some amazing objects and this is a brilliant way to generate lots of puppet characters quickly. You should discover lots of different ways that people see the characters.

Things to Notice

Sometimes you will feel inspired to direct If a scene gives you ideas and you find yourself wanting to give directions, or itching to get involved, or If the scene starts to run away with itself and you want to rein it in and shape it, these are signs that something is working. Keep these scenes.

Puppetry that gives you a feeling of wonder Look for moments that make you stare in amazement. Maybe you can't believe how well the puppet moves, or how cute it is when it speaks, or how beautiful it is when it floats on to the floor. It just looks so good, it is magical. When you identify a moment like this, you should look for ways of putting it in the show.

Strong puppet illusions Occasionally, a puppet illusion is very strong: the puppet looks like it is moving the puppeteer, it really looks like the puppet is talking, or you are convinced you can see a face in a plastic bag, and so on. This is what puppetry is all about. When you find these moments, keep them.

Puppetry sequences that are robust and repeatable Sometimes, you will discover something that works, and that works every time you do it. You can change the puppeteers and it works. You can change the puppet and it still works. When a puppet is robust like this, it will be able to do many things in your show.

Something that only a puppet can do Ask yourself how you would do this without puppetry? Would it be as good? A mime actor can pretend to break apart, but a puppet can actually break apart. An actor can dress up as a frying pan, but a puppet can actually *be* a frying pan. On the other hand, a puppet can pretend to sing, but a singer can actually sing. Either is possible, but which is better for your show?

'Popular' puppets Some puppets will get used a lot in the workshop, as puppeteers will tend to gravitate towards them. Others will get left out. Is it because they are difficult to use in improvisations? Maybe they will work with direction or maybe they are just not right for your story?

The land in the sky in a design workshop for *Citizen Puppet* (Blind Summit).

FAR LEFT: A different head on the puppet in a workshop for *The Table* (Blind Summit).

LEFT: Image from a workshop for *The Table*, which ended up being used for the flyer.

CAPTURING DESIGNS AND MAKING CHOICES

At the end of the R&D workshop, you should be in a position to pull together what you have discovered and create a cast of puppets, so that you or a puppet-maker can go away and start making them.

Make a Video Storyboard

Capture improvisations and good moments on video. If you miss something, get your puppeteers to go back afterwards and do it again so you can film it. You can review the video straight away, and you can also use a video editing programme to cut together a storyboard of the show. These days it is also very easy to share video with everyone online if you want to.

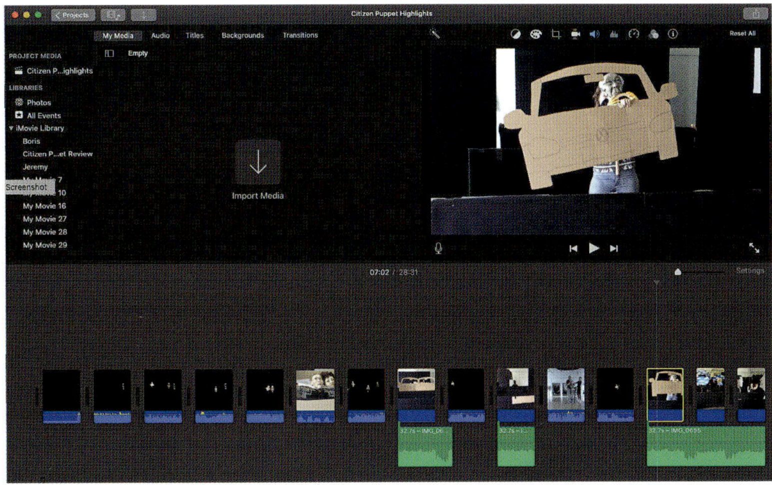

Storyboarding *Citizen Puppet* in iMovie.

Make a 'Cast Gallery'

Take photos of puppets, scenes or moments that catch your eye. If you miss something, go back and get the puppeteers to pose it again for you. Set up a photo session at the end of the day or at the end of the workshop, to make sure you have captured all the images that you liked. Put together a photo cast list of prototype puppets and their puppeteers.

You can now move the pictures around and try different puppets in different roles until you have the cast of puppets you want.

Casting gallery for *The Little Match Girl* (Blind Summit).

Characterize the Puppet Designer

Looking at your cast of puppets, see if you can come up with a genre that describes the aesthetic or the idea behind them. It might be something like 'Nightmare Punch and Judy', 'Political Power', 'Fairytale Children', 'Cubist', and so on.

Next, think about what sort of person would have made these puppets. Characterize an imaginary puppet designer. Using the examples above, you might say that the 'Nightmare Punch and Judy' puppets were made by a depressed and disillusioned Punch and Judy performer; the 'Political Power' puppets might have been made by a group of Extinction Rebellion activists; the 'Fairytale Children' puppets by primary school teachers, and the 'Cubist' puppets by a group of artists.

This will give you a coherent explanation as to why the puppets look the way they look, the puppet's backstory, and how the puppeteers should

ABOVE: Heads for *Citizen Puppet* (Blind Summit).

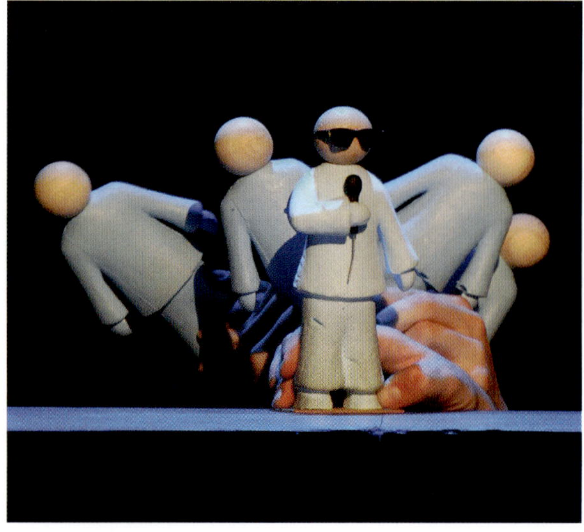

RIGHT: The Blue Men in *Low Life* (Blind Summit).

work with them. The aesthetic of the puppetry will tell you who is behind the puppets, what they care about, and what they think the show is about.

BOOTHS, TABLES AND SCREENS: THE PUPPET STAGE

When you decide what kind of puppets to use, you need to think at the same time about what type of stage they will need. A puppet stage is made of two parts: a mini-stage for the puppets and a life-sized stage for the puppeteers. A successful puppet stage frames the puppetry to bring the puppets into focus, and hides the puppeteers. The different kinds of puppetry have different ways of doing this.

String Puppet Stages

String puppets perform on a floor. They are operated from above and are lowered on to the stage on strings. They stand on a solid stage floor and can move freely around furniture and props and flying scenery flats. They walk in front of elaborate scenery, enter and exit from the wings and recreate in miniature all the detailed blocking and choreography of a grand theatre performance.

However, their strings mean that they cannot pass under anything. The ceiling of the stage and the tops of doors and flats need to be open for strings to pass through to the operator above.

Variations: The Classic Marionette Theatre

The traditional string marionette theatre is grand theatre in miniature, with a proscenium arch, wings, scenery and a stage floor. The puppeteers lower the puppets into the theatre through the roof and move them about to recreate a puppet version of grand theatre, opera or ballet.

The puppeteers may be visible behind the theatre or hidden by masking. In a specially built marionette theatre, they may be on a bridge built above the stage, concealed behind the walls of the auditorium.

Sometimes, a puppeteer may be able to access an understage area to get hold of the foot of a puppet for a moment to give it extra control.

Variations: 'Naked' String Puppetry

Naked string puppetry is string theatre in the round. The puppet performs on the ground in front of the legs of the puppeteer without any structure representing a theatre. The ground becomes the puppet's stage and the puppet appears to live in the real world. A simple bit of floor and some props can help locate the puppet.

This method is typical of street performances.

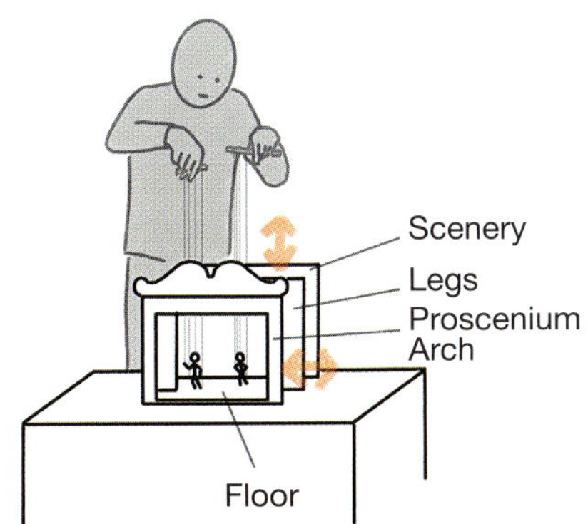

Simple string marionette theatre with visible puppeteer.

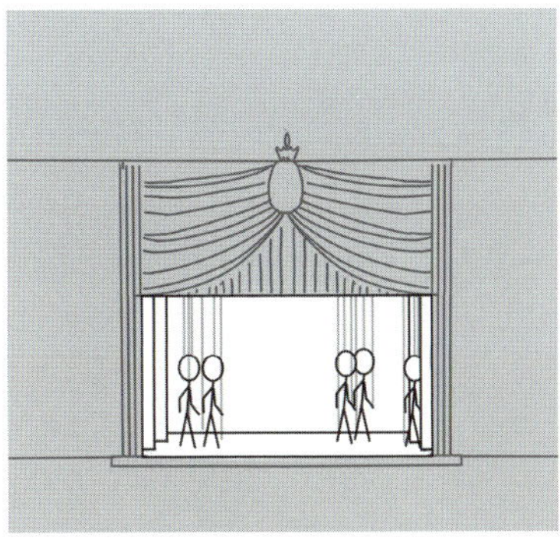

Purpose-built marionette theatre – front view.

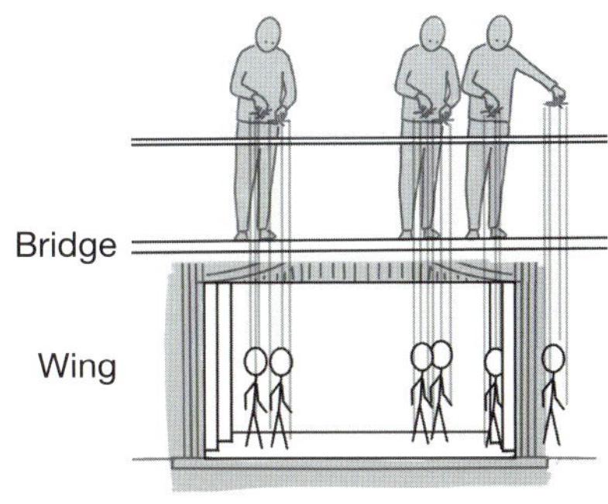

Purpose-built marionette theatre – behind the masking.

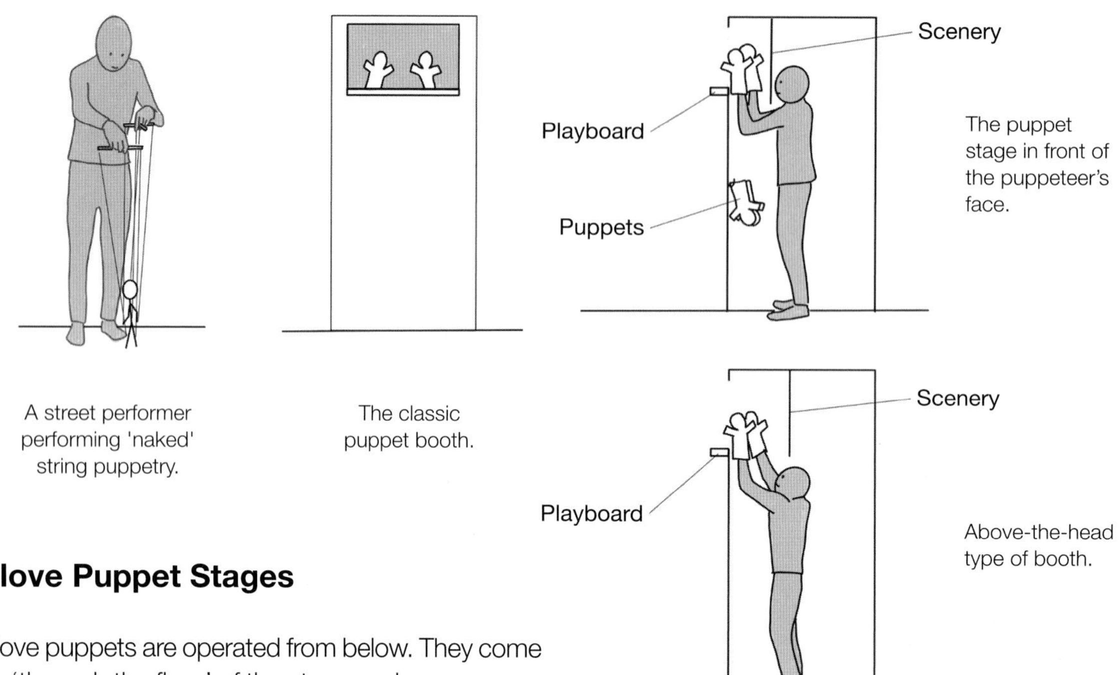

A street performer performing 'naked' string puppetry.

The classic puppet booth.

The puppet stage in front of the puppeteer's face.

Above-the-head type of booth.

Glove Puppet Stages

Glove puppets are operated from below. They come up 'through the floor' of the stage and appear over the top of a wall. The puppeteer hides behind the wall.

A glove puppet theatre is the reverse of the string puppet theatre: it can have wings, scenery and a ceiling, but no floor. Glove puppets cannot pass over anything and doors and scenery must be open at the bottom for the puppet to go through. Glove puppets are seen only from the waist up and most do not have legs. Where they do have legs (as, for example, Mr Punch does), they are simple appendages that are not operated but hang over the top of the wall to make the puppet look like it is sitting.

The wall is usually the front wall of a small shed called a 'booth', which hides the puppeteer. A puppet booth is highly portable and can be set up anywhere. Glove puppet shows are hugely popular, especially with children and on TV.

The Classic Puppet Booth

A puppet booth hides the puppeteer and provides a stage for the puppet. There are many variations, but the classic is the Punch and Judy booth, which is just big enough for one puppeteer and all their puppets. The puppet stage is either in front of the puppeteer's face or above their head. If it is above the puppeteer's head, then the puppets can make a full turn.

The Playboard

The playboard is a shelf that represents the stage. It is deep enough for the puppet to put something on it. Usually, a small curtain hangs in front of it so that the puppet can come out under it to address the audience 'in front of the curtain'.

False Floor

You can hide a puppeteer under the floor, behind furniture or under a table, and make the puppet either pop up from behind, or through a hole. If you have a hole then the puppet can be surrounded by a 'stage floor' to sit on, and it can't move because you will be left with a hole! On the other hand, if the puppet pops up behind something, then it can move along the back of it. With a double of the puppet, you could also make it disappear in one place and reappear in another place.

A glove puppet performing on a flat surface needs a hole for the puppeteer's arm.

If you take the puppet away you are left with a hole!

With playboard the puppet is in a show

Without playboard the puppet is in the world

Using the TV frame as a puppet booth.

In television or filming situations, a false floor can be built up on scaffolding, for the puppets to appear on.

Variations: TV Frame

In the early years of putting puppets on television there was a playboard in the foreground at the bottom of the frame. The Muppets pioneered a new way of presenting puppets directly to the camera so that the frame of the television itself became a puppet booth. This gives the illusion that puppets are 'at large' in the world. The puppeteers have access to monitors so that they can see where the puppet is in the frame and what it is doing.

'Boothless' Glove Puppetry

Certain puppeteers, such as Neville Tranter and Avenue Q, have very successfully brought glove puppets out of the booth. The lack of a booth reveals the workings of the puppeteer, and this can be part of the appeal.

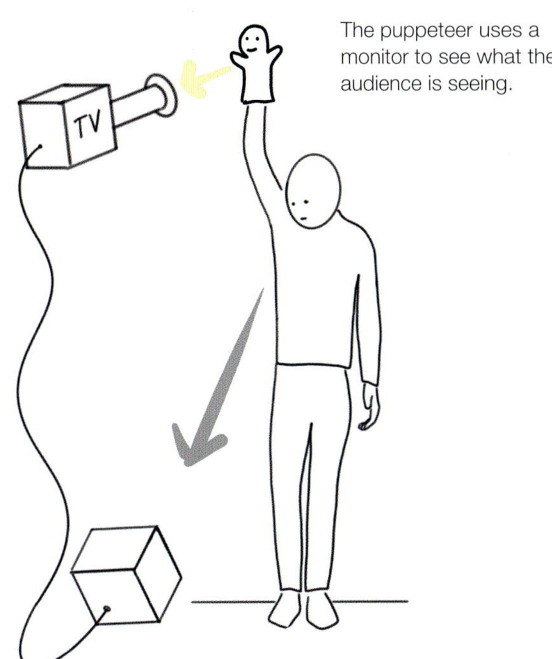

The puppeteer uses a monitor to see what the audience is seeing.

Rod Puppet Stages

Rod puppets are most often held on a table in front of the puppeteer or puppeteers operating them. The puppeteers form the background to the puppet, or at least stand in front of the background scenery. The puppet and puppeteer exist in different slices of space – the puppet in front and the puppeteer behind. The audience understands that they can see things in the puppet space – the puppets – but not in the puppeteer space. The puppeteers are 'hiding in plain sight'. If there is scenery behind the puppeteer, the audience can also see that.

This kind of puppetry can achieve the most realistic movement and the puppets can perform in the same space as people, making the method popular in contemporary theatre productions. The limitation is that the puppeteers have to be upstage of the puppets so as not to block the audience's view. This can make the blocking feel rather linear and stagey.

A table for the puppeteers is a stage for the puppet: *The Table* (Blind Summit).

The Classic Table Top

A raised platform, for example a table, acts as a stage for the puppet, while the floor acts as a stage for the puppeteer, giving each a distinct world in which to live. The raised platform for the puppet means that it is at an ideal height for the puppeteers standing on the floor.

Walking in the Air

Although they are rod puppets, traditional Bunraku puppets actually perform on a stage that is more like a giant puppet booth. A wall creates a raised 'floor' level and the puppets walk in the air behind it. Because the puppets are quite big, the head puppeteer wears elevated shoes.

Traditional Indonesian rod puppets also perform in a kind of booth.

Performing on the Stage Floor

Rod puppets can perform on the stage floor with a team of puppeteers behind them. This has become increasingly popular in Western theatre in the last thirty years, to create unusual characters and special effects.

Shadow Puppet Stages

Shadow puppets need a light source and a screen, as they are created by placing an object in a beam of light projected on to a surface. The puppet shadow is a negative image – an absence of light – and there are many ways to achieve this, with the light either behind a back projection screen or in front of a screen.

Images appear and disappear instantly, suspended on light beams. Light is however unforgiving and complicated to set up and manage. Shadows distort as they move from the centre to the edge of the light source and anything and everything that catches the light will appear on the screen.

Note: shadow puppetry uses a large number of puppets, often in quick succession. One of the challenges of working with a shadow stage is finding a way to set it up so that the puppeteer can reach the puppets quickly and discard them easily after using.

Variations: Back Projection

Back projection is the most recognizable version of shadow puppetry. The light is behind a screen and the puppeteer stands behind the light and puts puppets into the light to create shadows on the screen, which are seen from the front. Screens

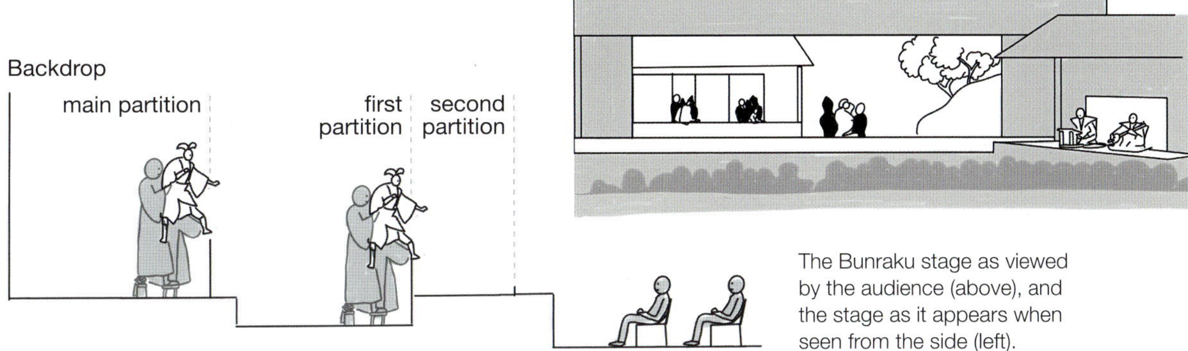

The Bunraku stage as viewed by the audience (above), and the stage as it appears when seen from the side (left).

can be made from paper, a shower curtain, cloth, or a specially made 'back projection screen' material, which is a kind of plastic. One of the problems of back projection is that there can be a 'hot spot' around the light source. This can be mitigated by using one of the specially made screens, which create the most even light.

Variations: Front Projection

In this method, the light is in front of the screen and the puppeteer can be watched by the audience as they put the puppets into it. The screen does not have to be see-through, so the shadows can be projected on to a wall, or indeed anything that takes light. This eliminates the hot-spot problem because the light is facing away from the audience.

Focused Light or Point Source Light

A focused light – one with a lens, such as a theatre light or a torch – will be focused only at one distance from the light, meaning that it is not possible to move closer or further away from it without going in and out of focus and creating a double edge. In this case, the best shadows are created by putting the puppets up against the screen.

A point source light stays in focus wherever the shadow puppet is placed, meaning that it is possible to move around in the light and play with scale. A naked 50W 12V halogen bulb is a very good point source (*see* Chapter 2). The naked bulb can be masked with a matt black metalwork hood or black metal masking known as cinefoil.

Portable Lights

Portable lights carried by puppeteers mean that the light source and the puppets can move, enabling the creation of beguiling special effects and tricks.

Switching Between Light Sources

With two light sources side by side, it is possible to switch instantly between two scenes on the same screen.

ABOVE: Back-projection shadow set-up.

BELOW: Front-projection shadow set-up.

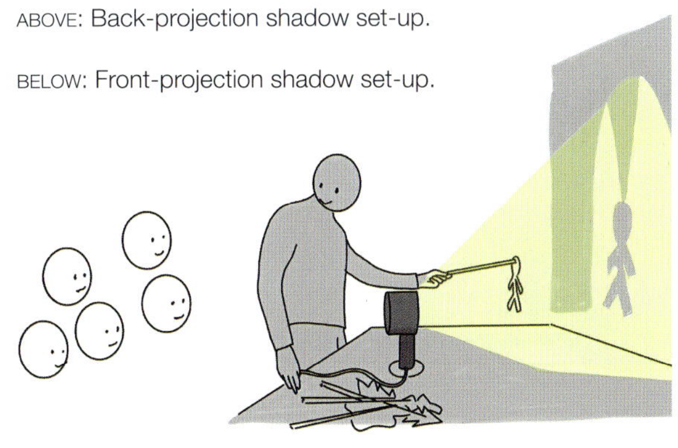

10

TALK TO THE HANDS: DIRECTING PUPPETRY

When you direct puppets, you are really directing puppeteers. If you want the puppets to do something, you will need to talk to the puppeteers to make them do it. One of the challenges is that the puppeteer's job is to be invisible, and make the audience look at the puppets. Your job, as puppet director, is to see the puppeteers, understand what they are doing, and help them to do it better.

Remember when you start the selection process that a puppeteer is anyone who says they are a puppeteer. There is no particular proficiency test. A puppeteer can be a singer, actor, dancer or other performer who prefers to channel their performance through puppets. Sometimes they do not yet know that they are a puppeteer. It is rare that everyone will come to rehearsal with the precise skills you are looking for, but if they have aptitude and enthusiasm, you will be able to teach them how to use the puppets. You need to be inventive when you are looking to select people for your team.

This chapter comprises some exercises that are aimed at recruiting and auditioning puppeteers, building a team and directing puppetry.

OPPOSITE: Peter and the Cat in rehearsal for *Peter and the Wolf* (Blind Summit).

LOOK FOR ENTHUSIASM IN APPLICATIONS

To start the selection process, ask applicants to send a CV, a headshot and a letter saying who they are and why they want to be considered. Of these, the letter is probably the most useful.

The CV should tell you where they have trained, what jobs they have done, and who they have worked with. Look for actor training, experience in physical theatre or comedy, and musicality. If they have these, they should be able to demonstrate discipline and a knowledge of the business – you will not have time to teach this in rehearsal.

The photo they choose to send will tell you how professional they are. It will reveal how they see themselves, what sort of acting roles they would go for, and how self-aware they are. It will be useful as a reference when you meet them, and for remembering them afterwards.

The letter gives the applicant a chance to show their enthusiasm, knowledge and interest in your work. These may well be the most valuable attributes they can offer. Look for what puppetry they have seen, what they understand about puppetry, and what experience they have. Have they done some research on you? How specific are they? An applicant who understands what they are applying for and genuinely wants to work with you will thrive in rehearsal, help their own career, and help you.

TEST THE ABILITY TO LEAD WITH THE PUPPET

The most important thing to find out about a performer who wants to be cast as a puppeteer is whether they can give up their centre to the puppet. Can they make you watch the puppet and not them?

This is a very simple exercise to do and gives everyone a chance to reveal this ability. Like all simple exercises, it is hard to do well, easy to do badly, and impossible to do perfectly.

You can use a box or a book to be a puppet head.

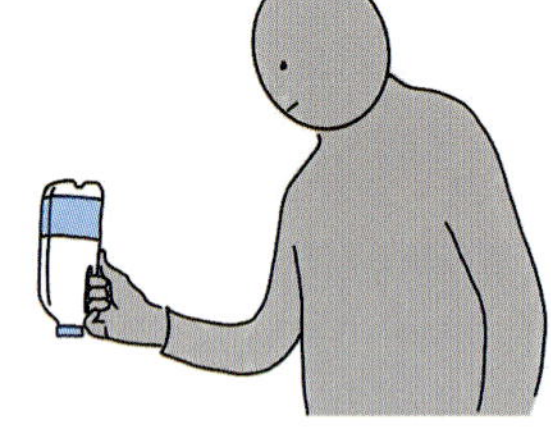

An empty milk carton also makes a good puppet head.

The Exercise

Set up the room with a stage area and an audience. If you have lots of people to see, divide your applicants into groups of 12 and give them a half-hour slot each.

All you need to do this exercise is a puppet 'head'. If you don't have a puppet head you can use an object such as a box, a milk carton or a book.

STEP 1: Bring the group into the room, introduce yourself and tell them that they don't need to have done puppetry before to do this exercise. Reassure them that they can just have a go and learn. Ask them to make an audience on one side of the room and explain that they are going to come up one by one and perform a simple task in front of the rest of the group.

STEP 2: Take a puppet 'head' and show them what you want them to do. They are going to make the head walk across the stage, as if it is on an invisible body.

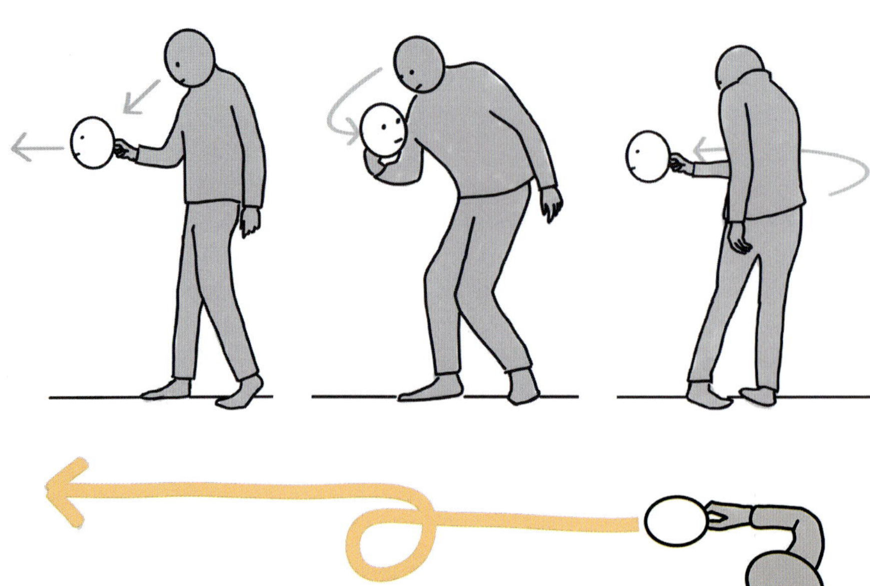

Auditioning potential team members: demonstrate how you want them to focus on the head (right).

Make the head lead a circle around you (middle right)...

... and continue to the other side of the stage (far right)

The journey across the stage.

STEP 3: Explain how you want them to do it: they should hold the head in their writing hand, focus on it at all times and make it 'lead' by making it move first. Show them the journey you want the puppet to make: entering from stage left, walking to the centre, stopping in the centre, turning around you, then exiting stage right.
STEP 4: Tell them what you will be looking for when they do it. You want to know what the head is looking at all the time. You want the head to lead all the movements. You want to see the head is 'alive'. The most important thing you will judge is whether you look mainly at the head or at them.
STEP 5: Ask each person to do it in turn and make a private note of their score out of ten (just to yourself). It should take about 15 to 20 minutes to see everyone.

Scoring the Participants

Do they do what you asked? Do they focus well on the object? Do they perform the journey as requested? Do they rush the exercise and leave bits out? Do they elaborate and do lots of things you don't need them to do? Do they know how to start and do they know when they've finished?
Do they seem comfortable on stage with a puppet? Does the exercise seem to free them as a performer or are they more interesting when they are not doing puppetry? Do you think they have done it before or is their first time? Do they seem excited by it? Amused? Interested? Some people are just happier when they are performing with a puppet, while others are confused by it.
Do they do more than you asked? Do they make an effort to bend their legs to make themselves move around in a more agile manner? Do they move the head with lively confidence? Do they make the head 'breathe'? Do they make the head look at specific things? Can you see some character in the head? Do you sense some sort of a story emerging from what they are doing?

Something to note

People can come back from this exercise A good puppeteer should be able to do this exercise without any trouble but on a bad day they can still mess it up. People do things wrong in auditions all the time. They might be too keen to show what they can do, or have learned to do it another way, or not understand what you have said. This exercise is a way of finding out people with potential, not a way of ruling people out.

LOOK FOR SPECIFIC SKILLS

This exercise is a way of looking for a deeper understanding of puppetry. You give everyone a go on one of the puppets that you are going to use in the show. If you don't have your puppets yet, choose a similar one or use a workshop puppet. This is a good way to follow the first audition exercise, to see how good someone's puppetry is, and what they do when they are under slightly more pressure.

The Exercise

Set up the room with a stage area and an audience. See people in groups of six or 12 and let them watch each other perform the task.

STEP 1: Show the puppeteers briefly how the puppet works and demonstrate a simple sequence of tasks: bring the puppet to life, make it look around the room, make it breathe, then develop an emotion using the breath. Take the emotion to the highest pitch it can go, and then pause. Explain to them what you are looking for and tell them you might direct them while they are doing it.
STEP 2: Invite them to go up one by one and have a go. If they do something that shows potential, direct them to see how they respond. Give them

about two or three minutes each on the puppet and then move on to someone else.

STEP 3: If you are using puppets that are worked by more than one person, make sure you swap the participants around so that everyone has a turn in each position.

It should take 30-40 minutes to see everyone. If you have time left over, you might want to ask particular people to have another go.

Things to Look For

How alive is the puppet? Does the puppet seem to think on its own? Is it breathing? Is it living? Are they able to give it a character?

Stillness Are they able to be still with the puppet? Are they able to keep it alive while it is still? Being able to use stillness is an essential part of puppetry.

Do they make you laugh or surprise you? Humour is very difficult (perhaps impossible) to teach. Look out for people who make you laugh in the audition. People who can make you laugh can usually provoke a range of other emotions too. You may not uncover someone's sense of humour at audition, but if you do, take note. Humour is a very useful tool in puppetry.

People who have a good effect on other performers Some people don't necessarily draw attention to themselves but have a good effect on the people they work with. If every time you see something good happen, the same person is involved, make a note of them. Puppetry is collaborative and these people are invaluable.

A willingness to be emotional A willingness to 'go there' is a very useful quality in a performer. They might not be in control of it at this stage, but if they can't risk genuine, loud emotion with a puppet, you need to know that.

BUILD A TEAM

Having found people with aptitude, skill and experience, you need to build a team that works together well. Good teams are made up of different types of people with different skills, different attitudes, and different strengths and weaknesses. The best way to build a team is to put them together in real situations and see how they do.

The Exercise

Invite puppeteers that you like to join a rehearsal for a morning or a day. Let them join in informally as part of your team, and see how they get on. Treat them as much as you can as if they are part of the team at their first day at work. Give them real problems to work on, and get them involved by working with them in the same way as you work with the other puppeteers that you know.

Things to Think About

Cast different personality types Good teams are not made up of all the same kind of people. Teams need a variety of different types. They need to get along with each other and yet also push each other to make the work better. They will spend a lot of time together.

Remember that people like doing different things Some people are natural ensemble players and others prefer written roles they can call their own. Some like to do a lot of homework alone and others want to do everything in the rehearsal room, with people around. Some people like to improvise, others like to be given lines. Some need to warm up when they get in to rehearsal, and others stretch before they come to work. Think about what sort of people you need for the work they are going to do.

Cast different levels of experience and skill You don't always need everyone to be the 'best'. Having someone who is new and keen to learn can give more experienced performers a new lease of life. More experienced performers bring knowledge and quick solutions to problems. Try to put together a team of people with complementary, non-overlapping skills.

Think about diversity Puppetry is a visual medium, so what the cast looks like is a very important part of what you are doing. Since it is not a realistic medium, the ethnicity and gender of the puppeteers do not need to be dictated by the puppets. The casting should reflect values you want to put across with the show.

PUT SCENES ON THEIR FEET STRAIGHT AWAY

To direct puppetry, you need to see it first. Getting a scene 'on its feet' straight away helps you see the parameters of the scene and feel what it is like when it is done with puppets. You don't need it to be done well; in fact, seeing the scene done badly is a very valuable exercise, as it takes pressure off the puppeteers and puts emphasis on clear storytelling. If, by a happy chance, the scene works when you do it badly, it will definitely work when you make it better.

The Exercise

Set up the room as a stage area and an audience area, and position yourself in the audience area.

STEP 1: Tell the puppeteers what you want them to do and how you want them to do it. Tell them to start by entering the stage, to do the main story points in the scene, and then exit.

Explain that you are going to set a stopwatch for how long you want the scene to take, and they should stay on stage until the time runs out and an alarm goes. If there is an event in the scene that must happen at a specific point, you can shout out when it happens.

If there are words that need to be said in the scene, you can do them in a number of ways. The performers can improvise to get the general meaning of the scene or – if you need the words to be more accurate than that – you can have someone read them out from the side of the stage. If you specifically need the puppeteers to say the words, you can have them hold the script in one hand and the puppet in the other. (They should look at the script all the time and not try and go back and forth between the script and the puppet. Going back and forth slows everything down.)

Make it clear to the participants that the point of getting the scene on its feet is not to get it right, or even to do it well. Instead, the idea is just to do it, to see what it is, so you can think about how to direct it.

STEP 2: Give the puppeteers a few minutes to prepare, and then ask them to run the scene in whatever way they can manage. If it is the first time they are doing the scene, they might need to discuss its main story points before they start. However, you should not give them too long to prepare, otherwise they will start to become anxious about 'doing it well', which is not the point of the exercise.

STEP 3: Run the scene with the stopwatch.

STEP 4: Once you have run it, you can discuss with the puppeteers what you saw. Discuss things you could add and things you want to cut.

STEP 5: Make any adjustments you want to make and run the scene again. Each time you run the scene, make it more detailed. Gradually, you will close in on a final version.

Tip for Doing the Exercise Well

Do it badly! The most important aspect of making this exercise work is that the puppeteers should have the courage to do it badly and underprepared. Doing the scene this way will reveal all sorts of things that can be improved. Elements that cannot be fixed should be thrown out.

What to Look Out For

Story What should happen in the scene? Did you see it happen? Is it obvious and clear to you watching it? Do you know who the puppets are? Where they are? And why?

Technical problems Could you see the puppets? Were the puppeteers holding them in the best way? Did they change their grip during the scene? Did the puppeteers get into awkward positions, fall over each other? Were there problems around the entrances and exits? Could they reach where they needed to? Ask the puppeteers to tell you what problems they had. Simple adjustments can often have a big impact.

Are the entrances and exits telling the story? Should the puppet walk on? If it pops up from behind a sofa, does the audience wonder what it was doing behind the sofa? Should it be on stage already at the beginning of the scene? These things can't be sorted out by the puppeteers because they cannot know what the scene looks like from the outside.

Signs can be used to give information.

Puppeting signs.

Old He Liyi in *Mr China's Son* (Blind Summit).

'LIVE DIRECT' A SCENE TO WORK IT OUT

When you are trying to make visual stories with puppetry, explaining your idea in advance can be very difficult. Describing elements that you want to see is very difficult. 'Live directing' a scene is a good way of sketching it out with the puppeteers for the first time in the space.

The Exercise

Set up the room as a stage and an audience.

STEP 1: Ask a puppeteer or puppeteers to go on stage and begin to improvise a scene with a puppet. You can give them a specific place to start and a specific scene if you want, or you can let them begin how they like. Tell them that you are going to give them instructions and they should try to follow without breaking their focus on the puppetry.

STEP 2: Let them begin to improvise. When you have an idea for something that you want to happen, give them directions to follow in the moment, a bit like a silent movie director. Say what you want to see. You might say something like, 'And now the puppet looks at the audience... then it looks at itself... and then it looks at the audience again... and then backs away... and turns to look at the back of the room... then looks at its feet....'

You can also direct the scene around the puppet, and the emotions and thoughts of the puppet: 'The puppet climbs on to the chair... she looks around her... everything is destroyed... she can't see anything living... someone else comes in now and says something to her....'

STEP 3: If the puppeteer is suddenly inspired to take over, you can stop directing. If they run out of ideas, you can jump in with directions again. You can direct other people to come into the scene with other puppets, or direct them to join on the puppet: 'Another puppeteer comes in now and starts to lift the chair….'
STEP 4: When everyone runs out of ideas, stop and review what happened.
STEP 5: Ask the puppeteers to try and repeat what they have done, but this time without direction.

Things to Note

Someone needs to record it When performers are being directed in this way, it is a bit like hypnosis and it is very difficult, in fact almost impossible, for them to remember afterwards what they have done. Make sure that you video the improvisation, have someone note it down, or make notes yourself as soon as you finish it.
The puppeteers get better at it With practice they will find that the puppeteers are able to follow instructions without looking up or breaking character. They also get better at remembering what they did afterwards.
There is only one point of view A limitation of this exercise is that it puts all the pressure on the director to come up with the ideas rather than drawing on everyone's creativity. For this reason, it is better for shaping a scene than for creating a scene.

SWAP IN TO SEE WHAT YOU WANT

One very good way to get across what you want to see is to show it. Instead of trying to explain what you are thinking, swap places with a puppeteer and let them watch you do it. This gives the puppeteer a chance to see the scene from the outside. It also gives you the perspective of being inside the scene.

The Exercise

Set up the room with a stage and an audience.

STEP 1: One puppeteer does a scene with the puppet, and everyone else watches.
STEP 2: At the end of the scene everyone says what they thought of what they saw. Did they understand it? Did they like it? Can they think of ways to improve it?
STEP 3: Anyone who has ideas to improve on the scene or the puppetry then swaps places with the puppeteer, repeats the scene and tries to make it better.
STEP 4: Discuss again what you saw. Again, anyone with an idea swaps places and does the scene again.
STEP 5: Keep swapping places until the scene gets to where you want it to be.

Things to Notice

Watching is as important as practising Knowing what you want the audience to see is as important as physically repeating the movement. Watching puppetry improves your puppetry as much as doing it.
Video may not give the best representation You can use a video camera to record what you are doing, but you do need to learn how to review the video. It is challenging to see yourself as an audience sees you. In addition, a video image tends to be flattened and to have a different emphasis from a live viewing.
The swap works both ways It is very helpful for the puppeteer to get a chance to see the effect of their puppetry from 'out front', but it is also useful for the people watching to pick up the puppet and see how different it feels from inside the scene, or rather behind the scene. Remember that the puppet is no one!

HANG OUT WITH THE PUPPETS

This is a great exercise when you want to reconnect with the puppets and be inspired. There are no expectations at all of the performers and you can indulge in the pleasure of simply moving puppets beautifully in space.

The Exercise

This exercise is best led without instructions, allowing people to join in or watch as they choose.

STEP 1: Put on some music, pick up a puppet and start to improvise with it yourself. Don't give any instructions, just start, and let people follow. It may take a while for people to join in.
STEP 2: Change the music track, and keep going.
STEP 3: Once everyone has joined in, take yourself out of the action, and watch the room in movement.
STEP 4: If you see something you like, video it.

Something to Notice

This exercise is a free exploration of objects and puppets moving in space It gives you as the director a chance to stand back and look at the natural dynamics of the puppets, and to see them afresh. What do they do to the space? What do they do to the puppeteers? What are they telling you?
The movement of puppets seems different when you do it to music How does music affect the movement, and how different does the music sound when you are watching and doing puppetry?

WHEN A SEQUENCE NEEDS CHOREOGRAPHY

Story is always the most important thing for an audience, but a well-choreographed sequence can be a crowd pleaser, and sometimes it is worth putting extra time aside to choreograph specific moments. Make sure, however, that it does not become so complicated that the technicalities dictate the pace of the action.

The Exercise

Before you start, be clear what you want to work on and how much time you are going to allocate to it.

STEP 1: Take the sequence that you need to make. For example, it might be three puppeteers making a puppet do a handstand.
STEP 2: Ask the puppeteers to try it first without breaking it down. Jump the puppet into the handstand, trying to get the same timing as a real person would have. Get the timing right before you start to break it down.
STEP 3: Now unpack the sequence movement by movement, using yourself as a reference, and recreate each movement with the puppet.
STEP 4: Then put the sequence back together so that you can do each beat.
STEP 5: Now do the sequence in very slow motion to get the rhythms and timing of the real action, but slowed down.
STEP 6: Increase the speed of the slow motion until you can do it at full speed, and it fits into the timing that you discovered at the beginning.
STEP 7: Revise the sequence as part of a warm-up in rehearsals, and before a show, so that it stays fresh in everyone's mind.

Something to Remember

No matter how well you do your specially choreographed movement, the audience will not enjoy it unless it progresses the story. Don't let it distract you from telling the story in the show. And don't let rehearsing it come before finding the story.

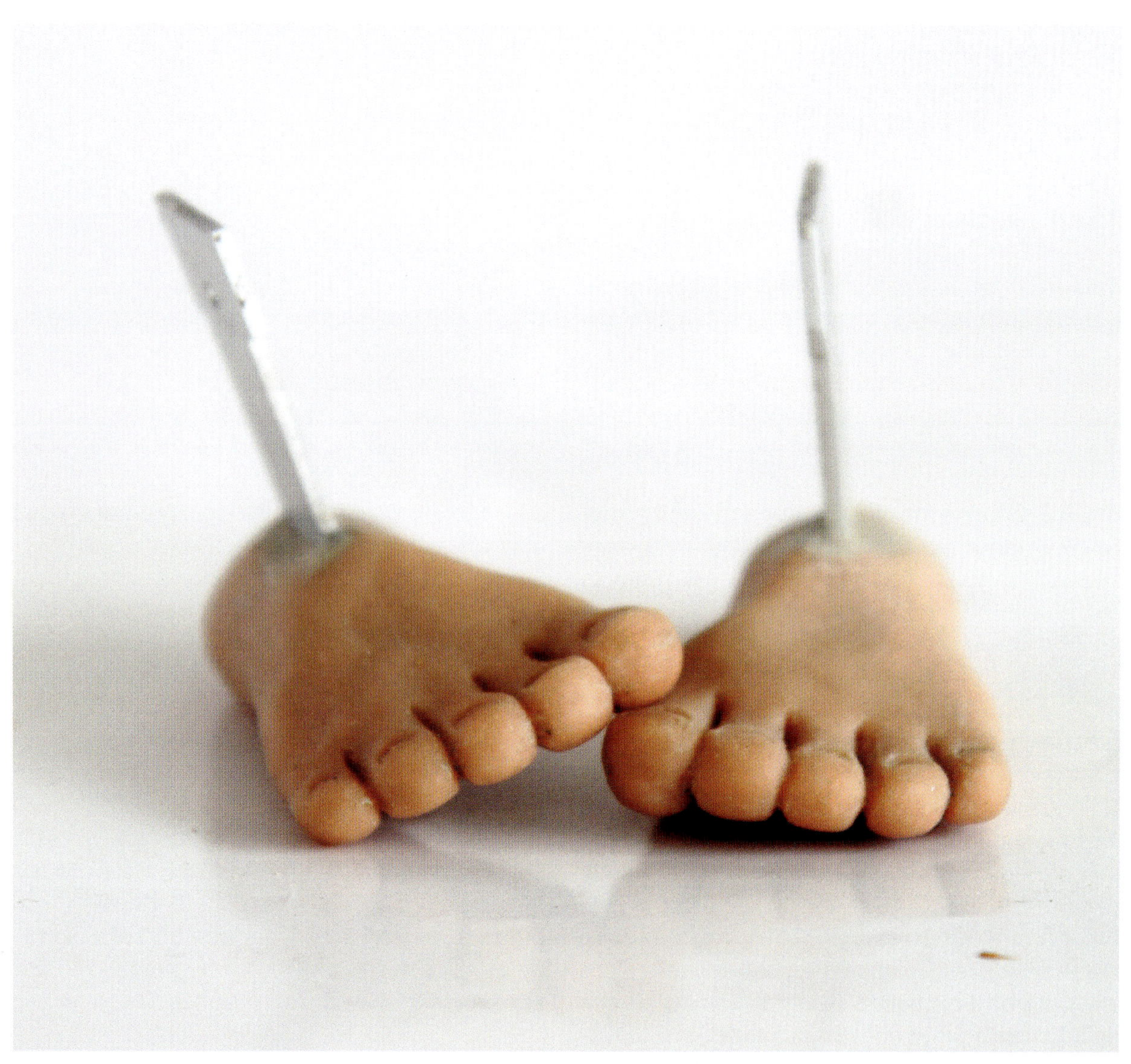

The End.

FURTHER RESOURCES

The following is a short list of starting places to learn more about puppetry, some places to buy things, and some shows to see. It is not exhaustive and is inevitably selective, but all the recommendations are based on personal experience.

RECOMMENDED PUPPETRY SHOWS

Avenue Q (on tour)
Dimanche (formerly *Backup*) by Focus Company and Chaliwaté Company (on tour)
Everything in the London Mime Festival
Madam Butterfly at ENO, Metropolitan Opera, Lithuanian National Opera, Vienna Stadtsoper
Meet Fred (on tour)
Stayagraha at ENO, Metropolitan Opera
The Caravan of Horror, Bakelite
The Lion King, London West End, Broadway
The Table (on tour)
War Horse (on tour)

PUPPET COMPANIES TO FOLLOW

Bakelite, Rennes, France
Basil Twist, New York, USA
Blind Summit Theatre, London, UK
Bread and Puppet, Vermont, USA
Complicite, London, UK
Dan Hurlin, New York, USA
Faulty Optic
Green Ginger
Gyre and Gimble
Handspring Theatre Company
Hensons (Jim, Bryan, Heather)
Ilka Schonbein
Improbable
Invisible Thread
Lone Wolf Tribe
Marcos Gonzalez
Teatro
The Last Great Hunt
Norwich Puppet Theatre
Philippe Genty
Potato Room Productions
Significant Object
Teatro y su Doble
The Little Angel
Theatre Rites
TOF Theatre
Tom Lee

PUPPETRY TRAINING

The Curious School of Puppetry (UK)
http://curiouspuppetry.com/

Royal Central School of Speech and Drama, London
Collaborative and Devised Theatre Course
https://www.cssd.ac.uk/courses/acting-cdt-ba

Royal Central School of Speech and Drama, London
Puppetry Course
https://www.cssd.ac.uk/courses/puppetry-design-and-performance-ba

East 15
Physical Theatre Course
https://www.east15.ac.uk/courses/ug00337/1/ba-physical-theatre

Eugene O'Neill Theater Center, Waterford, CT, USA
National Puppetry Conference
https://www.theoneill.org/pup

Institut International de la Marionnette
7 place Winston Churchill, 08000 Charleville-Mézières (France)
Tél. 00 33 (0) 3 24 33 72 50
institut@marionette.com

Blind Summit Theatre, London
Training workshops
www.blindsummit.com

PUPPET FESTIVALS

Canada
Festival de Casteliers, Montreal, Canada

Czech Republic
Skupa Pilsen's International Festival

France
Festival Mondial des Théâtres de Marionettes in Charleville-Mézières
Festival Marionettissimo in Tournefeuille, Toulouse
Saperlipuppet, La Chapelle sur Erde

Germany
Fidena Festival, Bochum, Germany
Figurentheater Puppet Festival, Munich
International Figuren Theater Festival, Erlangen, Germany
No Strings Attached Festival, Mainz, Germany
Synegura Festival, Erfurt

Latvia
Talinn Puppet Festival, Latvia

Poland
International Festival of Puppet Theatre for Adults, Bialystok, Poland
Kontrapunckt Festival, Poland

Romania
Pulzart, Sfantu Gheorghe, Romania (annually)

Russia
BTF Festival, St Petersburg, Russia

Slovenia
LUTKE, International Puppet Festival, Ljubljana, Slovenia (biennial, last held in 2020)

Spain
Fira de Titelles Festival, Llieda, Spain
MAF Santander
Qui Quiri Qui, Granada, Spain
Titirimundi, Segovia, Spain

Switzerland
Figura Festival, Baden, Switzerland

UK
Edinburgh Fringe, Edinburgh
Bristol Puppetry Festival, Bristol
Manipulate, Edinburgh (annually)
London Mime Festival, London (annually in January)
Skipton Puppet Festival, Skipton (annually)

USA
Chicago Puppet Festival

SPECIALIST MATERIALS AND SUPPLIERS

Cardboard: Kite Packaging (ask for pallet-size sheets)
Glue sticks: local stationers or DIY store, or online
Plastazote: SJG International (will send testers for free or low cost. Cut to order, so you need to specify density, thickness and colour, and whether skin on edge is OK.)
Scalpels and scalpel blades: local stationers or online.

PHOTO CREDITS

All photos by the author (Mark Down) apart from:

Anne-Marie Bickerton, page 12; Antonella Carrara, page 74; Bertha Elizondo, pages 100, 154 (bottom right), 166 (bottom); Fiona Clift, pages 40 (bottom left and right), 46; Helen Foan, page 114; Jerome Corbic, page 105; Lorna Palmer, page 128; Nick Barnes, pages 20, 27, 37 (bottom), 64, 104, 136, 139 (bottom right), 142, 148, 167; Odetta Riskute, pages 106, 111, 146, 150, 170; Patrick Baldwin, page 70; Richard Blomshield, pages 32, 97 (top); Stephanie Wickes, pages 6, 50, 140; Susana Neves, pages 38 (top), 113 (bottom right).

INDEX